TRUE TO LIFE

ENGLISH FOR ADULT LEARNERS

UPPER-INTERMEDIATE

Ruth Gairns
Stuart Redman

CLASS BOOK

CAMBRIDGE
UNIVERSITY PRESS

PUBLISHED BY THE PRESS SYNDICATE OF THE UNIVERSITY OF CAMBRIDGE
The Pitt Building, Trumpington Street, Cambridge, United Kingdom

CAMBRIDGE UNIVERSITY PRESS
The Edinburgh Building, Cambridge CB2 2RU, UK
40 West 20th Street, New York, NY 10011–4211, USA
477 Williamstown Road, Port Melbourne, VIC 3207, Australia
Ruiz de Alarcón 13, 28014 Madrid, Spain
Dock House, The Waterfront, Cape Town 8001, South Africa

http://www.cambridge.org

First published 1998
Seventh printing 2003

Printed in Dubai by Oriental Press

ISBN 0 521 57483 8 Class Book
ISBN 0 521 57482 X Personal Study Workbook
ISBN 0 521 57481 1 Teacher's Book
ISBN 0 521 57480 3 Class Cassette Set
ISBN 0 521 57479 X Personal Study Workbook Cassette
ISBN 0 521 58943 6 Personal Study Workbook Audio CD

CONTENTS

COURSE OVERVIEW

Unit	Language focus	Topics	Review
1 WHAT HAVE WE GOT IN COMMON?	determiners expressing connections/relationships expressing worries/concerns vocabulary: social issues; physical appearance; compound adjectives	finding things in common social/political issues physical appearance	problems with listening to spoken English
2 SLEEPING IT OFF	connectors: concession participle clauses present perfect simple vs continuous sleep vocabulary ailments and body problems	sleeping habits an art exhibition physical problems; ailments	Unit 1
3 HOW DO WE BEHAVE?	*wish* and *if only* + past perfect expressing thanks and pleasure *so* vs *such* (a) verbs of social communication focusing adverbs	behaviour in public social correspondence describing embarrassing situations	Unit 1 Unit 2
4 GETTING YOUR MESSAGE ACROSS	modals of past deduction *must've, could've, might've* + pp idioms: communication problems reformulating character adjectives phrasal verbs and idioms functional language	breakdowns in communication unrequited love describing character answerphones	Unit 2 Unit 3
5 BUILDINGS	noun groups: plural and compound nouns collective nouns countable/uncountable nouns adjectives as nouns past perfect simple and continuous present perfect review building vocabulary compound adjectives	a buildings quiz discussing amenities in your town unusual homes designing a language school	Unit 3 Unit 4
PROJECT: WRITING BIOGRAPHIES			
6 TRAVELLING CAN BE HARD WORK	emphasising structures making/changing arrangements present continuous and future continuous different uses of *would* phrasal verbs and idioms	customs on public transport formal and informal letters tour reps and package holidays	Unit 4 Unit 5
7 HOW DOES IT LOOK?	prepositions of place *look* + adjective *look like* + noun *look as if/though* colours and materials modal verbs: hypothesising adjective word order describing clothes	looking at paintings colour blindness a colour quiz describing clothes a questionnaire about clothes preferences	Unit 5 Unit 6
8 ADDRESSING THE ISSUES	*It's time* + past tense textual cohesion expressing willingness collocation vocabulary of politics, crime and the law	political scandal political issues discussing who to vote for TV censorship	Unit 6 Unit 7
9 MAKING THE MOST OF YOUR TIME	prepositions and adverbs tense and time nouns and adjectives + *-ing* or infinitive non-defining relative clauses time expressions	how you manage your time a time quiz writing an article under pressure	Unit 7 Unit 8

Unit	Language focus	Topics	Review
10 TELLING STORIES IN ENGLISH	linking spoken discourse attitude adverbs phrasal verbs and idioms purpose clauses crime vocabulary	anecdotes about famous people how to write short stories a story about poison	Unit 8 Unit 9
PROJECT: GROUP MAGAZINE			
11 EATING OUT	food vocabulary partitives simile and metaphor adjective suffix *y* reporting verbs verb patterns	a food quiz and discussion reading and writing reviews overhearing conversations	Unit 9 Unit 10
12 THEATRICAL INTERLUDE	question forms vocabulary: personal interaction adverbs of manner adverbial phrases pronunciation: accents describing speech	a scene from a Pinter play discussing accents and learning them acting a scene: stage directions	Unit 10 Unit 11
13 ON THE JOB	expressing obligation, permission and entitlement work vocabulary adjective + noun collocation appearance adjectives expressing probability	rights and wrongs in a work situation positive and negative aspects of jobs what to wear to interviews	Unit 11 Unit 12
14 ACCIDENTS WILL HAPPEN	present/past continuous (habits) *keep + -ing* form *used to/would* participle clauses verbs: *spill, scratch, rip* accidents, medical vocabulary	being clumsy or absent-minded insurance claims after accidents a dramatic operation	Unit 12 Unit 13
15 WAYS OF BEING BETTER OFF	expressing number/quantity uses of *whether* passives money and legal vocabulary paraphrasing	an experiment in honesty legal claims for compensation how to get a good deal when shopping	Unit 13 Unit 14
PROJECT: EDUCATION IN THE ADULT WORLD			
16 THAT'S A MATTER OF OPINION	conditional sentences: unreal past/present expressing opinions agreeing/disagreeing words with different meanings wedding vocabulary military service vocabulary	discussion about military service reacting to tricky situations marriage: who should propose to whom?	Unit 14 Unit 15
17 MANNERS	functional language: surprise, requests, enquiries, apologies and excuses describing change past tenses for distancing vocabulary: money and manners letter writing: style and layout	what to say in social situations changes in manners in society writing a formal letter of request	Unit 15 Unit 16

18 WHAT ARE THE ODDS?	degrees of possibility and
	   probability
	revision of *will* for prediction
	future continuous and future perfect
	revision of grammar and vocabulary
		probability factors of life
		predicting your personal future
		a board game to revise what you
		  have learnt
			Unit 16
			Unit 17

WHAT HAVE WE GOT IN COMMON?

> **Language focus**
> determiners: *both, neither*, etc. expressing connections and relationships
> expressing worries/concerns compound adjectives
> describing appearance vocabulary: social issues
> ellipsis

COMMON FEATURES
determiners; expressing connections/relationships

1 Work with a partner and imagine the sentences below are about the two of you.
Make any necessary changes to correct factual or grammatical mistakes.

Example:

    of us   *quite*
Both ~~the two~~ are ~~very~~ keen on sport.

or
Neither of us is very keen on sport.
or
I'm very keen on sport but my partner can't stand it.

Both the two are very keen on sport.
Neither of us has ever done anything illegal.
We come both from a village.
Both of us have a lot of spare time.
We have to both works for a living.
Both my partner and me can change a wheel on a car.
Neither my partner or I knows anything about astronomy.
Neither one of us is particularly interested in gardening.

Check the grammar mistakes with your teacher.
Do other pairs have the same things in common as you?

2 Now work in a new group of four. You have three minutes to find one new and interesting fact which is true about all of you (apart from the fact that you study English together). Don't tell this fact to other groups.

Examples: *You all have pierced ears.*
You all cry when you see Disney movies.
You all use the same brand of toothpaste.
You all believe in life after death.

3 ⊂⊃ You will hear two women asking questions to find out what two men have in common. What *do* they have in common?

4 ⊂⊃ Read the sentence beginnings, then listen to the recording again and tick (✓) the ones you hear.

> Does it have anything to do with ...?
> Has it got anything to do with ...?
> Is it anything to do with ...?
> Is it related to ...?
> Is it (in any way) connected to ...?
> Is it about ...?
> Is it to do with ...?

5 You are now going to play the same game. Two of you must now move from your original group to a new group. You have to guess your new group's common feature, using questions from Exercise 4.

6 Now work together as a whole class. Complete the sentence beginnings to make true sentences about your class.

Example: *All of us* .... **hate getting up in the morning.** ....

Be careful: some structures take a singular verb, some take a plural verb and one can take either. Check in the Language Reference on page 141 if necessary.

All of us/we all ...
Most of us ...
Practically every member of the group ...
None of us ...
Each person in this group ...
Several of us ...

COMMON IDEALS
vocabulary: social/political issues; expressing concerns

1 In small groups, check that you understand and can pronounce the words in the box.

> unemployment   crime   inflation   pollution   drug or alcohol abuse
> corruption   the quality of public transport   poverty   welfare funding

Discuss how these issues affect you personally. If you don't wish to talk about a topic, say 'I'd rather not discuss that'. Use these phrases to begin your discussion of each topic.

(Unemployment) affects me very directly because ...
(Crime) affects me to some extent because ...
(Corruption) doesn't affect me at all because ...

2 Do you think these issues are of great concern in your *country* and for your *government*? Are there any other issues which are more important?

Check that you understand the phrases in italics, then complete the sentences.

1. In my country ...... *is by far the most important* *issue.* *concern.*

2. People are also *increasingly* *worried* *concerned* *about* ...

3. People are *not very aware of* ...

Tell a partner what you wrote and why.

3 Read the paragraph, then shut your book and tell your partner what you can remember.

Do Europeans have opinions and tastes in common that distinguish them from the rest of the world? The answers are provided in one of the most comprehensive opinion surveys ever conducted. The survey, 'Europeans: Citizens of the World, Consumers of the World', questioned 18,000 people in 21 European countries, as well as 40,000 people worldwide on a range of topics. You are now going to read some of the findings.

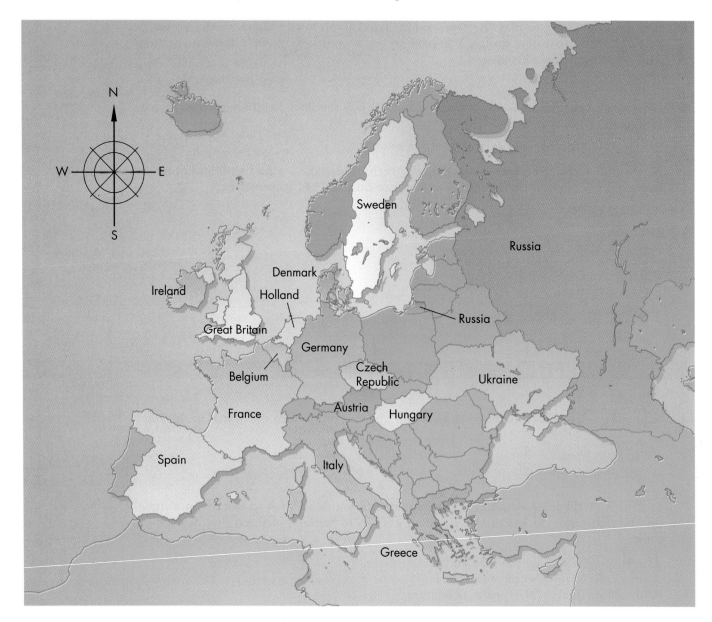

4 Work with your partner. Each choose *three different* nationalities from the box. Read the text quickly and underline anything you learnt about them. You have four minutes.

Germans	Italians	Ukrainians	the Spanish	the French
Russians	the Dutch	Belgians	Britons	Austrians
Czechs	the Irish	Hungarians	Danes	Swedes

Europeans: Citizens of the World, Consumers of the World

WORRIES

In western Europe, unemployment is by far the most important issue. When presented with a choice of 15 different areas of concern, every west European nation put unemployment either first or in the top three.

There were some national variations: Germany, Belgium and Britain put crime slightly higher than unemployment; France gave Aids a very high priority, placing it second after unemployment; Italians were worried about corruption, Scandinavians about pollution, and the Dutch about religious fundamentalism. For Russians, however, crime is by far the most important topic of concern, followed by inflation and personal lack of money.

In addition, Europeans felt that unemployment was the main cause of poverty. Elsewhere in the world, people were more likely to select lack of education as the main reason. Europeans also put great emphasis on insufficient welfare funding, unlike the rest of the world.

People from the former eastern bloc put slightly less emphasis on unemployment and more on drug and alcohol abuse. These countries also tend to be more concerned about the environment than they are about economic growth, as is Austria. Britain, France, Hungary, Belgium and Holland are more concerned about the economy.

CLEAN LIVING

Almost everyone in the Czech Republic had either bathed or showered on the day questioned – but they still come second to Hungary. The least likely to have had either a bath or shower are the Ukrainians and Russians, but this could be due to poor plumbing facilities rather than lack of hygiene. In western Europe, the lowest bath-plus-shower score goes to the Irish, and the highest to the Dutch, who rank just behind the Czechs. The keenest showerers are the Danes; the biggest bath fans are the British.

SLEEP

The earliest risers are the Czechs and the Hungarians – 46.8% and 42.7% respectively get up before 6 a.m. The ones who stay in bed are the Spanish and Irish – only about one in 15 get up before dawn.

Italians go to bed the latest – 55% stay up past midnight. Astonishingly, despite their early hours, 40% of east Europeans stay up past midnight. One can only hope for their sakes that it is not the same 40% that get up before dawn.

Another surprising fact is that the Dutch are the most likely to take a nap during the day – 42% had taken a nap during the day in question; well ahead of the alleged siesta-loving Spanish. The Irish are the least likely to have a nap, however.

MOOD SWINGS

Contrary to expectation, the British are quite hot-tempered, while the most softly-spoken nations are the Austrians and Germans – around one in ten had raised their voices in the last 24 hours.

Over 40% of Danes and Belgians had felt lucky, but only 6.5% of Greeks. Over three-quarters of the Dutch had felt happy, and the Swedes and Danes also scored highly. However, less than a quarter of Greeks and Russians felt happy. In western Europe, the saddest nations were the Italians and the British – one in four felt unhappy.

From *The European*

Tell your partner about your three nationalities. Does anything surprise you?

5 Are these sentences true or false, according to the text?

WORRIES
1. For Belgians, unemployment is the most important issue.
2. Europeans are more concerned about welfare funding than the rest of the world.
CLEAN LIVING
3. Hungarians are the cleanest, followed by the Czechs and then the Dutch.
SLEEP
4. Spanish people sleep more in the afternoon than the Danes.
MOOD SWINGS
5. The Dutch feel much happier than the Russians.

Compare your answers with a partner.

6 If you are European, what do you think of the findings? Do you think they are accurate?

If you are not European, what do you think the results of such a survey would be in your country?

SIMILAR BUT QUITE DIFFERENT!   describing appearance; compound adjectives; ellipsis

1 Who do you look like in your family? Tell each other in small groups.

Examples   *I've got my father's eyes.*
I look just like my sister – we're both tall and slim with the same shaped face.

2 With a partner, organise these words into the five categories in the table using a dictionary to help you. Give each category a heading.

short-sleeved   sun-tanned   well-built   shoulder-length   slim   wavy
clean-shaven   straight   high-heeled   polo-neck   tight-fitting   freckles
wrinkles   bald/balding   overweight   baggy   well-dressed   smart(ish)   curly
average-build/size   casual   dark-skinned   scruffy   skinny   presentable

1.	2.	3.	4.	5.

Add two more words to each category.

3 Look at the pictures of the people who are the same sex as you. Using vocabulary from Exercise 2 (and any other vocabulary), tell a partner how these people are similar to or different from you.

Examples: *The man on the left is well-built, **which I'm not**, and he's bald and **so am I**.*

*The first woman's got curly hair, and **so have I**, but she's wearing tight-fitting leggings, **which I never do**.*

4 In small groups, discuss these statements. Do you agree or disagree with them? Say why.

Sun-tanned people look more attractive.

Women worry too much about being slim.

Women are more attracted to clean-shaven men.

Cosmetic surgery is the best answer for people with wrinkles.

Most men don't worry about being overweight.

People who are scruffy don't care what others think of them.

People with curly hair always want straight hair, and vice versa.

High-heeled shoes make women look silly.

Well-dressed children are better behaved than scruffily-dressed children.

Tell the class which ones your group agrees with.

5 With a partner, write 50 words about one of the topics in Exercise 4. Show it to another pair for interest.

1 This lesson is about some of the problems you might have when listening in a foreign language. Start by making a list of the things you listen to in English both inside and outside the classroom. Which do you find the most difficult?

2 You are going to do a 'dictogloss'. First, read the text which tells you what it is. Ask your teacher anything you don't understand.

A *dictogloss* is a kind of dictation in which you hear a text but don't have time to write down everything you hear. Your task is to listen and take out the main ideas, and then put them together in correct sentences so you reconstruct the text. You don't need to use *exactly* the same words or grammar as the original, however.

So, the text you're going to hear is about listening to a foreign language, and these are the stages that you will follow:

1 *Listen* to the text to get the general idea. **Don't write** anything. At this stage, if you write you'll find it hard to concentrate on the meaning.

2 *Listen* again and **take notes**. Write **key words** and phrases, not complete sentences.

3 *Work with a partner. Together, try to **write out** the text using the notes you made.*

4 *When you have done as much as you can, **listen** to the text once more, and quickly note any **changes** you want to make.*

5 *With your partner, **polish** your final version of the text.*

6 *Now **compare** it with the tapescript on page 159. Where your text is different, is the English correct or not?*

3 ▭ Now do the dictogloss on the recording.

4 Which problems in the text do you have? Do you have any other problems when listening to a foreign language? Discuss in small groups.

5 ▭ Now listen to several people talking about these types of problems. Do they mention the same ones as you did? Make notes.

Did you have any problems understanding these speakers? If so, what were they?

6 In small groups, make a list of things you can do to help yourself with these problems in the table below. Then tell the rest of the class.

Listening to tapes and videos	Listening face-to-face
Don't try to understand every word you hear – try to get the general idea.	Ask the speaker to repeat what they said.

PERSONAL STUDY WORKBOOK

In your Personal Study Workbook, you will find more exercises to help you with your learning. For Unit 1, these include:

- exercises to practise a wide range of vocabulary
- listening to native speakers talking about how they are affected by different social issues
- a text about the use of 'animal insults' in different languages
- writing a letter to a penpal
- your first speaking partners activity

2

SLEEPING IT OFF

Language focus

connectors: concession
present perfect simple vs continuous
ailments and body problems

participle clauses
sleep vocabulary

1   How did you sleep last night?
Ask five different people.

2   Work with a partner. Make sure you understand the words and phrases in the box, using a dictionary and your teacher if necessary.

get a good night's sleep	suffer from insomnia	jump out of bed	fall asleep/be asleep
yawn	set the alarm (clock)	oversleep	have nightmares
count sheep	sleepwalk	snore	the alarm goes off
have a restless night	have a day off	sleep like a log	have a nap
a hot drink	be fast asleep	have a late night	lie very still
sleeping pills	lie on your back	feel drowsy	have a lie-in

Take turns to make sentences using at least two words/phrases from the box.

Example: *A hot drink before I go to bed helps me to get a good night's sleep.*

Continue until you have used up all the words.

3 Try the following sleep quiz with a partner.

THE SIMPLE SLEEP
quizzzzzz

We spend a third of our lives in bed, but how much do you know about sleep and dreams? Find out in our sleep quiz ...

1 How much sleep should you get each night?
 a 6–8 hours
 b as much as possible
 c it depends on the person

2 Sufferers of tired-all-the-time syndrome should:
 a get more sleep
 b aim to get regular sleep
 c cut down on sleep

3 If you have problems sleeping at night avoid:
 a exercise
 b coffee after lunch time
 c having a glass of wine in the evening

4 A good way to get quality sleep is to:
 a make your bedroom comfortable
 b eat a meal before bedtime
 c exercise during the day

5 If you can't sleep, it's best to:
 a lie very still
 b count sheep
 c get up for a while

6 Most of our dreams occur in REM sleep. REM stands for:
 a really early morning
 b rolling eye movement
 c rapid eye movement

7 Which is most likely to cause nightmares?
 a suffocation under the blankets
 b spicy food
 c stressful situations

8 People dream in black and white.
 a true
 b false

9 Children are more likely to sleepwalk than adults. If anyone sleepwalks, you should:
 a guide the sleepwalker back to bed without waking them
 b wake them up and talk to them about their worries
 c wake them up and put them back to bed

From BUPA *Upbeat* magazine

Check your answers by reading the text on page 153.

4 Look at the connecting words highlighted in yellow on page 153. Can you replace each connector with the words below? Refer to the Language Reference on page 141–142 if necessary.

– *Nevertheless* or *although* in place of *however* in Answer 1
– *But* or *however* in place of *nevertheless* in Answer 3
– *In spite of* or *even though* in place of *although* in Answer 7
– *Despite the fact that* or *despite* in place of *even though* in Answer 9

5 Complete the following sentences in an appropriate way.

1. My brother prefers a hard bed to sleep on whereas ...
2. I managed to fall asleep, despite ...
3. .... However, help is now available for long-term sufferers with a new aerosol spray.
4. In spite of the constant noise throughout the night, ...
5. I sometimes take sleeping pills, although ...
6. I still get occasional nightmares. Nevertheless, ...

1 Which of the following would you expect to see as part of an exhibition in an art gallery? Discuss in small groups.

> a self-portrait   a sculpture   a suit   a stocking   a pickled human brain
> a cushion   a manuscript   a landscape   a bag of salt   a pen
> a woman asleep in a glass case   a still life

2 Look at the picture and read the text. If this was in an art gallery near your home, would you go to see the exhibition? Why/why not? Discuss in small groups.

SORRY, I SLEPT THROUGH IT ALL

For one week in the autumn of 1995, the Serpentine Gallery in London was the venue for an extraordinary exhibition entitled 'The Maybe'. The centrepiece of the show was an actress, Tilda Swinton, who lay apparently asleep in a glass case for eight hours a day. Was she really asleep? Or was she listening with her eyes shut to the comments of the spectators?

Her performance was, however, only part of the exhibition which also featured the possessions of famous dead people including a suit belonging to a well-known comedian, Napoleon's rosary, some of Holst's original music, one of Queen Victoria's monogrammed black stockings and a pen belonging to Charles Dickens. Perhaps the most bizarre exhibit was the pickled brain of the inventor of the hand-cranked computer, Charles Babbage.

But what on earth did it all mean? 'Every object in the show is the property of a celebrity, but they're dead, and she's living,' said one critic. 'A highly entertaining reflection on the nature of dreams and dreaming, and the way we project our thoughts onto objects,' said another. 'Tilda ... enacts a little death ... and offers a sobering imitation of morality,' enthused a third.

And by the end of the week, 20,000 people had visited it, and most of them seem to have enjoyed it.

From *The Independent*

3 🔲 You will hear two people describe their reactions and other visitors' actions and reactions to the actress in the glass case. Which of the ones listed below are mentioned?

- staring at her
- laughing
- taking no notice of her
- feeling embarrassed
- crying
- watching her move and turn over
- watching other people's reactions
- following her round as she turned over
- speaking to her
- taking photos

4 Here are five items from the exhibition. Notice how past participles can follow directly after nouns as reduced relative clauses:

- a stocking *worn* by Queen Victoria (= *which was worn by ...*)
- a pen *used* by Charles Dickens to write 'The Mystery of Edwin Drood' (= *which was used by ...*)
- two pages of original sheet music *composed* by Holst
- the cape *worn* by Doctor Livingstone when he met Stanley
- a bag of salt *carried* to the Antarctic by Scott, found next to his body

Now expand these key words into clauses using suitable past participles:

- remains of a cigar / Winston Churchill
- cheque / the writer, Virginia Woolf to Quentin Bell
- watercolour paint box / the artist, Turner
- part of a plane / the American aviator, Charles Lindbergh
- manuscript / the poet, Wilfred Owen
- cushion / the psychoanalyst, Sigmund Freud

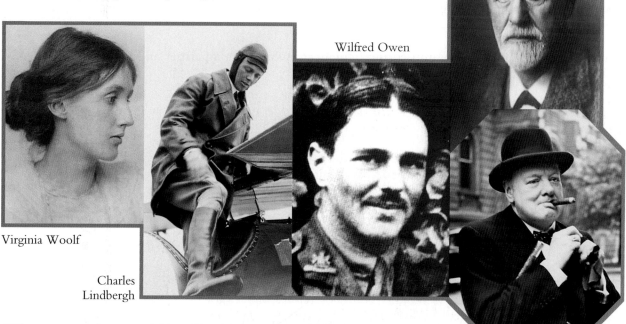

Sigmund Freud

Wilfred Owen

Virginia Woolf

Charles Lindbergh

Winston Churchill

5 Whose possessions would *you* like to see in an exhibition? With a partner make up some more examples using participle clauses after these nouns.

the earring(s) ...	the shirt ...	the letter ...	the manuscript ...
the gun ...	the car ...	the guitar ...	the camera ...
the lipstick ...	the suit ...	the dress ...	

Example: *the suit worn by Nelson Mandela when he was released from prison*

SLEEP AND OTHER PROBLEMS

present perfect simple vs continuous; vocabulary

1 Look at the list of problems in the box and check that you understand them.

jet lag	insomnia	dandruff	hiccups	asthma	sunburn
travel/motion sickness	a hangover	toothache	back pain		
a migraine	mouth ulcers	indigestion	cramp		

Do people cause these problems themselves (are they self-inflicted), or are the problems beyond their personal control? Discuss in small groups, giving reasons for your answers.

2 📻 Listen to people describing their efforts to overcome some of the problems in Exercise 1 and make notes in the box. Then compare with a partner.

	Problem	*How do you know?*
1.	....	....
2.	....	....
3.	....	....
4.	....	....
5.	....	....

3 Complete the tapescript on page 153, selecting the present perfect simple (e.g. *has worked*), or the present perfect continuous (e.g. *has been working*). In some cases, both are possible. Refer to the Language Reference on page 142 where necessary.

4 Organise the words in each box into correct sentences. Work with a partner and see which pair finishes first.

1.
I seeing even have
I sleep specialist
been everything
tried and have a

2.
how been to you
problems have long
having getting sleep?

3.
drinking this she
got weekend has
morning has a
because hangover
she been all

4.
because have
shampoo dandruff
I had for new months
I been medicated
using a have

5.
working airline
miles has for he
ten has of been for
over years the and
millions flown

5 Work with a partner. Choose one of the problems in the box in Exercise 1, and write a short text about it as in the listening exercise. Don't name the problem.

Show or read your text to another pair. Can they guess which problem you chose? Can they suggest any more solutions?

PERSONAL STUDY WORKBOOK

In your Personal Study Workbook, you will find more exercises to help you with your learning. For Unit 2, these include:

• vocabulary exercises on sleep and sickness
• an exercise on the pronunciation and use of different connectors
• an analysis of different tenses, in a text about hiccups
• people talking about nightmares they have had
• writing a letter of advice

Unit 2 SLEEPING IT OFF

REVIEW OF UNIT 1

1 Guess my job   connections and relationships

Work in small groups. One of you should think of an unusual job; the others have to ask yes/no questions to find out what it is. You have a maximum of 20 questions.

Try to include these questions:

- Does it have anything to do with ... (the law)?
- Has it got anything to do with ...
- Is it to do with ...
- Is it related/connected to ... (sport)?
- Does it involve ... (dealing with the public)?
- Do you have to ... (do shiftwork)?

When you have finished, change so that someone else thinks of a job.

2 What does it remind you of?   appearance vocabulary

What can you see in each picture? Work with a partner.

Example: *someone wearing a short-sleeved shirt*

What, if anything, do they remind you of? Discuss with your partner.
(Notice that the *plural* form of the nouns is used below. Why?)

Example: *Short-sleeved shirts remind me of my cousin – he always wears them, even with a suit.*
Freckles remind me of a kid I used to go to school with – she was covered in them.

HOW DO WE BEHAVE?

Language focus
wish and if only + past perfect   expressing thanks and pleasure
so vs such (a)   verbs of social communication,
focusing adverbs   e.g. interrupt, threaten

DON'T JUST SIT THERE – DO SOMETHING!   vocabulary

1 Work with a partner. What is the relationship between the people in the picture, and what is happening? Suggest two or three possibilities, then tell the group your ideas.

2 ▭ Listen to the speakers talking about the picture. Do they make the same suggestions as you did, and do they express them in the same way?

When you have listened, read the tapescript on page 160 and note down any new vocabulary describing the man's behaviour.

3 Match the words and phrases in the box with the definitions below, using a dictionary if necessary.

> threaten   warn   ignore   protect someone or oneself
> stick up for someone or oneself   intervene   interfere   interrupt

1. Stop someone from continuing what they are saying or doing by suddenly speaking to them.
2. Take action in a situation which is not your business, and where your action is not wanted by other people.
3. Say you will do something unpleasant to someone if they do not do what you want.
4. Tell someone about a possible danger or problem so that they are aware of it and can avoid it.
5. Keep yourself/others safe from danger or damage.
6. Support or defend yourself/others against attack or criticism, especially when no one else will do so (informal).
7. Take action in an argument or difficult situation because you want to stop things getting worse.
8. Pay no attention to what someone is saying or doing.

4 Read the three scenes relating to the people in the picture. Do scenes like these often happen on public transport in your country? Discuss in small groups.

Scene 1 (on a quiet train, 10.45 a.m.)

The man enters the train just behind the woman. He stands near her, staring at her as she reads her paper. Then he starts to make conversation. The woman is not interested and tells him to get lost, but as he becomes more insistent, she makes her reluctance and eventually her fear clearer.

Scene 2 (on a fairly busy train, 11.45 a.m.)

The man is standing next to the woman on the train and looks over her shoulder to comment on the story she is reading in her newspaper. He also says he knows her and that he met her at a party. The woman looks nervous and starts to move down the carriage. The man follows her. Each time she moves, he follows.

Scene 3 (an almost empty train, 10.30 p.m.)

The man goes and sits down next to the woman. He starts chatting to her but gets no response. Finally, he asks her for a kiss. Just one kiss, he says, and he'll go away.

From *The Evening Standard*

5 In your groups, discuss these questions about the scenes above. Try to use the vocabulary from Exercise 3.

1. If you were a passenger in the same carriage, would you say or do anything in each of the situations? If so, what?
2. What factors might influence your response in each situation?

6 These scenes were part of an experiment to find out how other passengers on the train would react; and the people in the picture are actors. Turn to page 154, where you can find out how other passengers reacted in the scenes, and why.

In groups, say what *you* think of each of the passengers' reactions and explanations.

1 Discuss these questions in small groups.

1. How often do you or members of your family write or receive the following? Give examples.
2. Which of them do you write because you *have* to, and which do you write because you *want* to?

- thank you letters/cards (for gifts/hospitality, etc.)
- letters of condolence and sympathy
- letters/notes of apology
- greetings cards (birthday, Christmas, religious festivals)
- letters/cards of congratulations
- postcards (from holiday places)
- other social letters

2 Work with a partner and complete the texts in pencil in a logical way. (More than one word can go in each gap.)

1

> 10 Green Lane Farm
> Hucclecote
> Glos GL31 4HU
>
> 10th June
>
> Dear Auntie Carole and Uncle Charles,
> _____ thank you very much for the generous cheque you sent me for my birthday. As you know, I have been hoping to get a car for ages as it would _____ be so much more convenient, and now I'll be able to afford one. When I've bought it I'll come and visit you.
> I hope you're both well and have a lovely holiday in France.
>
> _____
>
> David

2

> Thanks _____ a lovely evening on Saturday. The meal was wonderful and it was great to see you both in _____ good form.
> We _____ enjoyed meeting your crazy neighbours and look _____ seeing you here after we get back from our holidays.
>
> _____
>
> Jan and Terry

3

> *3 Farmington Road, Milton Keynes, Bucks*
>
> April 18th
>
> Dear Dieter,
>
> This is .... to thank you for looking after me .... well last week. I really .... the help you gave me; without it, the trip wouldn't have been .... great success.
>
> It was very kind of you to put me up in your own home and I felt I got to know a bit more about life in a German family. I .... enjoyed the trip to the mountains; we were lucky to have .... beautiful weather.
>
> Professionally, I was .... that we had such fruitful discussions and feel that we can now proceed to the next stage of the project without delay.
>
> Please .... regards to Bettina, and I look forward to seeing you in Milton Keynes in September.
>
> Until then, with kind ....
>
> Marion

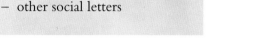 Now listen to the recording of the texts and note down anything different from your own answers.

3 With your partner, discuss these questions about the form and content of the texts.

1. Notice how the letters and card are laid out on the page: the position and form of the address, the greetings, the endings and the names. Are these the same in your language?
2. Look at the way *so* and *such* are used in the letters and card.
   When do we use *so*, *such* and *such a*?
   Why are *so* and *such* very common in these letters?
3. What is the purpose of these adverbs which are used in the letters and card?

just	simply	particularly	especially

What position do they take in the sentence?

4. Look at these phrases which often occur in this type of letter or card. Would you use a direct translation of these in similar letters in your language?

I'm writing to thank you for
Thanks for   } + noun or *-ing*
This is just to thank you for

It was { *great to* / *lovely to* } *(see you)*

We { *particularly* / *really* } { *enjoyed …* / *liked …* / *appreciated …* }

I was { *delighted that …* / *really pleased that …* }

Please give my regards to …
I look forward to …   } + noun or *-ing*

4 Write an appropriate thank you letter/card for one of these situations, using some of the language above.

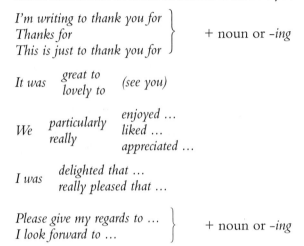

Give your letter to a classmate. What do they think of it?

1 Work with a partner and look at the photos below. Write down two possible embarrassing situations that might arise from each photo.

Example: *In picture 2, the person paying the bill realises they haven't got enough money.*

1

2

Show your ideas to another pair. Which do they think are most/least embarrassing?

2 📼 Listen to Paul talking about the first time he met his girlfriend's parents before he and Sally got married. Answer the questions and then compare with a partner.

1. Where did it take place?
2. How did he feel before he went there?
3. What three things happened which embarrassed Paul?

Listen again and follow the tapescript on page 160 if you like.

3 Look at these statements that Paul might have made about his experience. Correct any errors of meaning or grammar. Then compare with a partner.

1. I wish I had worn more formal clothes.
2. If only I didn't kiss Sally's mother at the station.
3. If only I'd known about Sally's father's past.
4. I wish I hadn't spent the weekend there.
5. If only I would have kept quiet during the meal.
6. I wish I'd been able to thank them for the dinner.

Now complete these rules:

We use *wish* and *if only* + past simple to talk about situations ...
We use *wish* and *if only* + past perfect to talk about situations ...

4 📼 📼 Listen to the speakers on the recording. What embarrassing things happened to them? With your partner, write down two things you think they could have said at the end of their story, using I *wish* ... or *If only* ... .

5 Do you have your own embarrassing story that you are prepared to tell others? Could you tell them about an embarrassing situation you saw? Tell each other in small groups.

REVIEW AND DEVELOPMENT

REVIEW OF UNIT 1

1 Common sounding | pronunciation: homophones and homonyms |

A What do the pairs of sentences have in common?
Read them aloud – what important difference is there?

1. a. She's sitting in the front row, over there.
   b. They had a terrible row and then split up.
2. a. He wound the scarf round his daughter's neck.
   b. It's an old wound I got in the war.
3. a. A tear fell down her cheek, onto her lap.
   b. Be careful – don't tear the book, it's valuable.
4. a. The dog's lead was hanging behind the door.
   b. The church roof is covered with lead.
5. a. Listen to the wind – it's more like a hurricane!
   b. It's an old watch, so I have to wind it every day.

A ROW IN THE FRONT ROW

B Some words have the same pronunciation but a different spelling.

Example: *That film was a terrible **waste** of time.*   /weɪst/
         *My **waist** is getting bigger and bigger.*   /weɪst/

CO Listen to the recording and complete the sentences with the words you hear.

1. I think she's suffering from ....
2. She .... it, but another came along quickly.
3. They sat quietly in ...., waiting for the doctor.
4. The .... has gone up enormously on this route.
5. He went out to buy a bag of ....
6. I sat down, feeling rather ....
7. I was never .... to do that.
8. It's .... we want, nothing else.

For each word, think of another way to spell it. What is the meaning now?

2 Beat the clock | speaking |

With a partner make a list of five pairs of things that are similar but different.

Examples: *crisps and peanuts   a computer and a typewriter   having a bath and having a shower*

Now work with two other learners. Tell them one of your pairs, and then give them 20 seconds to produce a satisfactory description of the similarity and difference.

Examples: *crisps and peanuts   Both of them are crunchy, come in packets and you eat them before or between meals, but crisps are made of potatoes and peanuts are nuts!*

REVIEW OF UNIT 2

1 Where do you suffer? | ailments and body problems

Read the items in the box and decide which parts of the body are most affected by the ailments. (Some words are from Unit 2, others are new, so use your dictionary if necessary.)

sunburn	asthma	a hangover	a cough	a migraine	ulcers
constipation	eczema	cold sores	hiccups	cramp	dandruff
indigestion	hay fever	jet lag	catarrh	blisters	

Work with a partner. Choose three of the ailments or problems and write some useful advice for sufferers, using the phrases below.

You should keep (well) away from (smoky places).
You should give up (spicy food).
It's best to avoid (alcohol).
One of the best things for it is (fresh air and exercise).
Whenever I get (X), I usually (use a cream).

Give your advice to another pair. Can they guess the ailment?

2 Recent evidence | present perfect + present perfect continuous

Look at the picture and make eight sentences using the present perfect or present perfect continuous. (Read the Language Reference on page 142 if necessary.)

Compare with a partner.

GETTING YOUR MESSAGE ACROSS

Language focus
modals of past deduction (*must've,* | idioms: communication problems
could've, might've + past participle) | character adjectives
phrasal verbs and idioms | functional language

WHAT ON EARTH DO YOU MEAN?
idioms: communication problems; past deduction

1 These sentences are all related to problems of communication. With your partner, put each one under the correct heading below.
Use a dictionary if necessary.

He must have misunderstood.
He didn't know anything about it.
He couldn't catch what she said.
He just couldn't grasp what she was saying.
He misinterpreted it.
What he said was very misleading.
He had to tell her to speak up.
He was completely incomprehensible.
He hadn't (got) a clue.
He was incoherent.
He must have got the wrong end of the stick.
He hadn't the faintest idea.
He was unintelligible.
He must have misheard the name.

He didn't understand correctly:

He must have misunderstood.

He didn't know:

He didn't know anything about it.

He didn't hear properly:

He wasn't able to communicate clearly:

Check your answers with the teacher. Make sure that you can pronounce the phrases correctly.

2 Choose at least six of the sentences and continue them, using *because, so, and* or *but.*

Examples: *He must have misunderstood because everyone burst out laughing.*
He didn't know anything about it, so he had to go to the library to do a bit of research.

3   In Exercise 1 several sentences use the construction *must have* (*must've*) + past participle.

Compare the examples below. How are they different in meaning, and why do you think *must have* + past participle would be common in the context of communication problems?

He must have misunderstood it.
He misunderstood it.
He can't have misunderstood it.
He could/might have misunderstood it.

4   With your partner, make deductions about what has happened: one firm deduction (*must've/can't've*) and one possible one (*could've/might've*) for each picture.

5   ▭▭ ▭▭ Listen to people talking about breakdowns in communication and answer these questions.

1. Where were each of the speakers and what was the situation?
2. Which people, apart from the speaker, were involved in the communication problems?
3. What was the breakdown?
4. How do you think each speaker felt or might have felt at the end?

Listen again and follow the tapescript on page 161.

6   Do you have your own story of a misunderstanding? Prepare it in your head, using a dictionary if necessary. Tell your stories in small groups.

Tell the class the funniest or most interesting story from your group. Do any of the phrases in Exercise 1 describe what happened?

1   Read the definitions.

> **unrequited** /ˌʌnrɪˈkwaɪtɪd/ *adj* **unrequited love**
> romantic love that you feel for someone,
> but that they do not feel for you
>
> *Longman Dictionary of*
> *Contemporary English*

> **unrequited** /ˌʌnrɪˈkwaɪtɪd/ *adj fml or*
> *humorous* (of love) not returned
>
> *Cambridge International*
> *Dictionary of English*

Can you think of two or three examples of unrequited love from films, books, plays, operas or television?

Example: *In* Fatal Attraction, *the character played by Glenn Close tries to kill the character played by Michael Douglas because her love for him is unrequited.*

Tell each other your ideas in small groups.

2   You are going to read an extract from a book about a couple who opened a language school for foreign students in London in the 1960s. One of their early students fell in love with his teacher. Read the letter he wrote to her and answer the questions.

1. What message is he trying to convey?
2. How does he express it?
3. What is your reaction?

> *Lady of my Heart,*
> *Know you why my eyes meet never yours in class? Is because I feel if they meet I will burst with electric explosion of my emotions. Lady, I walk through London and think of you only. The noise, the cars, the persons I not observe. One time a car almost me run over because I thought of you.*
> *Loved lady, concede me your number of telephone. We meet one evening when nobody is there. You are the most beautiful sun that never came through London's clouds. I will fold you in my strongness, I can insure you.*
> *Yours faithfully,*
> *F*

Discuss with a partner. If you like, you could correct or improve the letter together.

3 Now read the whole text to find out more about **F** – his appearance, his past experiences and his relationship with his teacher, Brita, after writing the letter.

Shut your book, and tell a partner everything you can remember about these things.

> F, a student in our school at about this time, was doing a postgraduate course at London University. He was small, with a tuft of wild, black hair, and eyes that would suddenly turn away from the person he was speaking to and gaze intently into space. Although he was voluble and childlike, he was very probably in his early thirties. When in the mood, he told fantastic stories about his experiences: how a plane in which he was travelling had crashed into the jungle, and he had escaped from natives armed with blow-pipes; how when a boy, he had been in the upper part of a skyscraper that had collapsed, and had been projected through the window into the bedroom of a building opposite where a man was strangling his wife. As he related these aerodynamic happenings, his hand and body moved as if he were soaring through the air, 300 feet from the ground.
>
> Among other things, he fell passionately in love with Brita, in whose class he was. Instead of compositions, he wrote her notes, slipping them into her *Essential English Book 1* at the end of lessons.
>
> Brita did her best to ignore his passion, but it was a little difficult. He began to put small boxes of chocolates and packets of cigarettes into her locker and coat pocket. Her attempts to give them back led to complications. F didn't carry a briefcase into which they might be slipped, and it was impossible to return them to him in the school as this would have resulted in the kind of public ping pong match which always takes place on these occasions.
>
> Brita: What shall we do with them?
> Brita's husband: Send them back by post.
> Brita: But that will hurt him!
> Brita's husband: That's the risk he's taken.
>
> So we dispatched a brown paper parcel to his lodgings near London University. Inside, there were seven boxes of Black Magic chocolates, and five packets of Du Maurier cigarettes, accompanied by a little note from Brita saying she could not accept them.
>
> F did not come to school for a couple of days but, thereafter, he transferred his attentions to Maria, another student in the same class. To our amusement, we noticed that she was soon smoking Du Maurier cigarettes and handing round Black Magic chocolates. Both of them seemed very happy.

From *Babel in London* by John Haycraft

4 Work with a partner. Match the adjectives describing character with the definitions.

> a. prone to exaggeration   b. deceitful   c. sensitive   d. hypocritical
> e. unpredictable   f. sincere   g. naive   h. fickle

> 1. someone who keeps changing their mind about people or things (negative)
> 2. someone who wants others to think they have better morals than they have; they say one thing and do another (negative)
> 3. a tendency to say things are better, worse or more important than they really are
> 4. when you trust people too much and believe what they say as a result of your innocence and lack of experience (negative)
> 5. someone who is honest and really believes what he/she says (positive)
> 6. someone who behaves dishonestly and tries to keep the truth hidden (negative)
> 7. someone who changes their behaviour so that you never know what they are going to do
> 8. someone who shows understanding towards other people's feelings or problems *or* someone who gets upset or hurt easily.

Now with a partner, write your own definition of these words.

> generous   unreliable   violent   passionate   sensible   kind

5 From your understanding of the text, which of the words in the boxes might you use to describe F, Brita and the characters in the film, books, etc. you discussed in Exercise 1.

Are there other adjectives you need? Use a dictionary to help you.

Discuss your answers in small groups; you may have different opinions.

1 Discuss in small groups.

1. What are the advantages and disadvantages of owning an answerphone?
2. What are the advantages and disadvantages of leaving messages on other people's answerphones?

2 🔲 Listen to the answerphone messages Sally received when she got home one evening and complete the sentences.

Alice rang. She apologised for ....

....

and would like to ....

Please ring ....

Phone number: ....

The Waterfront

Good meals in a friendly atmosphere
Telephone:
01888 334 5678

Derek rang to check ....

At the moment he is ....

He wants Sally to ....

Phone number: ....

Patience rang to say that ....

....

She wants Sally to ....

at ....

Phone number: ....

*John and Lucy Robins
invite you to the wedding of their daughter
Patience to Jonathan Briant
on
June 24th at 2.00
at St Swithins Church,
Sharpeton*   *RSVP*

Martin Bellingham rang. He is going to help Paula to ....

....

He can't ....but he'll come

....

He needs more information about ....

....

Phone number: ....

Compare with a partner.

3 📖 Look at the sentences and see if you can remember which of them were on the answerphone messages. Then listen to the recording and tick the ones you hear.

I won't be able to make it.
Hope you can make it.
I'm sorry to let you down.
I'm sorry I let you down.
I'm so sorry for not turning up.
Will you be in?
We've split up.
Could you pop round later?
Listen, I'd better go now.
The wedding is off.
The wedding's been called off.
I don't want to get stuck in the traffic.
I want to double-check everything is OK.
Thanks for ringing me back.
Thanks for ringing this morning.
Speak to you soon.

4 Work with a partner. You are going to act out the return calls Sally makes to the people on the recording. One of you should look at the cards below while your partner looks at the ones on page 154.

Before you begin each conversation, take a minute to think whether you can use or adapt any of the phrases in Exercise 3.

Role Cards Partner A

Situation 1
You are Sally, returning Alice's call. You've forgiven Sally for letting you down, but Sunday is a problem (think of a reason). You are prepared to go on another day if it's a restaurant near your home.

Situation 2
You are Derek, receiving Sally's return call. Sally is rather unreliable. She's let you down before so you're hoping it won't happen again.

Situation 3
You are Sally, returning Patience's call. Patience is your oldest friend and this isn't the first time she and Jonathan have split up. Be reassuring and understanding, but try to keep it brief – you have another important call to make.

Situation 4
You are Martin Bellingham, receiving Sally's return call. It's 11.00 and you were already in bed asleep and are not pleased to be woken up. You can't find a pen or piece of paper.

Tell the class how you resolved one of the situations.

PERSONAL STUDY WORKBOOK

In your Personal Study Workbook, you will find more exercises to help you with your learning. For Unit 4, these include:

- exercises on phrasal verbs, idioms and character adjectives
- listening to angry answerphone messages
- writing 'tactful' messages
- reading a poem
- doing another speaking partners activity

REVIEW OF UNIT 2

1 Wide awake and fast asleep | sleep vocabulary: collocation |

Look at the collocations. In each case, one of the words does not collocate. Which?

Example: *to be* –
  awake
  asleep
  half asleep
  sleepy
  ~~*sleep*~~

1. to have –
   a nap
   a good/bad night's sleep
   tiredness
   nightmares
   a day off

2. to set –
   the alarm
   your watch
   something on fire
   the TV
   the video

3. to suffer from –
   jet lag
   a cough
   travel sickness
   insomnia
   nightmares

4. to feel –
   sleepy
   drowsy
   asleep
   exhausted
   sluggish

5. to lie –
   down
   still
   on your back
   awake
   out

2 Sleeping people | speaking |

Noon by Vincent Van Gogh

Travellers by Eduard Ole

My Second Sermon by John Everett Millais

Choose one of the paintings, which you are going to speak about for two minutes. Prepare your ideas, using a dictionary or your teacher to check any new words. You can follow the framework below if you wish:

– a general description of what is happening in the picture
– any interesting details that strike you
– what you think the person is like, or what they may be feeling
– what happened before, and what may happen after
– your reaction to the picture

Find one or two learners who chose different paintings. Speak for two minutes about your picture, then let the other learner(s) ask you questions or comment on the picture themselves.

If you like, you could write about the picture and give the text to your teacher or other learners to read.

REVIEW OF UNIT 3

1 Thanks for the lovely lamp | speaking: expressing thanks and pleasure; *so* and *such*

With a partner, choose a picture of a gift and a relationship from the box.

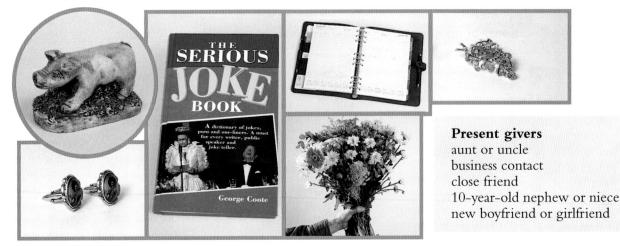

Present givers
aunt or uncle
business contact
close friend
10-year-old nephew or niece
new boyfriend or girlfriend

Now use the role cards below. Do the role play, sitting back to back so you can't see each other's faces.

> A: You are the present giver. The other day, you sent B the gift you chose. B is going to phone you.

> B: A sent you a gift (the one you decided on at the beginning). Telephone A to thank them, and remember to use *so* and *such* to show how enthusiastic you are. Then invite them to do something suitable (example: go out together).

You could record your conversation and listen to it afterwards. Does it sound natural? Could it be improved?

2 I did it my way | *wish* + past perfect

Look at these famous people and the sentences about them.

Bob Dole probably wishes he had won the US Presidency in 1996.

Lisa Marie Presley probably wishes she had never married Michael Jackson.

The athlete, Ben Johnson, probably wishes he had never taken drugs before the Olympics.

With a partner, think of three or more famous people, perhaps from your country. Write a sentence for each, saying what they probably regret, as in the examples.

5

BUILDINGS

Language focus

plural nouns, compounds
adjectives as nouns
present perfect review
compound adjectives

collective nouns, uncountable nouns
past perfect simple/continuous
building vocabulary

NOUNS ARE BUILDING BLOCKS

noun groups; building vocabulary

1 Look at the words in the box. What do they mean, and why do they all end in 's'? Work with a partner and use a dictionary to help you.

premises   outskirts   surroundings   facilities   refreshments   headquarters

[ ] Now listen to the recording and write down the sentences.
Check with your partner.

2 Here are some more questions about particular types of noun. Answer them in small groups.

COUNTABLE AND UNCOUNTABLE NOUNS

Correct any errors in these sentences. (Not every sentence has an error.)

1 We have many forms of transports in our city.

2 The traffic are very bad in most big cities.

3 I had a lot of troubles getting from the airport.

4 The council is making good progress with the school development project.

5 The atmosphere in the village was great, especially the nightlife, and the accommodations we were given were excellent.

COLLECTIVE NOUNS

These nouns describe a group of people. They can take a singular or plural verb.

What do you call ...
a group of people who control a country and make its laws?

the government

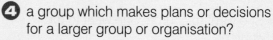

1 all the people who work in one organisation?

2 a group of people who decide in a court if someone is guilty or innocent?

3 all the people who attend a concert or play?

4 a group which makes plans or decisions for a larger group or organisation?

5 the group who are elected to govern a local area?

6 all the ordinary people in a country who are not in the government or acting in an official role?

COMPOUND NOUNS

Complete the sentences with the correct compound noun.

Example: Our factory is situated on an industrial *estate* .

1 Many young people prefer to stay in a *youth* .... because it's very cheap.

2 You aren't allowed to drive in a *pedestrian* ....

3 I need to go to the toilet – is there a *public* .... near here?

4 I left my umbrella on the bus and had to collect it from the .... *office*.

5 You can buy or rent a flat through an *estate* ....

6 There is a *taxi* .... outside the railway station.

7 We met outside the *law* ....

8 We always go to the indoor *shopping* .... when it's raining.

PLACES AND ARTICLES

What's the difference between ...?

1 He's gone to prison./He's gone to the prison.

2 She went to church./She went to the church.

3 She's going into hospital./She's going into the hospital.

4 He's gone to university./He's gone to the university.

5 I met him at school./I met him at the school.

There is a limited number of these expressions.

ADJECTIVES AS NOUNS

Certain adjectives can be used with a definite article to describe groups of people, often in a similar social or physical condition (e.g. *the rich*, *the poor*, etc.).

Example The government should do more for *people without much money.*
The government should do more for *the poor* .

Do the same with the sentences below, using a suitable adjective as a noun. Don't forget the definite article *the*.

1 The theatre has good access for *people in wheelchairs*.

2 We need more resources to help *people without jobs*.

3 The *people who were hurt in the accident* were taken to the casualty department.

4 *People with a lot of money* do not suffer so much in times of recession.

5 *People over 65* automatically get free public transport in my town.

6 Pavements in bad condition are very dangerous for *people who can't see*.

What's your score out of 30? Give one mark for each correct answer, and in the first exercise one mark for each correct sentence. Which group has the highest score?

3 Form new groups to practise the new vocabulary. Do the questions in any order.

1. Discuss the following in your home town:
   the atmosphere   public transport   tourist accommodation
   the nightlife   your local council/government

2. Do you have these in your town? If so, where are they, and what do you think of them?
   a hospital with a casualty department   an indoor shopping centre/mall   a youth hostel
   public lavatories   law courts   a prison   a university   a pedestrian precinct   taxi ranks

3. What are the facilities in your town for:
   the disabled?   the elderly?
   the blind?   the unemployed?

4. How is life different in your town in the centre and on the outskirts?

5. Do you feel financial resources for public services in your town are well spent?

NO PLACE LIKE HOME
past perfect simple and continuous; present perfect revision

1 People often buy unusual old public buildings which they convert and renovate to live in. Would you like to live in any of these? Why/why not? Discuss in small groups.

> a railway station   a public lavatory/loo★   a stable
> a police station   a railway carriage   a mill

★ loo is an informal word in British English for *toilet*; *lavatory* is a more formal word.

2 The man in the picture bought and converted an old ladies' lavatory to live in. Before reading the text, find these things in the photos:

> bricks   tiles   mock-Tudor design   a roof   a skylight

Now read the text and tell your partner if you would like to live there, saying why.

There's no place like home

Frank Webb is converting a former ladies' lavatory in Kew, south-west London, into a one-bedroom house.

As soon as I heard a ladies' loo was being advertised in a local paper, I wanted it. I've had to put up with endless jokes about spending a penny*, but I knew that I could make the building into a beautiful home. It might seem rather odd to want to live in a place which was once a lavatory, but there's something wonderful in knowing that thousands of people have used the building over the years.

I was divorced several years ago, and I had been looking for a place for myself, somewhere fairly small, but unique in some way. The loo was suggested to me by the wife of a friend. I think she was joking, but it was exactly what I'd been searching for.

Since I bought the lavatory, several ladies have turned up at the door, wanting to use it. I let them use my own bathroom. After all, there are still Doulton tiles on the outside wall saying 'Ladies' Lavatory'.

When I first stepped into the building it had been out of use for many years, but was completely intact. All the toilets, cubicles and washbasins were still there, in working order.

It was built by the council in 1905 for visitors to the fairground that used to be nearby, and for ferry passengers who had travelled down the Thames. It's a tremendously solid brick building and surprisingly warm in winter. I haven't had to do any work on the walls or roof, and there is even an attractive mock-Tudor frontage. I had to take down the cubicle partitions which were made of solid slate. A lot of graffiti had been scrawled over them in the course of its history as a public lavatory. I have taken photographs of everything, so I can show people what it was like.

One of the things I like best about the building is the light which streams in through the skylights and windows. I got rid of the rather institutional fluorescent bulbs and I'm making use of natural light as far as possible, replacing the old, frosted glass with more modern, opaque glass.

When I started the renovation work, I discovered a little safe in the wall, where an attendant had put a piece of paste jewellery and a note saying that it was lost property. I like the thought that my home has a history shared with all these other people.

From *The Daily Mail Weekend*

* *to spend a penny* is an old-fashioned expression used in British English meaning *to go to the toilet*, because it used to cost a penny to use a public lavatory.

3 Some of the information in the text has been organised chronologically in the diagram below. With your partner, find two mistakes in the diagram and correct them.

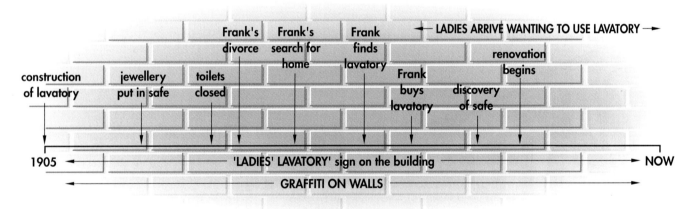

4 Without looking back at the text, complete these sentences using a suitable tense.

Example: *He wanted to buy the lavatory as soon as* ...*he saw it was being advertised.*

1. Before he bought the property, he ...... for quite a long time.
2. When he first saw the property, it ...... as a toilet for many years.
3. Since he moved in, several ladies ...
4. It was partly built for ferry passengers who ...... the Thames.
5. He had to remove a lot of graffiti which ...... since it was built.
6. When he opened the safe, he discovered that an ...

At least four of your answers should include the past perfect simple (*had* + past participle) or continuous (*had been* + present participle). Why? Discuss with a partner, then compare with the Language Reference on page 144.

5 Work with a partner. Choose one of the buildings in Exercise 1 (or one of your own) and imagine that you had bought and converted it to live in. Work out:

 - what had happened to make you want to move
 - where and when you found your property
 - how long you had been looking for somewhere to live
 - what attracted you to it
 - what you have done to it since moving in
 - something you have recently discovered about the history of the property

Find a new partner to interview you about your property, using the guidelines above. Of the two buildings you and your new partner have chosen, which is the most interesting?

DESIGN YOUR OWN SCHOOL

1 You are going to design your own language school. First you must choose the premises. Which of the two pictures would you choose, and why? Discuss with a partner.

Amora House

Dado Court

2 With your partner, create compound adjectives on the topic of buildings or districts starting with the words below.

Example: *centrally-**heated***

air-...   old-...

self-...   brand-...

semi-...   run-...

built-...   well-...

Use a dictionary to help you and check your answers with your teacher.

3 ⬚⬚ ⬚⬚ You're going to hear an estate agent describing the two properties. Look at the table below and put a tick (✓) if the statements are true about the properties, a cross (✗) if they are not true and a question mark (?) if they are not discussed.

	Amora House	Dado Court
– is in a built-up area		
– is in a residential area		
– shares the building with other companies		
– is centrally-heated		
– is air-conditioned		
– is in good condition		
– is near a bus stop		
– has snack bars nearby		
– has a lift		

Compare with your partner.

Did you hear any other information that would influence your choice of building? Which one would you choose now? Discuss with your partner.

4 Form committees of three or four people who have chosen the same property.

You are now going to decide how to use the space in the building for your language school. The plan (identical for both Amora House and Dado Court) shows you the state of the building at the moment. Read the information in the box, then plan your school.

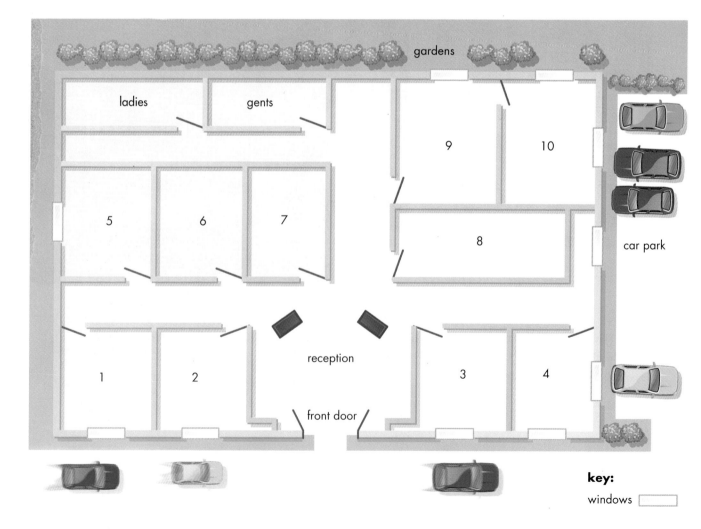

Unit 5 BUILDINGS

Choose from the following facilities:

classrooms	a snack bar
a lecture room	a library
a student common room	a study centre with computers
a staffroom (including teaching resources and equipment)	a language laboratory

Information:
1. To be financially viable, you must have a minimum of six classrooms.
2. The administration is situated in a separate area. You do not need to worry about this.
3. The reception area and toilets are fixed and cannot be moved.
4. You can remove a maximum of two partition walls between rooms or between a room and a corridor to make a larger area for some of your facilities.
5. You may wish to combine certain facilities within one room, but remember that this will restrict the space for each facility.
6. Your plan must include the *exact location* of everything.

5 Prepare a clear copy of your design, and present it to other groups. They may ask you questions or challenge you on your ideas. Be prepared to justify your decisions.

PERSONAL STUDY WORKBOOK

In your Personal Study Workbook, you will find more exercises to help you with your learning. For Unit 5, these include:

- a spiral word game on different vocabulary
- an exercise on plural nouns and uncountable nouns
- distinguishing between words that are similar in meaning
- a text and accompanying task to practise narrative tenses
- listening to the advantages and disadvantages of living in a ladies' lavatory

---

REVIEW AND DEVELOPMENT

REVIEW OF UNIT 3

1 I'm absolutely furious | speaking |

Read the letter from a problem page in a newspaper. As you read, underline anything which would be strange or unusual in your country or your home.

Dear Virginia,

Last month, an old friend of my husband's came to stay for the weekend with his wife, who we'd never met before. They were perfectly pleasant and brought a box of mints as a house present. I organised a party of 10 people, including another old school friend of my husband's I'd never met, who wrote to thank me for a wonderful evening.

I was quite exhausted by Monday morning and so was my husband, and the couple thanked us before they left.

I have heard nothing from them since and I'm absolutely furious. My husband says they are just casual people; they said thank you, after all, and not to get in a fuss. But I feel that if they can't be bothered to write a postcard of thanks at the very least,

I never want to see them again. I went to such a huge effort. We literally poured food and drink, including champagne, down their throats, and spent every waking moment driving them round to see places of interest. I feel completely unappreciated. Am I just being old-fashioned?

Yours sincerely,

Althea

From *The Independent*

Discuss in groups whether or not you sympathise with Althea, and why.

---

2 Regrets ... I've had a few ... | wish + different forms |

Complete the first column about yourself in the table below.

	You	DeNica
1. something you don't know how to do, which would be useful (example: make electrical repairs)		
2. something you haven't got and would like to have (example: a sailing boat)		
3. a quality or characteristic you haven't got (example: ambition; tolerance)		
4. something other people do that annoys you (example: making a noise late at night; interrupting you when you are busy)		
5. something you did that you regret (example: being unkind to your sister when you were young)		
6. an opportunity in your life that you missed (example: going to live abroad after leaving school)		

▢ Listen to DeNica on the recording. Write down the exact words she uses.

Notice in 4 how she uses *wish + would*. This is a common construction to express annoyance when someone or something continues to do something or won't do something.

Examples: *I wish David would come round and see us more.*
I wish it would stop raining.

Work with a partner. Tell them your wishes, using similar structures to DeNica.

REVIEW OF UNIT 4

Sorry? | asking for repetition or clarification; intonation |

A When you are talking to someone and you don't hear or understand them, what questions can you ask, or what can you say? With a partner, make a list of at least ten.

Examples: *Could you say that again?*
Sorry, I didn't hear what you said.

Tell your sentences to the rest of the class, and say which you think are more polite.

B ▢ Listen to the recording. Write down any ways of asking for clarification or repetition that you hadn't thought of.

C ▢ Listen again. At least three of the requests sound impatient or angry. Which ones?

Practise all the requests with a partner without sounding angry or impatient!

PROJECT: WRITING BIOGRAPHIES

1 In this project, you are going to find out about another learner and write a profile of them in about 200 words for everyone else to read. First find a partner to work with on this project.

2 Look through this list of possible contents for your biography. Which words in the list mean *important*?

> *Possible contents of your biography*
> name
> profession
> marital status
> current living arrangements
> crucial events in your life
> key influences in your life (childhood and adult)
> your major achievements
> regrets or frustrations in your life
> unfulfilled ambitions
> your main hopes/goals for the future
> leisure activities
> your attitudes to your family, relationships, work or other issues
> how other people see you

> ....
> ....
> ....
> ....

Together, add any other possible topics to the list.

3 Decide which of the topics (about five or six) you would be prepared to talk about, or would like someone to write about you.

Now tell your partner about the topics you have chosen. They should listen and write brief notes, like this:

> Mariko
> marital status: married to American, Dan (met travelling)
>   two children Masako (5), Elliot (3)
> achievements: passing university exams when pregnant
>   winning regional painting competition

4 With your partner, look at the beginnings of several different profiles. Which one(s) do you prefer and why?

If I had to choose one thing that really interested me about Hervé, it would be his childhood. I was amazed to discover that although he has nine brothers and sisters, he has only ever met six of them, because ...

Carlos was born in 1972. He went to school at the age of six, and was able to read by the age of seven ...

I have to admit I am really very envious of Tomiko: she has fulfilled her main ambition by travelling to every continent in the world ...

Marina is 21. She comes from a small village in the mountains called Spak. She lives with her brothers and aunt because her mother is a famous actress who ...

'My work is my life.' These were the words Johann used to sum up his attitude to his very absorbing and exciting job in designing ...

With your partner's help, write the opening sentence of the profile you are going to write about him/her.

5 Look at the extract from a profile and decide whether it is correctly written. What changes and corrections would you make? Work together.

> *... exam again, which it was a quite frustrating experience for her. However, she carried on studying by her own and finally she succeeded to pass her accountancy exams. She got a work very well-paid in a large firm where she still works now. She advised that she was very lucky because when she started there she was a junior staff, but several people have left their works and she got promotion very quickly ...*

6 Write your partner's biography. When you have finished it, show it to your partner. See if they agree with what you have written, and if they can suggest any improvements. Then give it to your teacher to correct.

You could display all the biographies on a wall for everyone to read, or perhaps make a group magazine for everyone including photos of all of you.

6

TRAVELLING CAN BE HARD WORK

> **Language focus**
> emphasising structures   making/changing arrangements
> (e.g. *the thing that annoys me is ...*)   present continuous and future continuous
> different uses of *would*   phrasal verbs and idioms

SEAT HOG!   ways of emphasising

1 You are going to listen to some people talking about the annoying behaviour of other passengers on long train and coach journeys. What do you think they might mention? Discuss in small groups.

2 🔲 🔳 Now listen to the recording. Make notes in the box, then compare with a partner.

	things they find annoying	*reason (if given)*
Speaker 1		
Speaker 2		
Speaker 3		
Speaker 4		

3 When we want to emphasise particular ideas and opinions, we can use a variety of structures. Here are two which are common in both spoken and written English.

I find it really irritating	when (people keep correcting me)
It annoys me	if (people leave the lights on)

🔲 On the recording, the speakers used other ways of emphasising their ideas, and these are particularly common in *spoken* English. Listen to the recording you chose again, and tick the sentence beginnings that you hear. Do you hear the words in brackets or not?

Sentence beginnings:
The thing that (really) annoys me is   people (doing) ...
The thing that (really) gets★ (to) me is   people who ...
What (really) annoys me is when ...
The thing (that) I find (most) irritating is ...

★makes me angry (informal)

Practise in pairs, completing the sentences with your own ideas about travelling.

4 Work in small groups. Use the structures in Exercise 3 to discuss what annoys you in the following situations, and give your reasons:

in your workplace   on the beach   in a restaurant   at the cinema

5 In your country, is it common for people to do the following on trains and coaches, and what is your opinion of these things? Discuss in groups.

- start up a conversation with strangers
- take their own food to eat on the journey
- hand their food round to other passengers
- take their shoes off
- tip people who may serve them
- lie down across the seats
- give up their seat to someone else (e.g. the young or the elderly)
- listen to personal stereos
- play cards/games
- take animals with them

I'LL BE ARRIVING AT ELEVEN
making and changing future arrangements

1 Read the texts. In each one, find at least three features (layout and/or language) which identify the style as formal or informal.

Margot,
Just a quick note to say that I'll be arriving at JFK on the 24th at 11.00 p.m.
Sorry it's so late, but as I'm meeting Bob and Jean in the afternoon,
I can't get a flight till 7.30. Still, I hope you'll be able to meet me,
because I've got a lot of stuff. If you're not there, don't worry, I'll get
a taxi.
Love, Derek

MERSON ELECTRONICS

Cavendish House Worple Way Bristol BS1 7QX

Tel: (01272) 691132   Fax: (01272) 691133

Pansing International
100 Industrial Rd
Singapore 1953

10 June

Dear Mr Lea

I am writing to confirm the arrangements for Dr Robinson's visit to your factory next month.

She will be arriving at Changi Airport on flight BA 873 at 15.00 on 8 July. I would be grateful if you could arrange for a car to meet her at the airport and take her to the Raffles Hotel where she will be staying for the first part of her trip. After that, she moves on to visit KJP Trading, and they will be responsible for her arrangements from then onwards.

She is due to meet your MD the day after her arrival, but she will also need two further days to talk to other members of staff and become acquainted with factory procedures.

I understand that she will also be attending a formal company dinner on 9 July, and she has asked me to inform you that she is a strict vegetarian.

Should you require any further information, please do not hesitate to contact me.

Yours sincerely

Jackson Lomax

Jackson Lomax

2   Read the text in the box, then do the exercise below.

> In the texts, both the present continuous and the future continuous (*will be* + *-ing*) are used to talk about an event arranged/scheduled for the future. In this use, they are often interchangeable, but speakers sometimes prefer the future continuous when they are giving important information to the listener, which may affect or involve them and which they may need to act upon.

Complete the sentences showing how the listener may be affected and what action they should take. Then compare your answers with a partner.

Example: *We'll be leaving at 7.00, so*   make sure you're here by 6.45.

I'll be wearing my best suit, so …

I'll be seeing John tomorrow, so …

We'll be staying at a hotel near you, so …

The coach will be leaving in a few minutes, so …

Mary will be paying for the meal, so …

3   ▭ You will hear Derek phoning Margot and Jackson Lomax phoning Mr Lea. They are discussing changes made in the arrangements since the fax and letter were sent. Write down the changes and the reasons.

4   With your partner, write a letter to Mr Lea confirming the new travel arrangements based on the phone conversation. Use the letter in Exercise 1 to help you, and add one more piece of new information to your letter.

Then show your letter to another pair. Do they think it is accurate and written in an appropriate style?

1 A 'tour rep' (representative) is someone who works for a travel company looking after tourists in a holiday resort. What kind of duties do they have?

2 Look at the phrasal verbs and idioms and decide how a tour rep might use them when talking about their job and possible problems. Use a dictionary if necessary.

to give up (doing) something
to calm someone down
to pick someone up
to see someone off
to throw someone out
  (of somewhere)
to get/be out of control
to sort something out
to show someone round
to get/have time off
to tell someone off
  (for doing something)
	Examples: to give up (doing) something
	Perhaps tour reps give up the job because it's
	* hard work.*
	to calm someone down
	Tour reps may have to calm travellers down
	* when they are angry or upset, if their flight is*
	* delayed, for instance.*

Tell your ideas to the rest of the group.

3 Read about the tour rep and see if your ideas in Exercise 1 are in the text.

1 My first day as a tour rep was a nightmare. I was 22 when I applied for a job as a tour rep. I was sent on an introductory 14-day training course in Majorca, but you don't really find out what the job is about until you are
5 actually up to your neck in it.
My very first day on the job I had a terrible experience. I was having a drink at about 2 am thinking, 'Thank goodness the first day is over', when someone arrived and told me that the hotel was trying to throw one of the
10 guests out because he had hit his wife over the head with a shoe and split her head open. I tried to mediate in French with the hotelier, but all he said was, 'I don't want him here; get the police.' So I called the police, but they **wouldn't** take him without identification.
15 Eventually I found his passport in his room among 20 bottles of whisky, and then the next day, I had to get him released because his wife **wouldn't** press charges. It was a nightmare.
They had warned us during the training course that
20 things **wouldn't** be easy, but I wasn't expecting problems quite so soon. During my last season, a forest fire came down the mountain during the night and surrounded the hotel. In another resort, things sometimes got a bit out of control. I **would** get hooligans throwing
25 furniture out of the window, refusing to leave the hotel. It was my job to tell them off for behaving like that.

Although every day was different, I **would** usually go to the airport each day to pick up new arrivals or see people off. The planes **would** arrive at any time, 3 am
30 or whatever, and **I'd** have to meet the guests and welcome them. In the mornings **I'd** visit the guests in their hotels, sort out their problems, then during the afternoon, go off on a tour, show people round, and finish off with a cabaret, karaoke night or welcoming dinner in the
35 evening. I was supposed to get one day off a week, but that didn't always happen.
If you're selling holidays, in many ways you're selling a dream, and people do get disappointed and can end up screaming at the reps. Usually they start by complaining
40 about everything – the beach, the bar, etc. I **would** try to calm them down, and most people were fairly reasonable in the end.
A lot of reps give up after one season; there are very few who carry on for years, but I enjoyed my three
45 years. On my first trip to Corsica, I met a waiter, and in my last summer, I married him. The staff **wouldn't** give me any time off, so I had to marry him on my day off. But the guests were very nice and gave us presents and said they'**d** come and visit us in England. Overall, I've
50 no regrets, and I **would** certainly do it again if I had the chance, and I **would** recommend others of an adventurous spirit to do the same.

From *The Independent on Sunday*

4 Think about being a tour rep yourself. What aspects of the job would *not* appeal to you? Are there other positive aspects (not mentioned) which *would* appeal to you? Discuss in small groups.

Example: *I would hate dealing with tourists who were drunk.*

5 Look at the examples of *would* ('*d*) and *wouldn't* in the text. With a partner, match the examples with these meanings.

1. = used with *if* in conditional sentences referring to imaginary or improbable situations
Example: *I would be annoyed if you did that.*

2. = *used to do* for repeated or habitual actions in the past★
Example: *When we were younger, we would always get home by 7.00.*

3. in the negative form = *refused to / was unwilling to*
Example: *I asked her nicely, but she still wouldn't help me.*

4. = past tense of *will* in reported speech
Example: *He told me he would phone me, but he didn't.*

★ *would* and *used to do* are interchangeable when talking about actions in the past, but *would* cannot be used to talk about past states:
He used to be fatter when he was younger. (correct)
~~He would be fatter when he was younger.~~ (wrong)

6 Work with a partner. Practise using *would/wouldn't* in these situations.

1. Think about holidays/days out you went on when you were younger. Tell your partner two or three things that you or members of your family often did.

Example: *My mother would always take far more clothes than we needed.*

2. Think about holidays again, and things that you or members of your family refused to do or were unwilling to do.

Example: *I wouldn't go to bed when my parents told me to because I wanted to stay up late.*

PERSONAL STUDY WORKBOOK

In your Personal Study Workbook, you will find more exercises to help you with your learning. For Unit 6, these include:

- an exercise on different future forms
- more practice of phrasal verbs
- pronunciation: linking
- a text about 'road rage'
- writing a picture story

REVIEW AND DEVELOPMENT

REVIEW OF UNIT 4

1 We've split up!   phrasal verbs and idioms

A Match the sentences on the left with an appropriate answer on the right. Only use each answer once. Compare with a partner, then memorise the extracts. Say the sentences on the left, and see if your partner can remember the responses.

I'll pop round and see you after ten o'clock.	I already have.
Could you double-check the holiday dates?	Yes, I'm always getting held up there too.
We got stuck in a traffic jam by the station.	That's a pity – oh, well, never mind.
I won't let you down again.	They'll probably get back together again.
We won't be able to make it, I'm afraid.	Can't you make it a bit earlier?
Derek and Jill have split up.	Yes, they're playing next week instead.
Didn't he turn up last week?	Is that a promise?
The match is off this evening.	No, that's the second time he's let me down.

B Choose one of the dialogues above and develop a conversation around it. Act out your conversation for another pair.

2 Can you work out what happened?   past deduction

With a partner, read the situations, then write a possible explanation for them using *could've, might've, must've* or *can't have* + past participle.

Example: Our dog heard something and barked, so we were very lucky.

Possible explanation: *There could've been a burglar who the dog heard and barked at.*

The branch broke under his weight.
I can't believe he passed the exam.
They think he left the gas on.
This bike has gone rusty – how did that happen?
They moved house in the middle of the night without telling anyone.

REVIEW OF UNIT 5

1 I know what I like   `speaking about buildings`

Work in small groups. Each of you should choose a different painting. Think about your painting, then be prepared to talk about it for two minutes. You could include:

– a description of the building and the surroundings
– what you like/don't like about the building and the painting
– the advantages or disadvantages of living in such a building

When you have spoken about your painting, ask the others in the group for their ideas.

2 Where's the best place to ...?   `buildings/places`

Look at the words and check any you don't know (meaning or pronunciation).

the outskirts of town   a shopping mall   police headquarters   a service station
an industrial estate   the law courts   a lost property office   a youth hostel
a safe   a mill   a public lavatory   a stable   a pedestrian precinct   a taxi rank
an estate agent's   a prison   a loo   a student common room   a library

Play this game in groups of three. One of you should think of a word from the box; don't tell it to the others in the group. They have to ask yes/no questions to guess the word.

Example questions: ***Do people*** *buy things there?*
 Has it got anything to do with *transport?*
 Is it a place where you *keep things?*

The person who guesses correctly thinks of another word, and you can play again.

HOW DOES IT LOOK?

> Language focus
>
> prepositions of place   *look* + adj, *look like* + noun
> *look as if/though*   colours and materials
> modal verbs: hypothesising   adjective word order
> describing clothes

MANET'S MASTERPIECE
prepositions; *look (like/as if)*; colours and materials

1 Look at the painting by Edouard Manet called 'A Bar at the Folies–Bergère' (1882). With a partner find the colours and materials below and identify the objects.

     greyish blue   pale pink   beige   dark green   marble   velvet   lace   glass

Now tell your partner your impressions of the painting. Do you like it? Why/why not?

2 Complete the questions below using the correct prepositions.

1. What can you see ...... the top left-hand corner?
2. What do you notice about the label ...... the bottle ...... the bottom left-hand corner?
3. What can you see ...... the background?
4. What is the barmaid wearing ...... her neck and ...... her arm?
5. What can you see ...... the counter ...... the foreground?
6. Whose elbows are resting ...... the balcony?
7. Who is wearing a dress with buttons ...... the front?
8. What can you see running ...... the middle of the painting?
9. There's a woman ...... the front row with grey gloves .... What's she doing?

Now answer the questions with your partner.

3 You can give your impression of how something seems using:

look + adjective   *The barmaid looks unhappy.*
look like + noun   *The vase looks like a drinking glass.*
look as if/though + clause   *It looks as if/though there's a mirror behind the bar.*

With your partner, make more sentences. You could talk about:

the barmaid   the man/the couple on the right   the place   the atmosphere   the decor

4 Read the text and try to remember the important information.

1   Manet's famous picture is set in the Folies-Bergère, one of the celebrated café-concert venues of late 19th-century Paris. They were places in which to meet people from all social classes, to eat, drink and entertain. The woman on the balcony looking through her opera glasses at the other people in the café symbolises this society where to see and be seen was all-important. In the top left-hand corner are the pink-stockinged legs and bright green shoes of an acrobat who is providing the entertainment, but nobody seems interested, least of all Suzon, the barmaid, who stands in the centre, lost in thought.

2   On the right-hand side of the picture is what looks like a reflection of Suzon talking to a customer. But is it? Logically, her reflection would not appear in this position, and her pose is different to that of the girl who looks out of the canvas. The reflected Suzon is deep in conversation with a man. Who is he? Perhaps this is a conversation that Suzon had a few minutes earlier. Perhaps it is the conversation she hopes she will have, meeting the man who will fall in love with her and take her away from the drudgery of her barmaid's existence.

3   Although Manet usually avoids any conscious symbolism in his pictures, the bottles on the counter do contain nuances of meaning. Champagne, the drink of high society, stands next to a bottle of English Bass beer, identifiable from the red triangle on its label, which is more often associated with the lower classes. The society of the café-concert was similarly mixed, with the upper middle classes and workers rubbing shoulders with each other, and enjoying each other's company. Notice also the nice detail on one of the wine bottles. The artist's signature and the date, 1882, appear on the label of the bottle in the bottom left-hand corner, rather like a vintage wine.

4   The composition of the painting is also very striking. The balcony provides a strong horizontal band that divides the composition in two. There is a strong vertical line running down Suzon's face and dress, so that each side of her is like a reflection of the other.

From *Annotated Art* by Robert Cumming

Cover the text and look at the picture. Tell your partner what you can remember.

5 Put the extracts below in an appropriate place in each paragraph, changing the punctuation where necessary. The paragraph numbers are in brackets.

much loved by artists (1)
and which she is now thinking about (2)
preferring instead to show modern life in a factual way (3)
Other strong horizontals are created by the bar counter and its reflection in the mirror. (4)

1 We usually associate the verb *tell* with speaking, but it also has the meaning of recognising or distinguishing one thing from another. Answer the questions in pairs.

1. Can you **tell the difference between** different brands of cola?
2. Can you **tell if** someone is lying to you by watching their eyes?
3. Can you **tell** black **from** navy blue in a shop when you're buying clothes?
4. Can you **tell** identical twins **apart**?
5. Can you **tell** if someone's hair is dyed?
6. Can you **tell** what type of job someone does just by looking at them?

Now make up two more questions using *tell* to ask another pair.

2 Imagine you couldn't tell one colour from another – in other words, you could only see in black and white. What problems might you have with any of these jobs?

> photographer   beautician   football referee   gardener   fashion designer
> police officer   train driver

Examples: *photographer*   *You might not be able to take good pictures in colour.*
            beautician   *You wouldn't be able to choose the right make-up for someone.*

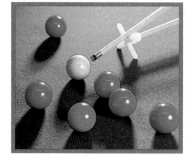 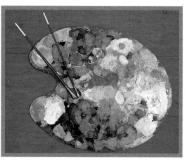 

3 What do you know about colour blindness? Discuss these questions in groups.

1. If you are colour blind, does it mean you can't see *any* colours?
2. Which colours cause most problems?
3. What type of person suffers most from colour blindness?
4. Are people born colour blind, or do they develop the condition?
5. Is there a cure for people who are colour blind?

4 🔲 Listen to a doctor talking about colour blindness. What are her answers to the questions in Exercise 3? Compare with a partner.

5 Working with a different partner, try this 'colour quiz'.

1 **What colour is** a pedestrian crossing?	7 **What colour do** traffic lights **go** for 'stop'?
2 What colour is an elephant?	8 What colour do leaves go in the autumn?
3 **What are the colours of** your national flag?	9 **What colour represents** the political party most concerned with protecting the environment?
4 What are the colours of a rainbow?	
5 **What colour do you associate with** 'nothing to declare' at customs?	10 What colour card represents a 'caution' in football?
	11 **What colour is formed by mixing** red and blue?
6 What colour do you associate with embarrassment?	12 What colour is formed by mixing yellow and blue?

Now write some more questions to ask another pair, using the language in bold in the quiz.

1 Work in small groups. Using a dictionary, organise the words below into the following categories and make sure you can pronounce the words correctly.

opinion	colour	pattern	material

tartan   purple   suede   plain   cord(uroy)   scruffy   stylish   pale lemon
spotted   check(ed)   mauve   denim   silk   fashionable   fur   lovely
brownish   wool/woollen   cotton   revolting   bright red   patterned

Now add two more adjectives of your own to each category, then compare in groups.

2 Notice that the adjectives in the table are organised to show the most common adjective order in English. For example:

a revolting spotted sweater (*not* a spotted revolting sweater)
a bright red silk blouse (*not* a silk bright red blouse)

Look at the articles of clothing. With a partner, describe each one using at least two adjectives and a noun, as in the examples above.

3 Look at the clothes. Which items could be worn together, and which items would look horrible together? Discuss with a partner, using the phrases in bold.

The (bright red silk blouse) **would go well with** the (red suede shoes).
The … **wouldn't go very well with** the … .
The … and the … **would look good/nice/strange/horrible together**.
The … and the … **would clash**.

4 Read the questionnaire and check that you understand all the vocabulary.

Section A: Colour

1 Which colours suit/don t suit you? Why?

2 Are there colours which suit women better than men, and vice versa?

3 Are there colours which suit older people better than younger people, and vice versa?

4 When you buy a new item of clothing, do you buy other items to match? (e.g a blouse to go with a skirt; a tie to go with a shirt)

Section B: Buying clothes

5 Do you buy clothes on impulse? Why/why not?

6 Do you prefer shopping on your own or with someone else?

7 What do you think of window shopping?

8 Do you often buy clothes that don t really suit you or don t really fit you? If so, why?

Section C: Associations

9 Are there particular clothes you wear for weddings or funerals?

10 Do you associate certain clothes with people from particular countries? If so, what?

11 Do you associate your friends with particular items of clothing? Give examples.

12 Do you care what clothes other people wear?

5 ▢▢ ▢▢ Listen to two people discussing question 9. Which clothes do they say are conventional? Which clothes have they seen or worn which are unusual?

Now discuss your own answers to the questionnaire in small groups.

PERSONAL STUDY WORKBOOK

In your Personal Study Workbook, you will find more exercises to help you with your learning. For Unit 7, these include:

• exercises on clothes vocabulary, adjective word order, prepositions and prepositional phrases
• the use of the adjective suffix *-ish*
• a text about 'car colours' and why they have changed
• responding to people who are describing unusual situations
• writing a description of a painting

REVIEW AND DEVELOPMENT

REVIEW OF UNIT 5

1 An extraordinary coincidence   past tenses

A The coincidence stories below are true. Read them, then tell your partner how you think the stories end.

1   Mrs M. Spraggett of Coventry was relaxing on the sofa when she was suddenly compelled to telephone her father. 'I never phone him unless I have something to tell
5   him, but I dashed to the phone. It rang and rang, and I kept thinking, "Dad, pick up the phone." Somehow I knew he was there.' Meanwhile, her father had been cooking some chips, and had sat down for a
10   minute to listen to the news, but had fallen asleep. He was woken by ...

1 Elsie Kerr of Camberley had an extraordinary piece of luck during the war. She had planned to spend the weekend at her friend Nancy's house, in Newcastle. But when she arrived in Newcastle,
5 she bumped into another friend whom she hadn't seen for years. The friend asked her to go dancing that evening. She hesitated, but in the end agreed to go, feeling a little guilty at letting Nancy down. That night, Newcastle was heavily bombed and
10 she and her friend took shelter. Imagine her horror when she left the dance hall to discover that the street where Nancy lived had been destroyed. Amazingly, because she had cancelled her visit to Nancy, Nancy and her husband had decided ...

From *The Daily Mail Weekend*

B Answer these questions with your partner. If the answer is yes, say if the meaning would be different.

Example: *In line 1, could you also say* had been relaxing?
Answer: *Yes, and in this case, the meaning would be the same.*

1. In line 8 of the first story, could you also say *had cooked some chips?*
2. In line 10, could you also say *had been falling asleep?*
3. In line 2 of the second story, could you also say *had been planning?*
4. In line 5, could you also say *hadn't been seeing?*

2 Building coincidences | pronunciation: connected speech |

A Listen to a short account of a coincidence relating to a building.

B Now do the dictation using the spaced version. Compare with a partner.

C Listen again, and repeat the sentences to imitate the speaker on the recording.

REVIEW OF UNIT 6

They wouldn't help me | uses of *wouldn't*; vocabulary |

Wouldn't can be used to show that someone or something was unwilling to do something.

In sentences 1–6, the professionals all refused to help in some way. Complete them with an appropriate verb and sentence ending. Don't use the verb *help*! Complete sentences 7–12 in an appropriate way.

Example *The mechanic wouldn't* ...**repair my car**..., so I **had to take it to another garage.**

1. The waitress wouldn't ...... me, so ...
2. The telephonist wouldn't ......, so ...
3. The doctor wouldn't ...... me, and ...
4. The plumber wouldn't ......, but ...
5. The surgeon wouldn't ......, and ...
6. The dustman wouldn't ......, so ...

7. The scissors wouldn't ...
8. The brakes wouldn't ...
9. The drawer wouldn't ...
10. The car wouldn't ...
11. The lid of the jar wouldn't ...
12. The rain wouldn't ...

ADDRESSING THE ISSUES

Language focus

it's time + past tense
expressing willingness
collocation

textual cohesion
political vocabulary
crime and the law

SCANDAL   crime and legal vocabulary; expressing willingness

1 Find a partner. One of you should read the case study below, while the other reads the one on page 154. Use a dictionary to check any new words.

Tell your partner about the story you read, and decide which story is the bigger scandal and why. Do you think either of the people should resign? Would they do so in your country?

Case Study 1
A finance minister in the current government has been accused of taking bribes. Newspapers have revealed that the minister received a large but unspecified sum of money from a foreign businessman just weeks after his company was awarded a major manufacturing contract. This is the second corruption scandal concerning a government minister in recent months, and a general election is due within six months.

2 With your partner, look at the pairs of words and phrases, and discuss the difference in meaning between them, using a dictionary where necessary.

1. being convicted of a drink driving offence/being charged with a drink driving offence
2. being stopped for speeding/being fined for speeding
3. pushing drugs/taking drugs
4. bribery/blackmail
5. shoplifting/burglary
6. fraud/tax evasion

Which of these do you think are most common in your country or district? Discuss with your partner.

3 Now read the profiles of four people who are candidates for election as your local leader (this could be a mayor, or council leader or other type of local official).

1. Doctor Rennison: local GP with 20 years' experience. Respected by broad cross-section of local population. Close links with all social service agencies. Intelligent, eloquent but is known to support euthanasia and was once involved in a police investigation about the mysterious death of an elderly patient. No firm evidence discovered.

2. Martha Holdsworth: solicitor with a lot of experience with the Citizens' Advice Bureau. Known for liberal views on legalising soft drugs. As a student was convicted of a minor drugs offence. Has been in a wheelchair for five years following a car accident. Is now a campaigner for better facilities in public buildings for disabled people. Extremely hardworking.

3. Eleanor Brown: gave up early career in journalism to bring up her three children. Now they have left home, is writing again for the local evening paper and runs a local charity organisation and AIDS support group. Became well-known locally when her home was burgled and she shot and wounded the burglar as he was trying to escape. This occurred shortly after the break-up of her marriage.

4. Tom Adams: local farmer/businessman with a reputation for getting things done, but known to upset people and make enemies. His business partner was charged with bribery of an agricultural official to gain special grants and subsidies, but Adams was not charged. Local man who loves the town and wants to preserve its character and traditions.

Which of them would/wouldn't you support or vote for, and why? Discuss in small groups, using the language in the box, and give your reasons.

I'd be I wouldn't be	willing happy reluctant/unwilling prepared very happy	to vote for someone who ...

| I'd
I wouldn't | support ... because ... | |

4 Have a ballot in the class to find the most popular candidate.

1 When people vote in elections, what kinds of things influence their decision? In small groups, look at the list below and add up to four more factors.

1. the way their partner or family usually vote
2. the appearance of the party leader/president
3. the electoral promises made by the party/leader
4. an important national issue e.g. educational policy

As a class, put all your ideas on the board. Are they the same as the ones on page 155?

2 In small groups, discuss the factors. Which influence *you* the most, and which influence people in your country the most?

3 ▭ You are going to hear three people from different countries speak about the factors which influence their voting choice. Make notes, then compare with a partner.

4 ▭ Listen again and fill in the gaps in the tapescript on page 155.

5 Look at these definitions.

issue SUBJECT /'ɪʃuː 'ɪsjuː/ *n* [C] a subject or problem which people are thinking and talking about • *environmental/ scientific/ethical/personal/family issues*

From *Cambridge International Dictionary of English*

leader /'liːdə /n [C] **1 IN CONTROL** the person who directs or controls a team, organisation, country, etc.: *The prize was awarded to President de Klerk and the ANC leader, Nelson Mandela.*

From *Longman Dictionary of Contemporary English*

policy PLAN /'pɒləsi /n [C] a set of ideas or a plan of what to do in particular situations that has been agreed officially by a group of people, a business organisation, a government or a political party • *They believe that the European Community needs a common foreign and security policy.*

From *Cambridge International Dictionary of English*

The adjectives in the table can be used with at least two of the nouns above (in some cases, all three). Look at the examples first, then complete the table with a partner.

	issue	policy	leader
controversial	yes	yes	yes
foreign	no	yes	yes
political			
strong			
economic			
vital			
global			
trade union			
party			

6 In five minutes, how many of these can you think of?

- a controversial issue in your country
- a strong world leader
- another country's foreign policy which affects your country
- a global issue
- a trade union leader
- a party policy not shared by any other party
- a vital political issue for you personally
- a good or bad economic policy

Compare your answers in groups.

TV CENSORSHIP
it's time + past tense; textual cohesion

1 You are going to read an article, but first look at the headline. What will the text talk about, do you think? Tell a partner.

It's about time we said 'no' to TV sleaze

2 Notice the structure *it's time* + past tense (or *it's about time/it's high time* + past tense for added emphasis) and read the definition on the right.

With a partner, complete these headlines about television issues, using your own ideas for the final one.

QUALITY, NOT QUANTITY

It's time ...... the number of cable and satellite channels.

OUR CHILDREN'S FUTURE

It's about time ...... our children from wasting their lives watching mindless TV programmes.

TV: ...
It's time ...

Which of the three headlines do you agree or disagree with most strongly, and why? Discuss in small groups.

If you say that **it is about time** or **it is high time** that something happened or was done, you are saying in an emphatic way that it **should happen** or be done now, and really **should have happened** or been done sooner. *It's high time the government displayed a more humanitarian approach towards victims of the recession ...*

3 The article below was written by Bruce Gyngell, the head of a terrestrial television company. Underline any points he makes which you agree or disagree with. In small groups, compare and discuss the points you underlined.

It's about time we said 'no' to TV sleaze

1 **Television is there to enrich our lives, not to shock or offend.** There are people who want pornography and subversive opinions:
5 I do not challenge their right to such material via magazines, videos and encoded television channels that people choose to receive by satellite or cable. But terrestrial television is
10 different because it goes so easily into people's homes and, after 60 years, is part of the furniture.

With programmes like **The Good Sex Guide**, which I banned from
15 Yorkshire TV*, we have reached the stage where so-called entertainment, once only to be found in seedy Soho** basements, is paraded on mainstream television as if it were respectable.
20 What are we doing to our sensibilities and moral values and, more importantly, those of our children, when day after day we broadcast an endless diet of sex and violence?

25 We have become afraid to censor. But, after a lifetime in television, I feel we have to take a stand. We have gone too far in the direction of 'freedom', and our terrestrial TV is in danger of
30 becoming a mire of salaciousness, negativity and violence. And it's not all right that the worst excesses are at night: children do watch then and do have VCRs (video cassette recorders).
35 We broadcasters have a duty to consider what we put out, to ensure it does not undermine society nor our audience's trust that it is safe to watch TV. That trust has taken
40 decades to build up and broadcasters are now in danger of throwing it away for the sake of a few late-night rating points.

As Sir David Puttnam recently said, 'We are in the midst of a revolution in
45 the way that moving images affect our lives. Will we use this to make our world a more harmonious and stimulating place? Or are we going to allow ourselves to slither down the road of
50 the circus – obsessed with spectacle – bigger, more expensive, more dangerous and, eventually, more bloody?'

★ *Yorkshire TV:* a regional TV company
★★ *Soho:* an area of London famous for nightclubs, striptease, etc.

4 What do the words highlighted in red refer to? Compare with a partner.

Example: *their* (line 5) refers to *people* in line 3
such material (lines 5–6) refers to *pornography and subversive opinions*

5 With your partner, choose one of the headlines that you agree on from Exercise 2, and write a paragraph expressing your opinion.

PERSONAL STUDY WORKBOOK

In your Personal Study Workbook, you will find more exercises to help you with your learning. For Unit 8, these include:

- an exercise on collocation
- correcting grammar and vocabulary mistakes
- pronunciation: sounds and spelling
- a text of famous quotations
- discursive writing: expressing a personal opinion

REVIEW OF UNIT 6

1 Sort them out | phrasal verbs + idioms |

Complete the phrases with a suitable particle.

| off   up   out   down   round |

lie .... in a public place

pick someone .... from a station or airport

calm someone .... who was upset or angry

start .... a conversation with a stranger

have more than two days ....

sort .... a problem

see someone .... on a long journey

show someone .... your home town/city or workplace

give .... your place to someone

tell someone .... for behaving badly

Work with a partner, and ask them when and why they last did these things.

Example: A: *When did you last lie down in a public place?*
          B: *Last Saturday. I went to the park and lay down by the lake and fell asleep.*

2 I'll be wearing my blue hat | tense revision |

For each group of sentences, match the beginnings on the left with a suitable ending on the right. Use each sentence beginning once.

The train usually leaves	as soon as the other one gets in.
The train will be leaving	at 6.15 every day.
The train will leave	in a few minutes, so hurry up.

I wear my blue hat	so you should be able to recognise me.
I'll wear my blue hat	on special occasions.
I'll be wearing my blue hat	then you can borrow my other one.

He works	all the time.
He'll work	when you get back, so don't bother to ring.
He'll be working	if we need more staff next weekend.

Now complete each of these sentence beginnings in a suitable way. (Remember that *spend* can be used to talk about time or money.)

I spend ...
I'm spending ...
I'll spend ...
I'll be spending ...

REVIEW OF UNIT 7

1 What's going on? | look + adjective, look like/as if/as though |

With a partner, describe the pictures, using at least two of these constructions in each one:

look + adjective
look like + noun
look as if / as though + clause

The man looks shocked.

The building looks like a church.

It looks as if there has been a fire.

2 Listen and answer | vocabulary |

Listen to the questions and write your answers.

Compare your answers with a partner, and look at the tapescript on page 165.

Tell your partner to close their book, then read the questions for them to answer.

3 The Fortune Teller | speaking |

Look at the painting by Georges de la Tour on page 155. With a partner, describe it in as much detail as possible.

9

MAKING THE MOST OF YOUR TIME

Language focus

prepositions and adverbs	tense and time
nouns and adjectives + *-ing* or infinitive	non-defining relative clauses
time expressions	

TIME MANAGEMENT vocabulary

1 How do you manage your time when you are working or studying? Tell a partner about things you spend too long on, and things you don't spend enough time on.

⬜⬜ Now listen to the speakers on the recording describing their time management problems. What problems do they have, and what solutions are suggested?

2 Here are nine important rules of time management. In groups, can you explain what any of them mean?

•••••••••••••• *Nine tools and rules* ••••••••••••••

1 Use your starter motor	6 The curse of perfectionism
2 Make routine your servant	7 Once past the desk
3 Every 'yes' is 'no' to something else	8 Appointments need to end as well as start
4 Distant elephants	9 Make time to plan
5 Salami	

3 The rules are explained in the following paragraphs, but they are not in the same order. Match each rule with the correct explanation, then compare with a partner.

A Make sure you schedule time to organise your activities. Some people find it helpful to plan their day first thing in the morning. For others, it may be better to plan in terms of a week. Ten minutes spent in planning will be saved many times over.

B A friend of mine was asked to give a lecture in Edinburgh. He knew it would take two days' preparation and a couple of days to travel to Edinburgh and back. It was not a lecture he particularly wanted to give, and in normal circumstances he would have declined immediately. But he was being asked a year in advance. It was so far away he almost said *yes* without thinking. Just in time he remembered: in a year's time it would still be four days' work and he would still have other priorities. Do not commit yourself to unimportant activities no matter how far ahead they are.

C A survey of students showed that the main difference between good students and average students was the ability to get down to work quickly. Do not spend time in that limbo of neither getting down to the work nor enjoying your leisure.

D Louise thought so carefully about every word, and worried so much about every sentence, that some of her best ideas never got published. Sometimes this painstaking care is essential, but for most activities, there comes a point when it isn't worth putting any more effort into it. Usually it is possible to spot when this point has been reached. This is the time to call a halt.

E Some people find large tasks so daunting that they never start them, or having started them, they become dispirited and give up. But if a large task is broken up into a series of small tasks and then tackled gradually slice by slice, it becomes much more manageable.

F If you can get into the habit of doing certain tasks at certain times of the day, you won't waste time worrying about the fact that you're not doing them.

G Whether you are meeting a colleague at work or a friend over coffee, don't just arrange a time to meet; you should also be thinking about a time to finish. There are two reasons for this. First, you know when you will be free for other activities. And second, if everyone knows when the meeting is scheduled to end, you will all make better use of the time.

H Most of us make the mistake of saying 'yes' to too many things, and end up living our lives according to the priorities of others rather than our own. We fail to recognise that doing one thing means that we are not doing something else. Think to yourself: 'If I say *yes* to this, what other activity will I take the time from?' Assertiveness is essential to good time management.

I When a letter arrives – typically one that we don't really want to answer – we sometimes read it and then put it aside. Later we read it again, start to think about it, then put it aside again. But during the time we have spent putting it off, we could have answered it. So when a task arrives, deal with it straight away, or decide when to deal with it and put it aside till then. It's pointless revisiting a task without carrying it out, so deal with what is on your desk, *once* only.

From *Manage Your Mind* by Gillian Butler and Tony Hope

4 Discuss these questions in small groups.

1. Are there any rules you disagree with?
2. Are there any rules here that you follow naturally?
3. Are there any rules that you would like to adopt in your own life?

5 The text includes a number of expressions that can be used to introduce positive suggestions and warnings. Notice that they are followed by an *-ing* form or infinitive.

Positive suggestions
It's worth (spending time ...)
It's good if you get into the habit of (doing ...)
It may be helpful to (plan ...)
It's important to (accept ...)

Warnings
It's not worth (spending time ...)
It's bad if you get into the habit of (doing ...)
It's pointless (doing ...)
It's a waste of time (going ...)

With a partner, write down some more 'rules' using the phrases above. Choose from the following:

– learning a foreign language
– sending business correspondence (letters, fax, e-mail)
– bringing up a child
– a topic of your own

TIME QUIZ

time expressions, prepositions and adverbs; tense and time

1 With your partner, think of three ways to say each of these times.

> 4.45 p.m.   21.55   6.30 p.m.

2 Try this time quiz, either alone, with a partner or in small groups. Your maximum time to do it is fifteen minutes. The quiz continues on page 68.

1 Tense and time
Match the time definitions a–f with the sentences 1–6.

1 She went to the police station because she'd lost her passport.
2 I've done my homework.
3 He's been making baskets for a couple of years.
4 We'll have done the job by the weekend.
5 I'm doing a great course which ends on Friday.
6 Money is the root of all evil.

a for all time
b activity finishing before another past event
c finishing before a point in time in the future
d an event completed at any time before now
e around this time, and temporarily
f from a point in time in the past up to now

2 Prepositions and adverbs
Replace the underlined phrase with a single word that has the same meaning. The first letter has been given to you.

1 Young people <u>these days</u> have a lot more money to spend than their parents did.
   n. . . . .

2 Have you been waiting <u>for a long time</u>?   l. . . . .

3 We arrived at 6.00 and Jackie got there two hours <u>after that</u>.
   a. . . . .

4 It rained <u>for the whole of</u> the weekend. t. . . . .

5 She's going to university in the autumn, but <u>in the meantime</u> she's working as a secretary.
   m. . . . .

6 They had an awful journey, but <u>in the end</u>, they got there safely.
   e. . . . .

3 Confusing pairs

Underline the correct answer in brackets.

1 I worked there (during/for) a long time.

2 They are a very reliable company: their flights always leave (on time/in time).

3 The others usually leave at 3.30, but I'll stay here (by/until) 4.00.

4 I'm coming back (in/after) three weeks' time.

5 The (current/actual) problems we face are no different from those of ten years ago.

6 We'll get the money (at last / eventually), but it might take quite a long time.

4 Times past

Fill the gaps to make each completed sentence similar in meaning to the one next to it.

Example: I *saw her a few days ago.*   I saw her the ..*other*. day.

1 She is no longer my wife.   She is my . . . . -wife.

2 I saw him the day before that.   I saw him the . . . . day.

3 They work in what used to be Yugoslavia.   They work in the . . . . Yugoslavia.

4 We left at 5, but Joan took a train before ours.   We left at 5, but Joan took an . . . . train.

5 I haven't been there recently.   I haven't been there . . . .

6 He's the man who had the job before I took over.   He's my . . . .

5 Time expressions

Correct any errors in the underlined expressions. Be careful: some are correct.

1 I got to the station just in the time.

2 I don't remember punk music – that was before my times.

3 Right! Time's up, everyone – put your pens down, please.

4 I've decided to stay in this school from the time being.

5 Could you do that on your own time rather than at work?

6 I go to the cinema from time to time.

For those who finish ahead of time ...

See how many compounds you can make with the word 'time' at the beginning or end:

Examples: **time**table over**time**   **time**-limit night-**time**

Check your score (one point for each correct answer).
24–30 Excellent! Well done!   19–23 Very good
14–18 Not bad   Less than 14 Never mind – there's still time to improve!

3 Work in groups of three or four with a stopwatch. Take turns to speak for one minute on the topics below. Don't repeat a topic anyone has talked about.

– a previous employer
– a former leader of my country
– what I hope to do eventually
– what I do in my own time
– the current social or economic situation in my country
– what my classmates do during the breaks in or between lessons
– my ex-boyfriend/girlfriend/husband/wife
– young people nowadays
– problems I've been having lately
– something unusual I do from time to time
– something before my time that older people are always talking about
– things I will have done by the end of this year.

1 Do you work best *under pressure*, or are you much happier with lots of time to do a job or task? Discuss in groups and decide which type of person you are.

2 Find a partner who is the opposite to you (based on Exercise 1). Together you are going to work under pressure. First read this short newsflash. Then shut your books and tell each other what you can remember.

```
NEWSFLASH
REPORT COMING IN - CUSTOMS OFFICIALS AT DOVER HAVE SEIZED DRUGS WITH STREET VALUE OF APPROX £1M.
NO CONFIRMATION YET WHERE DRUGS WERE FOUND AND WHO WAS RESPONSIBLE, BUT POSSIBLE CONNECTION WITH
RECENT DISCOVERY OF DRUGS IN ROTTERDAM.
```

▭ Now listen to a more detailed report of the news story and make notes. Compare your notes with your partner.

3 You are going to write the newspaper story of the drugs seizure. First notice how you can use non-defining relative clauses to help you in your writing.

Police officers, <u>who have been working on the robbery for two years</u>, are hoping to make an arrest today.
Street crimes, <u>which have increased dramatically in the last decade</u>, are becoming a great cause for concern.
The boy, <u>whose parents both have criminal records</u>, will appear in the juvenile court today.

The underlined clauses ('non-defining' relative clauses) are separated from the rest of the sentence by commas, and they give *extra* information about the people or things we are talking about. They can be used to add information within a sentence and avoid the need for two sentences.

For further information, see the Language Reference on page 146.

Add a suitable non-defining relative clause to these sentences, then compare with a partner.

One of the witnesses, ..., told the court that he saw the man only minutes before the robbery.

The police van, ..., drove away from the court at high speed.

The policeman's dog, ..., had its photo on the front page of the newspaper.

4 Now write the story from Exercise 2 with your partner. It must be between 115–125 words. You have twenty minutes only. Include one or two examples of non-defining relative clauses.

Read the story written by another pair. Note down any differences in the factual information included, and any language mistakes. Give it back to them.

5 Your editor has just informed you that you now have to reduce your story to a maximum of 100 words. You have ten minutes to edit and correct your story. You may also refer to the tapescript on page 166 for help.

6 Decide on the best headline and the best photo for your story, then pin your version on the wall. Move round and read everyone else's story. Which is the best?

MAJOR DRUGS HAUL

DRUGS RING SMASHED

POLICE SEIZE DRUGS WORTH OVER £1M

A NEW MEANING TO CHOCOHOLIC

PERSONAL STUDY WORKBOOK

In your Personal Study Workbook, you will find more exercises to help you with your learning. For Unit 9, these include:

- exercises on prepositions, adverbs and time expressions
- tense revision
- practice using relative clauses
- a text about effective time management at work
- people talking about the best time to do certain things

REVIEW OF UNIT 7

1 Yellow butter   `pronunciation: rhythm`

📼 Listen to the poem on the recording. Practise saying it at the same time as the speakers.

YELLOW BUTTER
Yellow butter purple jelly red jam black bread
Spread it thick
Say it quick

Yellow butter purple jelly red jam black bread
Spread it thicker
Say it quicker

Yellow butter purple jelly red jam black bread
Now repeat it
While you eat it

Yellow butter purple jelly red jam black bread
**Don't talk
with your mouth full!**

By Mary Ann Hoberman

2 Consequences   `could, might, would`

Work in small groups and make a list of at least five consequences of one of the following.

1. Imagine you had a third eye, in the back of your head.
2. Imagine you had a long tail.
3. Imagine you had no fingernails.

Use these structures in your list:

> You could/couldn't ...   You would/wouldn't ...   You wouldn't be able to ...
> You might ...   You might (not) be able to ...   It would mean ...

Tell another group your ideas. Can they add to your list?

REVIEW OF UNIT 8

1 It's not a crime in my country   `vocabulary`

Look at the words in the box, then answer the questions below with a partner.

> blackmail   speeding   euthanasia   subsidies   a charity   bribery   tax evasion
> pensions   burglary   pornography   fraud   taking drugs   censorship

1. How many of the words/phrases are crimes in your country?
2. How many of the words/phrases have a direct link with money?
3. How many of the words/phrases are usually associated with young people?
4. How many of the words/phrases are usually associated with elderly people?
5. Which single word/phrase represents the thing which makes you most angry? Why?

Discuss your answers with another pair.

10

TELLING STORIES IN ENGLISH

> Language focus
> linking spoken discourse, attitude adverbs, e.g. *surprisingly*, *luckily*
> e.g. *actually*, *to be honest* phrasal verbs and idioms
> purpose clauses crime vocabulary

YOU'LL NEVER GUESS WHO I MET ... linking spoken discourse; attitude adverbs

1 If you could meet any famous living person, who would it be, and why? Tell a partner.

2 Look at the bubbles. The words in bold are all common linkers in spoken English. How do you think the sentences might finish? Work with your partner.

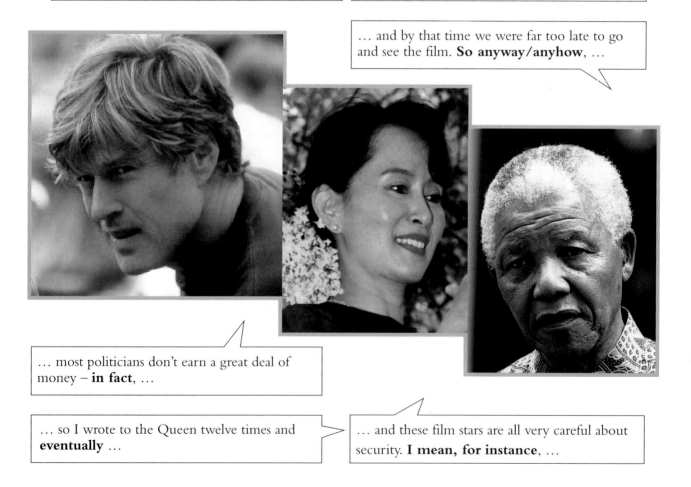

... and I thought Robert Redford would be very tall. **Actually**, he *'s even shorter than me.*

... I'd been invited to a party for the opening night of the play, and **to be honest**, ...

... and by that time we were far too late to go and see the film. **So anyway/anyhow**, ...

... most politicians don't earn a great deal of money – **in fact**, ...

... so I wrote to the Queen twelve times and **eventually** ...

... and these film stars are all very careful about security. **I mean, for instance**, ...

3 ▱ You are going to hear a true story about meeting a famous person. Stop the recording after each bleep. Use your understanding of the linkers to predict what the speaker says next. Listen more than once if necessary.

4 Work in small groups. You are going to tell each other a story (true if possible, but if not, invent one). It should be about seeing or meeting someone who is famous locally, nationally or internationally. Tell each other:

– where and when you saw this person;
– who you saw, and any contact that took place;
– what else happened, and how you felt.

If possible, use one or two of the linkers from Exercise 1.

5 ▭ ▭ Now listen to two more true anecdotes and answer these questions.

1. Where did the story take place?
2. Why was the speaker there?
3. Which famous person did they see?
4. Did they have any contact with them or speak to them?
5. Did they have a positive feeling about the person afterwards? (yes/no/don't know)

6 Another common way of linking ideas in spoken or written English is to use adverbs which introduce a reaction to something you have just said. Complete these sentences, then compare with a partner.

I asked her for her autograph, but **unfortunately** …

He didn't have much acting experience. **Surprisingly, though,** …

He had been playing for nearly two hours, **so naturally,** …

It was very difficult to get tickets for the concert. **Luckily,** …

Ideally, I'd like to get a job in the film industry. **Obviously,** …

WRITING SHORT STORIES THAT SELL
story vocabulary; phrasal verbs and idioms

1 Imagine you were going to write a short story based on this photograph. Think about these questions:

1. What's the story about?
2. Where does it take place?
3. What happens?

Discuss your ideas in small groups, then tell the class.

2 Imagine you are going to write the story for publication in a collection of short stories or a magazine. Check that you understand the underlined phrases in the box, using a dictionary if necessary.

> decide who your characters will be
>
> <u>work out</u> the plot
>
> <u>do a</u> first <u>draft</u> of your manuscript
>
> <u>send it off</u> to a publisher or a magazine
>
> <u>come up with</u> an idea
>
> <u>make up your mind</u> to write a story
>
> <u>get some feedback</u> from a friend
>
> <u>go over it</u> again and make revisions
>
> <u>do</u> any <u>research</u> necessary
>
> <u>think up</u> a title

Put the sentences in order, then compare and discuss with a partner (they may have a different order which is also correct).

Study your sequence for two minutes, then shut your books and see if you can remember it with your partner.

3 Read the introduction below, then go on to the next instruction.

Six guidelines for successful and saleable short story writing

How do you write a good short story? There is, of course, no single complete answer to this question. If you ask twenty writers the best way to set about short stories, you will get twenty answers. This is because short story writing, like any other art form, is not governed by a set of rules. There are however guidelines; let's look at the six most important ones:

Work in twos or threes. Look at the text on page 75 and divide it up between you. (If there are three of you, read two sections each; if you are a pair, read three.) Then shut your books and tell each other what you read.

4 Quickly read the sections you didn't read before. Was there anything important that you weren't told?

5 Think about a short story idea you came up with at the beginning of the lesson. Has the text given you any ideas about it, and would you like to change it in any way? Discuss in your original groups.

Now look at the Group Magazine Project on page 79.

1

Most short stories simply don't allow space to develop characters very far. Perhaps the best guideline is to say that short stories are theme-driven. So **find a theme**, and think about where it takes you. And the simpler the theme, the better. Examples might be: love, jealousy, loneliness, loyalty, greed, generosity. If you think about loyalty, for example, where does that take you? There are lots of possibilities: the wife stays loyal to her husband in spite of infidelity; the husband stays loyal to the memory of his wife years after her death. Equally, themes could be problem situations, such as shoplifting, divorce, unemployment.

. . . .

2

In order to move the story along, your characters should have to **resolve some conflict or situation**. Some experts provide great lists of conflicts: man versus nature, man versus man and so forth. But conflict situations do not have to be that dramatic. Any situation that presents a problem or forces a character to take a decision provides a conflict – and it is how your character resolves the conflict that provides the story material.

3

To avoid a complicated story, **don't have too many characters**. In the space of, say, 2,000 words, you just do not have room to handle a lot of characters. It is probably true to say that most successful short stories have three or less, but this is not a hard and fast rule.

. . . .

4

Whatever idea you have come up with, **keep it simple** is the advice given in creative writing classes the world over. Try writing your basic plot in a maximum of 40 words. If you cannot get it into that number of words, it certainly is a danger sign, so you should look carefully to see if the plot needs simplifying.

. . . .

5

Now **where do we start**? Many people tell the story as it happens, in chronological sequence, with the hero or heroine waking up at the beginning of the day. Typically, these stories start:

Sheila woke as the sun streamed through the bedroom curtains. She just knew that today was going to be special ...

This just isn't very exciting, so ignore the chronological sequence and start just as the moment of crisis is about to break, when the central character is faced with the conflict and has to set about resolving it. Imagine a story with jealousy as its theme – one in which Mary is jealous of another woman she has seen with John, and John has broken his dinner date with Mary. How about this?

'Damn them,' said Mary to herself, as she threw the smoked salmon into the waste bin and helped herself to her fourth glass of wine.

As an opening, it raises questions in the reader's mind: Why is Mary angry? Why is she throwing away the smoked salmon? And why is she drinking heavily?

. . . .

6

Everyone says the opening paragraph has to attract attention and command interest. This is true enough, but it is the last paragraph or two that often create the lasting impression. And your short story fails if it doesn't have a **satisfactory ending**. The ending should resolve all the factual questions raised by the story: how will character X overcome this problem? How will character Y react? But it is a bonus if you can leave your readers asking themselves: I just wonder ...? This way, you can leave your readers to write their own postscript.

Adapted from *Writing Short Stories that Sell* by Mike Wakefield

1 You are going to hear a short story about a poisoner, but first, with a partner and a dictionary, check that you understand these words and can pronounce them.

> poisoning   an antidote   to write a confession
> to deserve something   a druggist (US) / pharmacist (GB)
> evidence (of a crime)   to blackmail someone   to bluff
> to prevent something (from happening)   an undetectable poison

2 You can use the following connectors to talk about the purpose or reason for doing something.

> She gave me the money { *to* / *in order to* ★ / *so as to* ★ } help me.
>
> She did it { *in order not to*★ / *so as not to*★ } upset me.
>
> I put the light on *so that* { I could see better. / it would be easier to read. }

★ These forms are slightly more formal.

With your partner, complete these sentences in a suitable way.

Example: *You lock a door in order to* ... **keep people in or out.**

1. Some people try to blackmail others so as to ...
2. In order to prevent a murder, you might ...
3. People sometimes bluff in an interview to ...
4. The police need evidence of a crime in order to ...
5. A criminal might write a confession so as to ...
6. You might ask a druggist/pharmacist for advice so that ...

3 Think carefully about these questions, then discuss them in small groups.

1. Can you think of any reasons why you might justifiably give someone poison?
2. Is murder ever justifiable? Why/why not?

4 ▭ Listen to the first part of the story, then discuss these questions with a partner.

1. Who is Sangstrom, and what is his problem?
2. Why do you think the druggist says 'I already have' at the end?
3. How do you think the story will continue?

If you can't answer the questions, listen again.

5 📻 Listen to the rest of the recording. With your partner, retell the end of the story, putting the pictures in the correct order.

A

B

C

D

E

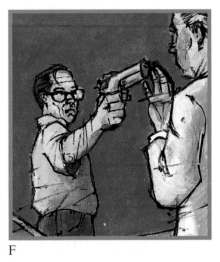

F

6 Think again about the qualities of a good short story from the text on page 75. Do you think *this* story has those qualities? Why/why not? Discuss in groups.

Can you write a summary in 40 words?

PERSONAL STUDY WORKBOOK

In your Personal Study Workbook, you will find more exercises to help you with your learning. For Unit 10, these include:

- a vocabulary quizword
- an exercise on punctuation and pronunciation (intonation)
- more work on phrasal verbs, idioms and link words
- four opening paragraphs for a novel
- listening to an Italian folk tale and writing a summary of it

---

REVIEW OF UNIT 8

1 It's time we did something about it `It's time + past tense; speaking`

Complete these slogans using a suitable subject + verb.

You get what you pay for

We need the best politicians money can buy. It's time ...... them a really good salary.

SAVE OUR FAMILIES

It's high time ...... all guns – let's rid society of this horror.

LEAVE THEM ALONE!

It's about time ...... prying into the private lives of famous people.

Now complete these slogans in your own words:

TRAFFIC NIGHTMARE

Our cities are intolerable. It's time ...

NO MORE ADDITIVES!

Do we really know what we are eating? It's high time ...

LESS WORK, MORE LEISURE!

Why do we work ourselves into an early grave? It's about time ...

In small groups, compare your answers. Do you agree with the completed slogans? Why/why not?

2 What an issue! `vocabulary: compounds`

With a partner, explain the difference between these pairs of compound words and phrases.

1. a controversial issue/a controversial policy
2. a local election/a general election
3. a police investigation/police evidence
4. main issue/minor issue
5. tax evasion/a tax exile
6. a parking offence/a driving offence

REVIEW OF UNIT 9

1 What do you remember? `time expressions`

Work with a partner. One of you should look again at the time quiz on pages 67–68, and test your partner on Exercises 2–6. Then swap and let your partner test you.

2 The man next door `non-defining relative clauses`

Work with a partner. Take it in turns to create sentences from this beginning and ending, which include a non-defining relative clause in the middle around the topics you are given. Look at the example first.

Example: *The man next door, (AGE), was arrested yesterday.*
The man next door, who is in his sixties, was arrested yesterday.

(APPEARANCE)
(CLOTHES)
(CAR HE DRIVES)
(JOB)
The man next door, (FINANCIAL SITUATION), was arrested yesterday.
(FAMILY)
(CHARACTER)
(BEHAVIOUR)

PROJECT: GROUP MAGAZINE

Before you start writing your short stories, you need to discuss some 'ground rules'.

1 Work in small groups. One of you should make notes on your group's opinion of the points below.

Magazine project ground rules

1. Should the stories be written by individuals, or should you work in pairs to produce a short story together? Or is it possible to have both individual stories and collaborative stories? What are the advantages of writing individually or writing in pairs?

2. Should the stories be written in class time (this will probably be necessary if you are working on stories in pairs) or should the first draft be written in your own time? Both have advantages, but if you write in class, your teacher will be there to guide you.

3. Should the stories in the magazine have a single theme (for instance, loyalty, bravery, man and woman) or should they all have different themes? Or might they be based around the picture on page 73, or another picture?

4. How long should the stories be? (The story on the recording on page 76 is less than 700 words; but short stories can obviously be longer, or shorter.)

5. When the stories are finally written, should they be put on a wall display, or into a booklet form? Should you have a prize for the best story? Are there other people outside your class who would be interested in your magazine?

The notetaker should tell the rest of the class their group's ideas.

You now need to reach an agreement together.

2 Look back at page 75, 'Writing short stories that sell'. Which is the most useful advice given there? Is there any advice you will ignore?

You now need to do your first draft, either individually or in pairs, as you agreed in Exercise 1. Write it clearly, because other people are going to read it before you finalise it.

3 Look at this extract from the first draft of a short story.

... so she went to Spain, determined to become successful and return home in triumph. But she couldn't get a job or a flat and ended up sleeping on a friend's floor. (1*) Then she saw a job advertised in the paper; it didn't look very interesting but she went out to phone. (2*) She only had one large note worth about $10, so she went and sat in a café to get some change. (3*) The waiter brought her a drink and came back with a huge bundle of notes. He hadn't looked properly – he must have thought it was worth $50. It was a huge amount of money to her and she sat there staring at it. In the end...

What kind of details would make this story more interesting? Look at the questions written by a reader and the feedback at the end.

1* How did she feel about this?
2* Did she find a phone easily?
   Did she really want to phone?
   Why didn't she phone from her friend's house?
3* What was the café like? (We don't have much
   idea of the atmosphere in the story.)

I like your story – you have chosen a good
conflict situation. I want to know what she does.

Can you suggest some improvements based on the reader's questions?

Now read the text on page 156. Is it better or not?

4 Swap your first draft with another learner/pair of learners. Look at their draft, and tell them what you *like* about their story. Then make any suggestions you think will improve the story.

Can you understand the story?
Has it got an interesting beginning and a satisfactory ending?
Are any parts too long or too short?
Arc there any details missing which would make the story come alive?

5 Get together and discuss and work on the suggestions. Then write a final draft and read it through carefully to check your English.

6 Make your wall display or put your magazine together. If you are making a magazine, your teacher will show you some covers to choose from, or you may wish to design one of your own.

Read and enjoy each other's stories.

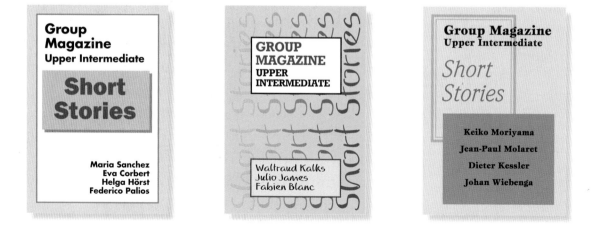

11

EATING OUT

Language focus

food and cooking vocabulary   partitives, e.g. *a slice of bread*
simile and metaphor   adjective suffix *-y*
reporting verbs   verb patterns

1 Choose two of these statements and discuss them in small groups. You have ten minutes.

– Fast food is destroying our food culture.
– Eating meat is wrong.
– Bottled water is a waste of money if tap water is clean.

2 Now try this food quiz with a partner or in small groups.

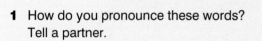

FOOD QUIZ

1 How do you pronounce these words? Tell a partner.

> recipe   prawns   rare   pastry   raspberry
> salmon   lettuce   pie   ingredients

2 Which of these vegetables are not in the picture below? Draw your own picture of the ones not included.

> french beans   courgettes   broccoli
> aubergines   celery   spring onions
> leeks   spinach

3 Five of these verbs describe cutting actions, which are shown below. Label the pictures, then write down the meaning of the odd one out.

slice	grate	carve	simmer	peel	chop

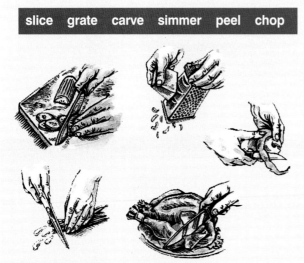

4 Which words on the left are often used with the uncountable nouns on the right to make them countable? There is more than one correct answer in some cases.

Example: *You can have a piece of cake/lemon/toast.*

a piece		sugar
a slice		cake
a pinch	of	lemon
a drop		toast
a spoonful		milk
a squeeze		salt

5 Complete these sentences in a suitable way.

1 ...... is/are a common source of protein.
2 ...... doesn't/don't contain many calories.
3 ...... is/are a common source of vitamin C.
4 ...... is/are very fattening.
5 ...... is/are a common source of carbohydrate.
6 ...... contains caffeine.

6 Which words would serve as opposites for the underlined words in these sentences?

1 The meat was very <u>tough</u>.
2 The apples were very <u>sweet</u>.
3 The soup was very <u>tasty</u>.
4 We ordered some <u>fizzy</u> water.
5 The dessert was very <u>light</u>.
6 The meat was quite <u>lean</u>.
7 The bread was <u>fresh</u>.
8 The prawns were <u>fresh</u>.

7 ▭ Listen to the questions on the recording and write your answers here.

1 ....
2 ....
3 ....
4 ....
5 ....
6 ....
7 ....
8 ....

There is a total of 50 marks – one for each correct answer, and in Exercise 5, one mark only for each partitive (e.g. a piece of cake/lemon/toast counts as one mark). How did you do?

3 Alone or with a partner, prepare a short talk (about two minutes) on one of these topics, using some of the words or phrases from the quiz.

How to make a well-known dish
A diet I have been on
Food in my country
A terrible experience I have had with food or drink

Decide what you want to say and make notes if necessary, but don't write out the whole talk.

4 Divide into small groups of three or four, and take it in turns to give your talks. As you listen, think of questions you would like to ask the speaker at the end.

1 Can you remember a particularly good or bad restaurant that you have been to recently? In small groups, tell each other about the experience.

2 Look at these dishes with a partner. What do you think they are, and how have they been cooked or prepared? Don't worry if you don't know all the words at this stage.

Example: *The first dish is a kind of seafood – I don't know what it's called in English, but we call it 'calamares' – and they're stuffed with rice and fried in oil and garlic.*

Now read one of the restaurant reviews while your partner reads the other. Which of the dishes are mentioned in your review? Tell your partner about the meal and where the reviewer ate it.

FERRY DISGUSTING!

You might think a five-hour sea crossing isn't the best place to have a gastronomic feast, and you would be right – but not because of the rough seas. I nominate 'Jerry's Ferries' for the prize for the worst meals ever cooked at sea! I needed a two-week tour of French restaurants to get over it.

We boarded the ferry at breakfast time and headed straight for the restaurant. Our charming waitress brought us a pot of good strong tea, but things deteriorated quickly after that – with toast which was cold and leathery. We ordered sausages, grilled tomatoes and scrambled eggs; the sausages were greasy and tasteless and the scrambled eggs were rubbery and very unpleasant. So full marks only for the tea!

By lunchtime we were starving as we'd only eaten a tiny amount at breakfast, so we decided to give the more expensive restaurant a try. A mistake. We both thought fish would be a wise choice at sea, but how wrong we were. The 'spicy grilled trout' tasted like shoe leather and was accompanied by lumpy mashed potato and a tiny green salad with no dressing. The desserts included an apple pie with surprisingly good pastry but the apple was a soggy green mess.
Next time, I'll take my sandwiches.

A hum of quiet enjoyment

By John Wells

We got there early and the restaurant was still empty, but from the moment the next party followed us in I knew we were in the right place. No one raised their voices, but the place hummed with quiet enjoyment, and the food matched the atmosphere.

There was a choice of nine starters, all of which sounded highly appetising. Among them were marinated squid with french beans, and potato pancakes with parma ham and celery. I started with leek and potato soup which was smooth, creamy and served at exactly the right temperature. My wife had steamed mussels with curry, cream and herbs, and described it as *very* herby and absolutely delicious.

There were seven main courses. I had roast pheasant which was a huge tender meaty leg, and it came on a bed of crisp rosti potatoes with broccoli. My wife's fish stew, made from cod and red mullet, was equally good, and we both finished off with a lemon soufflé which was light as a feather and very lemony.

The service throughout was quick, charming and unobtrusive, and an added bonus was the bill which was very reasonable for such high-quality food. Dinner for two with wine and coffee came to £57.50, service not included. We left a very generous tip.

Adapted from *The Independent on Sunday*

Now read the other review quickly.

3 Many adjectives are formed by adding *-y* to the noun, and the meaning is often *having* or *containing* the quality of the noun. For example:

Salty food contains a lot of salt.
Curly hair has a lot of curls.

From all the adjectives ending in *-y* in the two texts, how many of them have the meaning above? Make two lists with a partner (adjectives ending in *-y* with the meaning above and adjectives ending in *-y* which are different), and then make sure you understand the meaning of all of them.

-y (= with a certain quality)	*-y* (other examples)
spicy	**tiny**

4 Similes and metaphors describe things by comparing them with something else: similes use the words *like* or *as* in the comparison, metaphors do not. These are examples from the reviews:

The *scrambled eggs* were *rubbery*. (metaphor)
The *spicy grilled trout tasted like shoe leather*. (simile)
The *soufflé was light as a feather*. (simile)

Can you create appropriate negative similes for the food on the left, using the pictures on the right?

the coffee		
the peas		
the pasta	was/were	
the scrambled egg	smelt	like
the mashed potato	tasted	
the pastry	looked	
the steak		
the cheese		
the wine		

leather
bullets
old socks
rubber
cardboard
vinegar
a sponge
cotton wool
washing up water

With your partner, make up some similes or metaphors of your own about food.

5 Imagine the second restaurant was not excellent but awful. Rewrite the review to create the opposite effect, using appropriate adjectives, similes and metaphors. Work with a partner. (You are free to use vocabulary from the first text in Exercise 2.)

1 Do you often *overhear* other people's conversations? If so, where? Do you enjoy it, or do you try not to listen? Discuss in small groups.

2 ▭ Look at the picture of the people in the restaurant. You are going to overhear parts of *three* conversations. Which couple is having which conversation? Discuss with a partner.

3 ▭ Now listen again and answer the questions below using complete sentences. Notice that the question shows you the correct structure to use after the reporting verb.

Example: *Who tried to persuade someone to do something?*
    The woman tried to persuade the man to buy a new suit.

In Conversation 1:
1. Who tried to persuade someone to do something?
2. Who refused to do something?
3. Who regrets doing something?

In Conversation 2:
4. Who encouraged someone to do something?
5. Who suggested doing something?
6. Who agreed to do something?

In Conversation 3:
7. Who accused someone of doing something?
8. Who denied doing something?
9. Who promised to do something?

Compare your answers with a partner.

4 Can you remember how these verbs were used in Exercise 3? Put them in the correct columns below, without looking back at the exercise.

promise   encourage   regret   suggest   refuse   deny   persuade   agree   accuse

verb + inf	*verb + obj + inf*	*verb + -ing*	*verb + obj + prep*
promise to do	*encourage somebody to do*		

Now add these verbs to the correct column or columns. (More than one answer is possible.)

thank   avoid   offer   threaten   prevent   advise

Look at your completed table for two minutes, then close your book and ask your partner to test you like this:

YOUR PARTNER: *To accuse?*
YOU: *You could accuse someone of stealing something.*
YOUR PARTNER: *Yes, that's right.*

5 Look at the restaurant picture again. Imagine what might be happening in the fourth conversation. In pairs, write a short summary using some of the verbs from Exercise 4.

Show your summary to another pair. Do they think it is believable?

PERSONAL STUDY WORKBOOK

In your Personal Study Workbook, you will find more exercises to help you with your learning. For Unit 11, these include:

- practice using reporting verbs
- exercises on collocation and partitives
- pronunciation: intonation and 'shadowing'
- a text about food on the Internet
- rewriting a story to make it more interesting

REVIEW AND DEVELOPMENT

REVIEW OF UNIT 9

1 Getting into good habits   word/phrase + *-ing* form or infinitive

Choose one of these topics, then write down some rules to follow and bad habits to avoid, starting with the expressions below.

keeping a diary   keeping your home clean   going on a diet
giving up something, e.g. smoking, drinking, etc.   training a dog   babysitting

> It's definitely worth ...
> And it's a good idea to get into the habit of ...
> Most of all I think it's important ...
>
> On the other hand, I think it's pointless ...
> and a waste of time ...

Read your suggestions to a partner. Do they know which topic you chose? What do they think of your ideas?

2 Time yourself   compounds and time expressions

Work with a partner. You have two minutes to write down:

– as many compound words as you can including the word 'time', e.g. *timetable*;
– as many time expressions as you can including the word 'time', e.g. to be *on time*.

When the time is up, give your list to another pair to check. Use a dictionary if necessary. Who has the longest list?

3 He's not my husband!   stress in context

A The main stress has been marked in the first line of each dialogue below. Can you mark the main stress in the second lines.

Example: A: *You were in France for a <u>week</u>, weren't you?*
           B: *Oh, no, we were there for a <u>long</u> time.*

1. C: Is that bald man over there your <u>husband</u>?
   D: Oh no – he's my ex-husband.

2. E: Did you meet Henry <u>before</u> the war?
   F: It was after the war, I think, wasn't it, Henry?

3. G: Are these the <u>current</u> month's figures, Derek?
   H: No, sorry, they're the previous month's, I believe.

4. I: Did you catch the <u>7.00</u>?
   J: No, we managed to get an earlier train.

5. K: Did you manage this project <u>yourself</u>?
   L: No, it was my predecessor who ran it, in fact.

6. M: Is that lady in blue the <u>principal</u> of the college?
   N: She's the former principal, actually.

7. O: Is that what they did <u>in the past</u>?
   P: Mmm, and it's still done nowadays.

8. Q: Have you been to <u>the mountains</u>?
   R: Well, I haven't been there lately …

⊂⊃ Listen to the recording and check your answers.

Practise the dialogues in pairs, paying attention to the stress.

REVIEW OF UNIT 10

1 The trouble with Barry   speaking and dictation

A Read the first lines of the short story and discuss with your partner what the situation is and what you think might happen next.

> Barry glanced out of his office window at the car park below. Two police officers were getting out of a car, making their way towards reception. Barry froze.

B ⊂⊃ Listen to the recording. Were your ideas very different?

C ⊂⊃ Listen and write down the extract. Compare it with the tapescript on page 168.

D With your partner, work out how the plot might continue. Write out a summary of your plot in 40 words; then show it to another pair.

2 Quizword   crime vocabulary

Complete the quizword. If you do it correctly, you will find one word vertically down the centre which spells out another crime. Use your dictionary to find out what it means and how to pronounce it.

These are crimes in which someone ...
1. tries to get money by threatening to tell someone's secret.
2. sexually attacks another person.
3. tries to kill someone using arsenic, for example.
4. deliberately sets fire to a building or car.
5. breaks into a private house and steals things.
6. gets money by tricking or deceiving people.
7. kills someone intentionally.
8. sells illegal substances, such as cocaine or heroin.
9. steals something.
10. takes goods from a shop without paying.
11. drives faster than they are allowed to.
12. gives something valuable, like money, to persuade an official to do something for them.

THEATRICAL INTERLUDE

Language focus

question forms
adverbs of manner
pronunciation: accents

vocabulary: personal interaction
adverbial phrases
vocabulary describing speech

A NIGHT OUT

1 A man of 28 lives with his widowed mother. Think of the advantages and disadvantages of the situation for each of them, then discuss your ideas in small groups.

2 ▭ You are going to listen to the first scene of a play called *A Night Out* by the British playwright, Harold Pinter. Read the stage directions in italics on page 90, then listen to the first part of the scene and follow it in your book.

Think back to the advantages and disadvantages you discussed in Exercise 1. Can you see any evidence of these in this first extract? Compare in groups.

Act One Scene One

The kitchen of MRS STOKES' *small house in the south of London. Clean and tidy.*

ALBERT, *a young man of 28, is standing in his shirt and trousers, combing his hair in the kitchen mirror over the mantelpiece. A woman's voice calls his name from upstairs. He ignores it, picks up a brush from the mantelpiece and brushes his hair. The voice calls again. He slips his comb in his pocket, bends down, reaches under the sink and takes out a shoe duster. He begins to polish his shoes.* MRS STOKES *descends the stairs, passes through the hall and enters the kitchen.*

Mother: Albert! Albert! Albert, I've been calling you. (*She watches him.*) What are you doing?

Albert: Nothing.

Mother: Didn't you hear me call you, Albert? I've been calling you from upstairs.

Albert: You seen my tie?

Mother: Oh, I say, I'll have to put the flag out.

Albert: What do you mean?

Mother: Cleaning your shoes, Albert? I'll have to put the flag out, won't I?

Albert puts the brush back under the sink and begins to search the sideboard and cupboard.

What are you looking for?

Albert: My tie. The striped one, the blue one.

Mother: The bulb's gone in Grandma's room.

Albert: Has it?

Mother: That's what I was calling you about. I went in and switched on the light, and the bulb had gone.

She watches him open the kitchen cabinet and look into it.

Aren't those your best trousers, Albert? What have you put on your best trousers for?

Albert: Look, Mum, where's my tie? The blue one, the blue tie, where is it? You know the one I mean, the blue striped one, I gave it to you this morning.

Mother: What do you want your tie for?

Albert: I want to put it on. I asked you to press it for me this morning. I gave it to you this morning before I went to work, didn't I?

---

3 Using a dictionary, work with a partner to check any new vocabulary in the box.

> to feel guilty about something   to nag someone   to reassure someone
> to be suspicious of something/someone   to get irritable with someone
> to get on someone's nerves   to be nosy   to get away from someone

📟 Listen to the rest of the first scene. Then in pairs, complete the sentences about the people in the scene using the correct pronouns: *he, she, him, her, his.*

1. ...*She*... is nosy.

2. .... is feeling guilty.

3. .... is getting irritable with ....

4. .... is suspicious of ....

5. .... is making .... feel guilty.

6. .... is trying to get away from ....

7. .... is afraid of losing ....

8. .... keeps nagging ....

9. .... is getting on .... nerves.

10. .... is trying to reassure ....

Can you add any other sentences about their relationship?

4 Look at these five different types of question from the scene. For each example in Box A, find another example in Box B.

Box A
Cleaning your shoes, Albert?
You're dressing up tonight, aren't you?
What have you put on your best trousers for?
You're going out?
Didn't you hear me call you, Albert?

Box B
What do you want your tie for?
Aren't those your best trousers?
You seen my tie?
You're going to Mr King's?
There'll be girls there, won't there?

What does each pair have in common? In each question, does the speaker already know the answer? And if they already know the answer, why are they asking the question?

Example: *Cleaning your shoes, Albert?*   *The mother can see him cleaning his shoes, so she knows the answer; she's probably trying to get him to tell her why, and where he's going.*

5 Choose an extract from the scene, either on page 90 or 168–9, and rehearse it with your partner. Think first about the character and mood of the person you are going to play.

When you are ready, read your section to another pair.

I LIKE YOUR ACCENT!
pronunciation; vocabulary

1 ⊂⊃ Listen to this short passage read in three different accents, and answer the questions below.

Put the new potatoes in the bottom of the bowl.
Then put in the sliced tomatoes and chopped onion.
After that, add some herbs like parsley and basil, and that's it.

1. Can you identify any of the accents?
2. Underline any words or sounds which are pronounced differently by at least two speakers. What is different?
3. Which speaker's voice tends to fall more at the end of sentences?

2 ⊂⊃ Listen to each passage again and try to copy the accent. Work with a partner, then listen to others in the group. Who is closest to the original accent? Do you find one accent easier to imitate? Why? Which accent do you prefer?

3 Check that you understand the words in italics below. Discuss in groups.

1. In your country, are there *distinctive regional accents* or different *dialects*? If so, what are they?
2. Can you *imitate* any of them?
3. Do accents in your country vary according to social class? For instance, do you have *posh, educated* or *working-class* accents? What do you think about this?
4. How would you describe your own accent in your *mother tongue*? Do you feel you have a *strong* accent, a *slight* accent or no accent at all?
5. Do you have friends or family who have moved elsewhere, *lost their original* accent and *picked up* a different one?
6. In your country, are there people on TV who *impersonate* famous people? Do they simply *mimic* the voice and accent, or do they also copy their *mannerisms*?

4 ▭ ▭ Actors often have to imitate particular accents. Listen to these actors describing their experiences.

1. What accent does each speaker have to learn?
2. What features of the new accent do they have to learn? For example, are there particular sounds which are a problem?

Which of these strategies or techniques do the speakers mention? Listen again if necessary.

– listening to and trying to copy people with the accent
– listening to films or tapes of people with the accent
– going to a voice coach or teacher for help
– writing down difficult sounds phonetically
– memorising a typical sounding phrase
– concentrating on specific sounds

5 Do you use any of the techniques suggested by the actors to help you to improve your English pronunciation? Do you have any other techniques you could add to the list above? Discuss in small groups.

IT DEPENDS HOW YOU SAY IT   adverbs of manner; adverbial phrases

1 Try this short test on adverbs and adverbial phrases. Correct any mistakes connected with the words in italics, then check your answers using the Language Reference on page 148. (Be careful: some of the sentences are correct.)

> **Adverbs of manner and adverbial phrases**
> 1. She spoke very *fastly*.
> 2. He whispered *soft* in his ear.
> 3. They all volunteered *enthusiasticly*.
> 4. She slammed the door *furiously*.
> 5. She waited *nervous* by the phone.
> 6. She spoke to me in a *silly* voice.
> 7. He looked out of the window *gloomy*.
> 8. He walked down the corridor whistling *cheerfully*.
> 9. She introduced herself very *friendlily*.
> 10. He got up from his chair *wearyly* and closed the door.
> 11. They looked at each other *suspiciously*.
> 12. He replied *irritabley* in response to her criticism.
> 13. He stared at the screen in a *puzzled way*.
> 14. He read the first line of the passage *difficultly*.

2 With your partner, practise saying the first eight sentences in the manner of the adverb in each one.

Example: *Say the first sentence fast.*

3 You are now going to read part of a scene from a play, but you must provide the stage directions (in brackets) to indicate how the lines are spoken. Read the scene first, then, with a partner, fill the gaps using the words in the box. The first one has been done for you.

> suspiciously   nervously   ~~wearily~~   in a puzzled way   gloomily
> irritably   enthusiastically   cheerfully   surprised   sympathetically
> tenderly   whispering

The story so far ...

Martin and Gary share a flat together. Martin has been going out with Stephanie for several years, and next Saturday is her birthday. On the same day, Martin and Gary's favourite football team are playing an important match 100 miles away. Gary has managed to get two tickets and has asked Martin to go with him. Martin has agreed to go, but now realises he might have a real problem with Stephanie ...

Scene: *Evening. Inside Martin and Gary's untidy flat. Martin is lying on the sofa, watching TV and reading a sports magazine. The doorbell rings. Martin gets up (* **wearily** *), turns off the TV and wanders over to open the door. Stephanie comes in, removing her coat and throwing her bag on the floor.*

Stephanie: (........................)
Hello, darling! Had a good day?

Martin: (........................) No, not particularly.
I spent the morning tidying the flat ...

Stephanie: (looking at the mess ....)
I beg your pardon?

Martin: (........................) OK, OK, let me explain – I went to work and when I got back, Gary had been in and left it looking like a battlefield.

Stephanie: (........................) Oh, poor Martin. No, really, I don't know why you put up with him. He never does a stroke of work.

Martin: Well, he does have his good side. I mean, he's very good at getting the best tickets for the big matches ...

Stephanie: (........................) Football matches, Martin? What are you talking about?

Martin: (........................) Oh, nothing, nothing. By the way, what do you want for your birthday?

Stephanie: I want you to take me to that lovely Thai restaurant. You remember, don't you? (........................) It was so romantic there ...

Sound of someone opening the front door. Martin jumps up.

Martin: (........................) Oh, great, fantastic! – that'll be Gary. I'll make some coffee.

Gary: Hi, Martin ... Oh! (........................) well, hello, Stephanie – I didn't expect to see you this evening ...

Martin: Hi, Gary. (*walking out to the kitchen,* ....) Don't mention the tickets. I haven't told her yet.

4 ⏹ Work in groups of four. Three of you should read the scene. The fourth person should listen to see if the others are following the stage directions accurately. Then change roles. Now listen to the recording and compare it with your version.

5 In your group, decide what happens in the rest of the scene.

Examples: *Gary forgets what Martin said, and mentions the football match. Stephanie challenges him and gets very upset. Martin has to make a compromise.*
or
Stephanie wants Martin to ring the restaurant now to book a table for Saturday. Martin eventually has to confess.

Make up your own ending if you prefer. Write the rest of the scene, and include at least five directions to the actors. Then act the whole scene for another group.

PERSONAL STUDY WORKBOOK

In your Personal Study Workbook, you will find more exercises to help you with your learning. For Unit 12, these include:

- exercises on adverbs and adverbial phrases
- practice using question forms
- pronunciation: copying different accents
- a text about the man who helps famous actors to learn accents
- actors talking about learning different accents
- writing a dialogue

REVIEW AND DEVELOPMENT

REVIEW OF UNIT 10

1 What on earth do they need that for?   purpose clauses

A Work in small groups. Take turns to choose a word from each bubble, and complete the sentences in your own words.

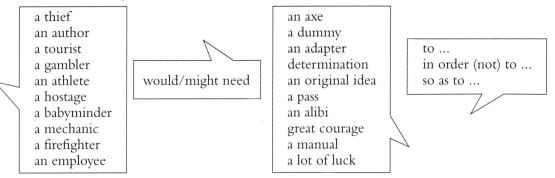

a thief	an axe	
an author	a dummy	to ...
a tourist	an adapter	in order (not) to ...
a gambler	determination	so as to ...
an athlete	an original idea	
a hostage	a pass	
a babyminder	an alibi	
a mechanic	great courage	
a firefighter	a manual	
an employee	a lot of luck	

would/might need

Example: *A thief might need an alibi in order to avoid being charged with a crime.*

B Make up similar sentences, using the prompts below or your own ideas. See what your partner thinks of them.

a comedian   a trapeze artist   a language learner   a farmer   an inventor
a hospital patient

2 Tell it in your own way　　`attitude adverbs; speaking`

Adverbs are often used to show someone's attitude to events or situations. The adverbs in this exercise (in bold type) also link one event with another.

Look at this example and decide the most suitable way to continue the extract.

Example: *… and we watched in horror as he fell from the first floor window.*

                    he was badly hurt, and we sent for the ambulance.
Astonishingly, *he didn't know where he was.*
                    he landed on his feet and was shaken but uninjured.

Work with a partner. Complete the extracts from the stories below in a suitable way.

1. … and I saw a man giving away $20 bills to strangers in the street. **Naturally**, …

2. … I saw her struggling with the heavy suitcase. **Unfortunately**, …

3. … and there we were, stuck in the desert with no petrol. **Strangely, though**, …

4. … **Obviously**, we needed help – but where would we find it at this time of night?

5. … **Incredibly**, she emerged from the crumpled car and limped towards us.

6. … **Miraculously**, we found it just before the tide came in, otherwise it would have been lost forever.

Compare your ideas with another pair.

Choose one of the extracts, and together write a story around it which will take precisely *one minute* to tell. Practise telling it to make sure your timing is correct.

Find a new partner, and tell them your story. What do they think of it?

REVIEW OF UNIT 11

1 Listen and answer　　`pronunciation; food vocabulary`

▭ Listen and write down your answers to the questions. When you have finished, check them with the tapescript on page 170. Then repeat the exercise with a partner. One of you reads the questions from page 170, the other answers. Pay careful attention to your pronunciation of individual words and the rhythm of the sentence.

2 What kind of person are you?　　`verb patterns`

Answer these questions, giving examples.

1. Do you often offer to do things for other people?　YES/NO
2. Do other people often offer to do things for you?　YES/NO
3. Do you often encourage other people to do things?　YES/NO
4. Do other people often encourage you to do things?　YES/NO
5. Do you often thank other people for doing things?　YES/NO
6. Do other people often thank you for doing things?　YES/NO

Were your answers mostly positive or negative? Was there any difference between the answers to the odd numbers (1, 3, 5) and the even numbers (2, 4, 6)? What conclusions can you draw from this? Discuss in groups, then answer these questions with examples.

7. Do you often blame other people for getting things wrong?　YES/NO
8. Do other people often blame you for getting things wrong?　YES/NO
9. Do you often refuse to help other people?　YES/NO
10. Do other people often refuse to help you?　YES/NO
11. Do you often prevent other people from doing things they want to do?　YES/NO
12. Do other people often prevent you from doing things you want to do?　YES/NO

How do your answers compare with those to the first six questions? Discuss in groups.

ON THE JOB

Language focus

expressing obligation,
permission and entitlement
work vocabulary
adjectives for appearance

if ever/whenever
adjective + noun collocation
expressing probability

IS IT RIGHT? IS IT FAIR?   obligation, permission and entitlement; work vocabulary

1 With a partner, discuss any difference in meaning or style in each of the pairs of words and phrases.

Example: Retire *and* resign *are different*: retire *means to give up work when you are at the end of your working life (60 or 65, say) and* resign *means to give up your job because you want to.*

retire	and	resign
go on strike		get the sack
be made redundant		be dismissed
employ someone		take someone on
be promoted		be laid off
have to do something		be forced to do something
have the right to (do) something		be entitled to (do) something
be allowed to do something		be about to do something
apply for a job		give up a job
maternity leave		paternity leave
compulsory		voluntary

2 Read through the questionnaire on page 97, and quickly write down *Yes, No* or *Not sure/it depends* at the end of each question.

3 Now work in small groups. Choose questions where you have different answers, and discuss your opinions.

4 ▭ ▭ Listen to some people discussing one of the questions on the questionnaire. What does the man think, and why does the woman disagree?

5 ▭ The questionnaire, and tapescript on page 156 include different ways of expressing obligation. Listen again and complete the gaps in the tapescript.

Questionnaire

Attitudes to work situations

1 Should employers be allowed to limit job applications to men, *or* women, *or* people of a particular age?

2 Should unemployed people be forced to accept any job they are offered?

3 Do you think workers ought to be allowed to go on strike, including the armed forces and emergency services?

4 When workers are made redundant, do you agree with the principle, 'last in, first out'? (In other words, the last people to be employed ought to be the first ones to be laid off.)

5 Should people be promoted on the basis of ability or seniority (in other words, the length of time they have worked in the company), or a combination of the two?

6 Should all fathers be entitled to paternity leave? If so, how much?

7 Do you think retirement at the age of 60 or 65 should be compulsory, or should people have the right to carry on working if they wish?

8 Do you think the retirement age for men and women ought to be the same?

WHAT TO WEAR TO GET THAT JOB
adjectives for appearance; expressing probability

1 When you attend a job interview, is it always important to be well-dressed? What have you worn to any interviews you have attended? Discuss in small groups.

2 With a partner, use a dictionary to help you with the meaning and pronunciation of the words in the box, and divide the words into three groups:

- words used largely with a positive meaning
- words used largely with a negative meaning
- words which can be positive or negative

smart	assertive	dreary	daring	conservative	quite stylish showy
fashion-conscious	businesslike	adventurous	elegant	provocative	inoffensive

3 Look at the five pictures. Which adjectives from Exercise 2 would you use to describe each one? Are there any adjectives you wouldn't use to describe any of them?

4 Find out how some experts from different professions would react to applicants wearing these outfits at a job interview (for a job in their profession). Read two of the texts while your partner reads the other two, and complete your section of the table below with these symbols:

★★ = very enthusiastic and *would definitely* offer the candidate a job on the basis of their appearance

★ = positive and *would probably* offer the candidate a job

? = mixed feelings but *might still* offer a job

?? = mixed feelings and *would be unlikely* to offer a job

X = very negative and *definitely wouldn't* offer a job

	Picture 1	Picture 2	Picture 3	Picture 4	Picture 5
Designer					
Banker					
Headmaster					
Doctor					

The designer

Picture 1: Fine. A lot of designers look like that, quite minimalist. Black and grey are very popular.

Picture 2: Yeah, no problems. She looks fine, smart, and the trousers are good. I prefer women to look comfortable in what they're wearing.

Picture 3: She'd have to have the personality to carry this off – it's interesting and outgoing. It makes a statement and wouldn't be out of place in our company.

Picture 4: Not very nineties – more like a seventies air hostess. I'm not sure what her design work would look like – probably not very exciting.

Picture 5: She looks very comfortable, which is a plus. I wouldn't rule her out, but she would have to wear something smarter for a client meeting.

The banker

Picture 1: She's smart, she's fashionable; I'd employ her.

Picture 2: Hmm, trousers. They're smart and elegant, but trousers are still a tricky issue at work. Definitely not interview wear, anyway, though I hope I'm broad-minded enough not to be put off totally.

Picture 3: Not right for our bank. I think the shiny jacket shows a lack of judgement about the interview.

Picture 4: What a very smart, elegant young woman! She's clearly going places. You can't fault her outfit at all: neat hair, coordinated jewellery. And red! A good assertive colour. She'd do very well.

Picture 5: She doesn't look very assertive. I'd probably give her the benefit of the doubt, but I'd worry she isn't projecting herself as a dynamic, young executive.

The headmaster

Picture 1: High heels don't make much sense in a school and a short skirt with tights is asking for trouble, quite frankly. Tights are likely to ladder or snag on the desks.

Picture 2: Has all the virtues: flat shoes and smart style that doesn't cry out. Just one snag: these are expensive clothes. That's not the message a teacher wants to give (and most couldn't afford them).

Picture 3: This is rather provocative and showy. It would be wonderfully appropriate in the right environment, I'm sure, but definitely not right for school. It looks like she's trying to make some sort of statement.

Picture 4: Overdressed for an interview, let alone the classroom. It's executive clothing, something industrial companies would no doubt swoon over. Incredibly bright and colourful, but too smart for here.

Picture 5: Perfect. She's taken a lot of trouble with her hair, she looks comfortable, the shoes are flat and the skirt is not too short. I'd give her the job.

The doctor (in a hospital)

Picture 1: This is the best of the lot. It's very smart and sensible, and the skirt wouldn't be too tight if you had to climb over beds to get to a patient.

Picture 2: I've no problem with a suit like this. Many female junior doctors do wear trousers. It's more practical and it's not frowned upon by enlightened members of the establishment.

Picture 3: Extremely practical because you could wipe the PVC down easily if there was blood on it! The outfit is inappropriate, though, if you're dealing with bereaved or worried relatives.

Picture 4: If you were in a GP practice or desk job, there would be no problems with this. It's conservative and wouldn't offend anyone. Hospital doctors, however, get their clothes in a mess, so it's too fussy.

Picture 5: This is fairly conservative, boring and dull. If a junior doctor came to work wearing this, she wouldn't offend anyone. A good choice.

Adapted from *The Independent on Sunday*

Compare and discuss your answers in small groups.

5 Do you agree with the opinions of the four professionals? Do you think it is reasonable to make judgements about people based on what they are wearing?

6 Using the probability expressions from Exercise 4, say how you would react to the woman in the five pictures if she was attending a job interview to be:
- someone in your own profession;
- a nightclub manageress;
- a receptionist in a modern art gallery;
- a candidate for a political party.

1   Most jobs have a downside (a negative side). What do you think they might be for these jobs? Discuss in small groups.

Nanny   Public relations officer for a travel agent   Head teacher

2   The adjectives in the box on the left are often used with the nouns in the box on the right. Can you match them correctly? Write the phrases in your notebook.

disruptive	deprived	situation	patience
complete	physical	customers	language
abusive	great	background	behaviour
embarrassing	awkward	violence	stranger

Which of these phrases might be used by the people above, talking about their jobs? Discuss with a partner.

3   📟 Listen to three people talking about the worst aspects of their jobs. Write down anything negative you did not mention in Exercise 1. Compare with a partner.

4   The nanny says, 'If ever I walk in on a row, I just sing loudly'. Look at these constructions:

If (I) ever
If ever (I)   + present simple, (I) present simple
Whenever (I)

In these sentences, *if ... ever / if ever ...* and *whenever* mean *every time that something happens.*

Which of the three people might say the following?

– If ever I start feeling down about my job, I just think of the kids and then I'm thankful I don't have a boring desk job.
– Whenever the phone rings early in the morning, I always assume it's bad news.
– If anyone ever sends me a letter of thanks or praise, my whole mood changes for the better.
– Whenever I feel like a change, I put him in the pushchair and go down to the park.

5 In pairs, make up sentences using *if ... ever / if ever ...* or *whenever* about the people in the pictures. They can be about the downside of the job or its more positive aspects.

traffic warden

publican

nurse

lifeguard

hairdresser

flower arranger

Example: (*traffic warden*)   *Whenever people start to get abusive, I don't let it worry me; I just think about lying on a beach, or something nice like that.*

Tell your sentences to other learners. Can they tell which job you are talking about?

6 Think about your own job, or that of a friend or relative. Make notes on the positive features of the job and the downside. Do the positive features outweigh (= are greater than) the negative features, or vice versa? Discuss in small groups, giving your reasons.

PERSONAL STUDY WORKBOOK

In your Personal Study Workbook, you will find more exercises to help you with your learning. For Unit 13, these include:

- vocabulary exercises
- an exercise testing the use of modal verbs of obligation
- pronunciation: word stress
- guessing the meaning of new words in a text
- discursive writing: organising an argument

REVIEW AND DEVELOPMENT

REVIEW OF UNIT 11

1 I like ... food   vocabulary: -y suffix

Underline *like* or *don't like*, then complete each sentence truthfully, using a suitable adjective with a -*y* suffix. When you have finished, compare and discuss your answers with a partner.

Examples: *I like/don't like* ....**stony**...... *beaches.*
               I like/don't like ....**sandy**...... *beaches.*

I like/don't like .... beaches.

I like/don't like .... weather.

I like/don't like .... places.

I like/don't like .... meat.

I like/don't like .... food.

I like/don't like .... hair.

I like/don't like .... water.

2 I'm starving! | vocabulary: expressions/idioms |

Read the dialogues and with your partner and a dictionary,
check the meaning of the expressions underlined.

1. A: I could do with a bite to eat.
   B: Yeah, me too – I'm starving. My stomach's rumbling.

2. C: Fancy a drink?
   D: No, thanks, I'm teetotal.

3. E: Would you like some more spaghetti?
   F: No, thanks, I'm full up.

4. G: Oh, I'm dying of thirst.
   H: Do you fancy an orange juice?
   G: Yes, that'll do.

5. I: I'm not going to invite your cousin again: he eats like a pig and drinks like a fish.
   J: Yes, and he needs to go on a diet!

Practise the dialogues together until you can say them without looking.

REVIEW OF UNIT 12

1 It's a question tag, isn't it? | question tags |

A We use question tags:

1. to check when we aren't sure about the answer (a real question). In this case, the tag rises.

Example: A: *You're German, **aren't** you?*
          B: *No, I'm Austrian, actually.*

2. to ask for agreement (an unreal question). In this case, the tag falls: the listener is expected
   to say 'yes'.

Example: A: *This hat really **looks** good on her, **doesn't** it?*
          B: *Yes, great.*

Look at the form:

She speaks English, doesn't she?
positive   negative auxiliary

He can't swim, can he?
negative   positive auxiliary

Now complete these questions with the correct tags.

1. Delia drives a Volvo, ...?
2. You haven't been to Rome, ...?
3. It won't rain tomorrow, ...?
4. They should have rung, ...?
5. Lovely day, ...?
6. He's got a dog, ...?
7. He has to leave at 9, ...?
8. They used to live abroad, ...?

B With a partner, add two question tags to each dialogue where appropriate, and
decide if they should rise or fall. (There may be more than two possible places where
you can put them.)

1. A: What's up?
   B: I haven't got any money in the bank.
   A: Well, never mind. You get paid tomorrow.
   B: Yes, but I'll be broke again next week.
   A: You really need to win the lottery.

2. C: They're very strange people.
   D: Oh, do you think so?
   C: Well, they keep snakes. Anyone who keeps
      snakes has to be a bit unusual.
   D: Oh, come on. There's nothing wrong with that.
      Uncle Donald used to have a snake.
   C: Precisely. Uncle Donald wasn't exactly *normal*.

14

ACCIDENTS WILL HAPPEN

Language focus

present/past continuous (habits)
used to/would (past habits)
verbs, e.g. *spill, scratch, rip*

keep + *-ing*
participle clauses
accidents; medical vocabulary

ARE YOU CLUMSY OR ABSENT-MINDED? expressing present and past habits

1 Do you know what *clumsy* and *absent-minded* mean?
If not, look at these dictionary definitions.

> **absent-minded:** likely to forget things, especially because you are thinking about something else.
>
> *Longman Dictionary of Contemporary English*

> **clumsy:** awkward in movement or manner.
> A **clumsy** person often has accidents because their actions are not controlled or careful enough.
>
> *Cambridge International Dictionary of English*

> A **clumsy** person moves or handles things in a careless awkward way, often so that things are knocked over or broken.
>
> *Collins COBUILD English Dictionary*

Work with a partner, and use a dictionary where necessary. Which of these sentences describe the typical actions of a clumsy person? Which describe an absent-minded person? Be careful: some sentences refer to neither.

1. I've smashed three glasses this week.
2. He tripped over running for the bus.
3. I crept along the path.
4. He's mislaid his keys.
5. She spilt the coffee down her new dress.
6. He leapt over the gate.
7. I bumped into the table.
8. She bruised her leg on the desk.
9. He left the gas on.
10. He vanished behind the trees.
11. She didn't turn up for the meeting.
12. I scratched the side of the car.
13. She ripped her shirt.
14. I've left my book at home again.

2 Are you (or were you) clumsy or absent-minded? If so, what sort of things do/did you do? Discuss in small groups, using any vocabulary from Exercise 1.

---

3 🎧 Listen to the two people on the recording and complete the tapescripts. Then compare with a partner.

My problem is ...., important things, such as my front door key or my credit cards – that sort of stuff. And it's really irritating because I know they're important but .... in the house – I don't have one place you see where I keep these things – and within hours, minutes even, I can't remember where they are. My wife .... looking for things I'd mislaid, but now she refuses to lift a finger to help me.

I remember as a teenager I .... and my body was covered in bruises all the time where I .... and falling over. And at home I .... and smashing glasses – my mother would never let me do the washing up or anything like that, and for a while it got so bad that she .... of value so that I couldn't get my hands on it and break it.

4 Answer the questions with your partner.
1. What forms does the man use to describe his absent-minded habits?
2. Why do you think he uses *these* forms, and not the present simple (e.g. 'I mislay things'; 'I put them down')?
3. What forms does the woman use to describe the clumsy habits she used to have?
4. Both speakers include *used to* + verb and the woman uses *would* + verb. Are these two forms interchangeable in all the examples here?

Check your answers in the Language Reference on page 149–150.

5 Do any of the people below have habits that annoy or irritate you? If so, complete the sentences, then compare and discuss them in groups.

News journalists are always ... *prying into the private lives of famous people.*

The problem with parents is that they're always ...
I hate motorcyclists – they're forever ...
Some politicians make me angry. They keep ...
When we were children, my brother/sister was forever ...
We used to have a teacher who kept ...

6 🎧 🎧 Listen to the recording. Are the speakers clumsy or absent-minded? What examples do they give? Make notes, then compare with a partner.

UNUSUAL CLAIMS
accident vocabulary; participle clauses; writing

1 Look at the picture. What do you think caused the accident? Think of two possible explanations, then tell a partner.

2 Sometimes when people have to describe an accident for an insurance company, their story of what happened can become confused, with funny results.

Read these real extracts and find the accidents which suggest that the driver wasn't paying attention.

Dear Sir,
The accident happened like this ...

<u>Arriving home</u>, I drove into the wrong house and crashed into a tree I don't have.

I pulled out from the side of the road, glanced at my mother-in-law, and drove straight into the river.

I thought my window was open, but I found out it wasn't when I put my head through it.

<u>Approaching</u> the junction, I saw a sign suddenly appear in a place where no sign had ever appeared before. I was unable to stop in time to avoid the accident.

I told the police I was not injured, but on <u>removing</u> my hat, I found that I had a fractured skull.

I was thrown from my car as it left the road. I was later found by some cows.

<u>Attempting</u> to kill a fly, I ran over a cat and struck a telegraph pole.

My car was legally parked as it backed into the other vehicle.

The indirect cause of the accident was a little guy in a small car with a big mouth.

I had been driving for forty years when I fell asleep at the wheel and collided with a lorry <u>coming</u> in the opposite direction.

From *The Bloomsbury Guide to Letter Writing*

Work in small groups and compare your answers, then tell each other which explanations you like best. Choose one or two of the very illogical accounts. What do you think the person meant to say?

3 How often can you replace words or phrases in the extracts with the word *hit*, without changing the meaning? Make a list of these words, then compare with a partner.

Example: **to crash into something = to hit something in a vehicle with force**

4 Participle clauses may contain present participles, e.g. *seeing*, or past participles, e.g. *seen*. Here are three ways in which we use present participles in these clauses.

- To give more information, often replacing a relative clause:
  *The man **driving** the lorry couldn't stop.* (= who was driving)
- To show that events happened simultaneously, replacing *when*:
  ***Seeing** the child, I swerved at once.* (= **when I saw** him)
- To show that one event is the result of the other, or explains the cause/reason for the other (often formal):
  ***Realising** that I couldn't help them, I decided to leave.* (= **because I realised** that ...)

Now look at the underlined participles in the text. How would you paraphrase each one? Are they examples of the first, second or third participle clauses above?

5 Imagine you were one of the people involved in the accident on the right. Write down what happened using vocabulary from the text and participle clauses where appropriate.
Then find someone who wrote about a different person, and read their account.

1 One of the most remarkable true stories in medical history includes the vocabulary in the box. Can you tell the first part of this incredible story using these words? Work with a partner and use a dictionary if necessary.

Hong Kong	holiday romance	to the airport	motorbike	take–off
knocked Paula off	bruised arm	jumbo jet to Heathrow	surgeon on board	

2 Read the first part of the story, then find a different partner. How accurate are your predictions so far? Explain to each other any differences between your story and the text.

Drama at 9,000 metres

Separated and waiting for a divorce, Paula Dixon decided to spend a holiday with her sister who lived in Hong Kong. She went with her friend, Barbara Murray, and on their first evening in Hong Kong, Paula met Thomas, a thirty-year-old factory manager from Stuttgart, Germany.

They had a whirlwind romance, and shortly before the end of the holiday they made plans to get married. Paula would go back to England but soon return to Hong Kong, and live with Thomas.

On the day of their return, Barbara took the bus back to the airport, but Thomas gave Paula a lift on his motorbike. On the way, a car pulled out from a side road, hit the bike and knocked Paula off. She was shaken, and her left forearm was bruised and bleeding, but apart from that she felt okay, and she insisted on continuing to the airport. Once on board, she asked one of the attendants for some paracetamol and a bandage. The attendant was immediately alarmed and a call went out for a doctor. It was answered first by Tom Wong, a newly qualified doctor who was returning to his job in Scotland, but also by Angus Wallace, a 46-year-old Scotsman who was a professor of orthopaedics and accident surgery in Nottingham.

Wallace examined the woman. The arm was painful, but she complained of no symptoms other than the bruised forearm. And even if the arm were fractured, the surgeon decided the injury was not serious, and she could still continue on the flight. 'We can take off and treat her arm when we're in the air,' he told the cabin crew.

3 〔⫌〕 Look at the picture and listen to the rest of the story. What happens? Tell your partner.

4 📼 Listen again if necessary, and answer these questions. Compare with a partner.

1. What happened when Paula took her shoes off?
2. What did the doctor think the problem was at first?
3. How did he know it was very serious?
4. Which of the objects in the picture did he use in the operation?
5. How did Paula feel after the operation?
6. What happened to Doctor Wallace?

5 Work with your partner. The words in the box are all related to medical matters. How many of them were in the reading or listening texts?

a bruised arm	to be in pain
a fractured rib	to be in agony
a swollen ankle	to be shaken
a collapsed lung	to be in shock
a bandage	a surgeon
a plaster	an operating theatre
a first aid kit	an anaesthetic
painkillers	instruments
breathing difficulties	life-threatening
symptoms	life-saving
internal bleeding	

6 Shortly after she arrived in Hong Kong, Thomas bought her an engagement ring, and she decided to write a short letter to Angus Wallace. With a partner, write the letter she sent and then compare your letter with others in the class.

PERSONAL STUDY WORKBOOK

In your Personal Study Workbook, you will find more exercises to help you with your learning. For Unit 14, these include:

- using different constructions to describe annoying habits
- an exercise on synonyms
- practice using participle clauses
- a text about dangerous objects in the house
- people talking about childhood memories

REVIEW AND DEVELOPMENT

REVIEW OF UNIT 12

1 Attitudes to the theatre | speaking |

Read the questionnaire and check any new words in your dictionary. Fill in your answers, then discuss them in small groups, giving your reasons.

totally agree				totally disagree
1	2	3	4	5

1. Theatre has a more immediate and direct effect on the audience than cinema or television.
2. Watching a play being performed live in the theatre is a completely different experience from watching on television.
3. Reading a play is as valuable an experience as watching a play being performed.
4. Theatre appeals to only a minority of the population.
5. The formal aspects of an evening at the theatre are off-putting.
6. The community, both at local and national levels, should subsidise the theatre.

From *From Page to Performance* by Don Shiach

2 The best and the worst | adverbs and adverbial phrases

What would be the best way and the worst way
to do these things? Discuss in small groups.

Example: *tell someone you loved them*
the best way: tenderly
the worst way: in a boring voice

- tell someone they had failed an exam
- ask for a refund in a shop
- drive over a mountain pass
- ask your boss for a pay rise
- shut a door
- choose a husband or wife
- speak in a job interview

REVIEW OF UNIT 13

1 Work quiz | listening and vocabulary

📼 You will hear ten definitions or explanations of words and phrases connected with
work. Listen and write down your answers, then compare with a partner.

Now try to define the words and phrases in your own words. How quickly can your
partner give you the word or phrase being defined?

2 The inevitable cutbacks | modals: obligation, advice, possibility

Arun (in the picture) runs a local shop in a suburb of London, but recently his business
has suffered. Read the text and make notes on these questions.

1. Why is the business suffering?
2. What action has he considered to meet this challenge, and why?
3. How does he feel about this situation?

Compare your answers in small groups.

My business has suffered terribly recently because a large supermarket has opened near here, and it sells many of the things that I stock, such as newspapers, food, etc. And the trouble is, they can sell food at a much more competitive price because of their size, and also offer a much wider range of goods.

I've tried to fight them in a number of ways. For instance, I've reduced the price on some goods, which means a lower profit margin for me, but I'm not sure if I can ever compete with supermarkets on price. My one advantage might be to stay open longer when the supermarket is closed and get more business that way.

I've also thought about laying off one of the two women who work part-time. This would mean a financial saving for me but the quality of service would suffer at the same time, and that may not be in my long-term interest.

Obviously, I'd like to offer a wider range of goods but it just isn't practical. Ultimately, I just have to accept the competition and I can't blame people for looking for bargains, but I do feel bitter that I've built up a business over ten years which could all be swept away in a matter of months.

What do you think Arun has got to do? What do you think he ought to do? What
other things could he consider doing? Discuss in small groups.

WAYS OF BEING BETTER OFF

HOW HONEST ARE WE?

expressing quantity; using whether

1 You are walking along a quiet street and find a wallet containing £30 (about $50). What would you do? Discuss in small groups. (If something like this *has* happened to you, tell the group what you did.)

2 In an experiment, researchers dropped a number of wallets containing £30 and waited to see how people would respond when they found the money. Read this short text to find out how they set up the experiment. Then shut your book and tell a partner what you can remember.

In a recent experiment carried out by the *Reader's Digest* magazine, a team of researchers dropped 80 wallets – ten each in four big cities and four medium-sized towns in England, Scotland and Wales. Each wallet contained a name, two telephone numbers, family photographs, tickets, receipts and £30 in cash. The researchers left them in shopping centres, train and underground stations, supermarkets, car parks and on pavements. Then they watched to see what would happen. Each person who returned a wallet was offered £30 as a reward. The researchers carried out a similar experiment in 12 American cities and towns, and 18 other European cities and towns.

You are going to predict the results of this experiment, but first rewrite the phrases from each column in order, from *the most* to *the least* in column 1, and the *biggest* difference to the *smallest* in column 2. Some phrases in each column have the same meaning. Work with a partner.

Column 1	Column 2
a few people	very little difference
hardly anyone	a fairly significant difference
the vast majority	a big difference
quite a lot of people	hardly any difference
very few people	a huge difference
nearly everyone	a significant difference
a handful of people	a slight difference

3 Now try to predict the results of the experiment. Answer the questions, then discuss your answers in groups.

1. Can you guess how many people returned wallets in Britain?
   a) the vast majority?   b) more than half?
   c) less than half?   d) only a handful?
2. Do you think people in the medium-sized towns were more honest than people in the city? If so, were they:
   a) much more honest?   b) slightly more honest?
3. Of the people who returned the wallet, how many were happy to accept the reward?
   a) nearly everyone?   b) quite a lot?   c) a few?
4. Do you think that men are:
   a) much more likely to return the wallet than women?
   b) more likely to return the wallet than women?
   c) less likely to return the wallet than women?
   d) far less likely to return the wallet than women?
5. Would you expect any difference at all between Britain and the rest of Europe? If so, would you expect:
   a) a huge difference?   b) a fairly significant difference?   c) very little difference?
6. Would you expect any difference at all between Britain and America? If so, would you expect:
   a) a very big difference?   b) a fairly significant difference?   c) hardly any difference?

4 ⬜ Listen to one of the researchers describing the results and write down the correct answers to the six questions above. Compare your answers with a partner. Are you surprised at any of the results?

5 ⬜ ⬜ Why do you think people did return the wallets? In groups, think of three or four reasons. Then listen to the researcher describing the reasons. What are they and which was the most common?

6 Think about the situation again and discuss these questions in small groups.

1. Does it make any difference whether a wallet contains £30 or a lot of money, e.g. £300?
2. Does it depend on whether you find a wallet in a crowded place or a deserted place?
3. Would a telephone number in the wallet help you decide whether to give it back or not?
4. Does it make any difference whether a wallet is an expensive one, or cheap and shabby?

The questions above contain *whether* rather than *if*. In which of them could you use *if* in place of *whether*? Discuss your answer with a partner, then check in the Language Reference on page 150.

JOIN THE RUSH TO SUE   passives; legal vocabulary

---

1 The following verbs on the left and nouns on the right are often used together when talking about legal cases involving money. How many correct combinations can you find?

Example: *You can be awarded damages/compensation/£1m.*

be awarded	a settlement	libel
reach	a dispute	£1m
ruin	damages	a verdict
settle	compensation	someone's life
sue someone for	a decision	out of court
appeal against	someone's reputation	negligence

2 🎧 Listen and answer the questions, then compare with a partner and check with the tapescript on page 172.

3 Read the article and underline the correct 'active' or 'passive' construction in brackets.

Mouth burnt on a pie?
Join the rush to sue

More and more Britons are using the law to settle disputes. We may still be a long way behind the United States, but the rush to the courts has lawyers rubbing their hands with delight. Here are some recent examples.

The scalding apple pie

Darren Miles received £750 compensation from McDonald's when the hot filling from an apple pie fell out and scalded his arm.

Mr Miles fears he may be permanently scarred as a result of the accident. His lawyer said that the pie had not been fit for its purpose – (to eat/to be eaten) immediately after sale.

'If a child had (injured/been injured) in this way,' he said, 'it could have been a lot more serious.' McDonald's settled out of court without accepting responsibility.

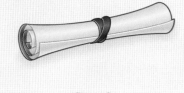

The burglary victim

A burglary victim (told/was told) to pay £4,000 damages – to the burglar.

Ted Newberry, aged 82, shot burglar Mark Revill from inside his garden shed near his home in Ilkeston. Later Revill (jailed/was jailed) for the burglary, but he (sued/was sued by) Newberry for damages, claiming that the injuries had been traumatic and had 'ruined his life'.

Awarding the damages, Mr Justice Rougier said that Newberry's action constituted negligence.

The stressed worker

Social worker John Walker (awarded/was awarded) £175,000 in compensation when he successfully claimed that his employers were negligent in subjecting him to too much stress. As a result of the stress, Mr Walker had two nervous breakdowns and had to take early retirement.

It was the first successful civil action of its kind. A spokesman for Mr Walker's union said it was a landmark case. 'When we meet employers to discuss these matters, I believe we will now (treat/be treated) much more seriously.'

The rugby referee

A High Court judge (ruled/was ruled) that rugby referee Michael Nolan was liable for damages after a young player (paralysed/was paralysed) during a match that he was controlling.

Mr Justice Curtis said that Mr Nolan had not shown reasonable care and skill in preventing the injury when a number of players (collapsed/were collapsed) on top of one another.

The court had heard that the game was bad tempered and violent, and had already suffered a high number of collapses before the injury to Ben Smoldon, aged 21, who is now crippled for life as a result of the incident.

From *The Independent*

4 What do you feel about the decision to award these people compensation? Do you agree with the decisions, and the amount of money awarded? Discuss in groups.

5 Check the passive constructions you underlined with a partner and then with your teacher.

When we use a passive construction, the 'agent' (the person or thing that does or causes the action) is often not mentioned. There are several possible reasons for this:

a. We **don't know** who or what the agent is.
b. We **know** who or what the agent is, but we don't need to state it, either because the agent is obvious or because the agent is less important than the action.

Can you name the agent in the passive examples in brackets in the text?

6 Work with a partner. Choose one of the boxes below and write the compensation story, similar to those in the text you read in Exercise 3.

   a. You will need to add further details about ages, times, amount of compensation, etc.

   b. Link the information together in a logical way. Notice how the texts above begin with a general statement about the compensation.

   c. Include examples of the passive where appropriate.

> 1. A group of workers/forties and fifties/chest illness/unable to work or lead a normal life/contracted the illness after exposure to chemicals/factory/20–25 years ago/sued factory owners

> 2. 15-year-old boy/rollerblading on pavement/hit a bicycle against a tree/boy fell/broke both legs/sued for negligence/owner left bike in a dangerous position

> 3. After operation on baby/parents found five-centimetre needle in baby's knee/not removed during operation/baby OK/parents sued hospital for negligence

Compare your stories in groups.

WHAT'S YOUR BEST PRICE?

1 If you bought the following goods in your country, could you try to negotiate your own price with the sales assistant? Discuss in small groups.

> a melon from a supermarket
> a melon from a market stall
> a watch from a jeweller's
> a watch from a market stall
> a new car from a showroom
> a coat from a boutique
> a TV from an electrical shop
> a holiday from a travel agent

2 Some people believe you can always negotiate a better deal. The text on page 113 gives some tips on how to do it. While reading the text, write down a paraphrase for the underlined words or phrases (the first two have been done for you). Then compare your explanations with a partner.

3 Discuss in small groups.

   1. What do you think of the different strategies mentioned in the text? Which one(s) would be possible and/or successful in your country?

   2. Have you used any of these strategies to get a discount? If so, tell the others.

   3. Do you find it difficult to haggle★ with a sales assistant? If so, why? Do you enjoy haggling?

★*haggle* to bargain or negotiate your own price. An informal word.

EVERYTHING IS NEGOTIABLE!

1 SHOULD I PAY CASH?

Many expensive products are bought using credit cards or interest-free credit terms, both of which can cost the shopkeeper quite a lot of money. It is therefore worth asking for a discount (= **a reduction**) if you can pay cash.

2 THE RIGHT WAY TO ASK

Avoid sounding apologetic, doubtful or desperate. Asking 'Do you give discounts?' won't elicit (= **succeed in getting the right information from the other person**) a great response. Expect a positive answer and you'll probably get one. For example, try saying, 'If you knock ten per cent off , I'll buy it.'

3 JUSTIFY A DISCOUNT

You can do this in several ways. One is to find a fault with the merchandise, e.g. a small mark on a dress or pair of trousers, and use it as a way of negotiating a better price. Another is to ask for a reduction if you are buying in bulk.

4 ASK FOR EXTRAS

Some shops prefer to offer additional products rather than reduce the price, so try asking for extras, e.g. one customer who spent £600 on an expensive camera asked the salesman to throw in a tripod worth £30. The salesman agreed immediately.

5 ESTABLISH RAPPORT

Eye contact is important to establish a feeling of trust, and a little humour during negotiation also goes down well and may influence the salesperson in making them more sympathetic towards you.

6 DO SOME RESEARCH

Find out the standard price for any goods you intend to buy, and any other information which may be useful in getting the best deal. For example, with the appearance of a new model, car salesmen are very anxious to sell the old model and will often be prepared to accept very low offers to get rid of old stock.

Whether you're buying a car or a coffee pot, there are bargains out there. Just bear in mind what Mike Hartley-Brewer says: 'People write a price on a ticket, but who's to say it's the one we have to pay?'

4 📖 Listen to a woman haggling over the price of a pair of earrings in an antique jewellery shop. Which strategies in the text does she use and how successful are they?

5 Now look at the photos and as a class decide quickly on a sales price for each one.

6 Work with a partner. Choose one of the objects, and think how you could negotiate a better price. Then find a new partner who will be a salesperson. Tell them which object you want to buy, and try to negotiate a price.

PERSONAL STUDY WORKBOOK

In your Personal Study Workbook, you will find more exercises to help you with your learning. For Unit 15, these include:

- exercises on collocation and topic vocabulary from the unit
- an exercise on the passive
- practice with ways of expressing quantity
- a text about credit cards
- people describing how their life would change if they were richer

---

REVIEW AND DEVELOPMENT

REVIEW OF UNIT 13

1 Members of the opposite sex | vocabulary: adjectives |

Read through the questionnaire and complete section d) in each question with a word or phrase of your choice.

Give your copy of the questionnaire to a partner.

Look through the questionnaire in front of you and underline any of the answers you agree with in each question. Compare and discuss your answers in groups.

WHAT DO YOU LIKE IN THE OPPOSITE SEX?

1. In their general dress, I like members of the opposite sex who are:
a) fashion-conscious
b) conservative
c) smart
d) ....

2. I also like members of the opposite sex who wear clothes that are:
a) adventurous
b) casual but stylish
c) provocative
d) ....

3. In terms of character I like them to be:
a) patient
b) assertive
c) easy-going
d) ....

4. In their approach to life I like members of the opposite sex to be:
a) enthusiastic
b) daring
c) conservative
d) ....

5. In their attitudes I like them to be:
a) broad-minded
b) conservative
c) extreme
d) ....

2 Rights and wrongs | passive structures; discussion |

Read the sentences and correct any grammatical errors. Compare with a partner.

1. Airline pilots should force to retire at 50.
2. Parents should allow children to decide whether or not their mother should go out to work.
3. Children should entitle to work ten hours a week from the age of 12.
4. If you are refused a job, you should be have the right to know the reason.
5. If employees give promotion, they should always get a higher salary.
6. You should always be given travelling expenses to attend an interview for a job.
7. If some workers in a company go on strike, they shouldn't allow to try to prevent other employees from going to work.

Now discuss your opinion of the sentences in small groups.

REVIEW OF UNIT 14

1 Coming down the mountain | participle clauses |

With a partner, complete these sentences in a logical way.

1. Coming down the mountain, we ....
2. A boy carrying a heavy rucksack ....
3. Not knowing anything about first aid, I ....
4. The rope supporting the climbers ....
5. Finding their path blocked, ...
6. The rescue helicopter flying overhead ....

2 Listen and answer | pronunciation/vocabulary |

The words in the box often cause pronunciation problems. Work with your partner. Can you pronounce them correctly, and do you remember what they mean?

> disinfectant   bruise   injury   fracture   collide   vehicle   collapse   skull   bandage
> surgery   agony   deteriorate   breath   breathing   symptoms   anaesthetic

▭ Listen and answer the questions.

Now look at the tapescript on page 172. Practise your pronunciation by reading the questions to your partner, who should answer them with their book shut.

PROJECT: EDUCATION IN THE ADULT WORLD

1 Have you heard of these different exams in English? Have you done,
or thought about doing any of them? Discuss in small groups.

- Cambridge First Certificate in English (FCE)
- Cambridge Advanced English (CAE)
- Oxford Higher
- ARELS Higher

2 ⊂⊃ Listen to the woman describing the four exams and work with a partner. One of
you should make notes on FCE and the Oxford Higher; the other should make notes
on CAE and the ARELS Higher. At the end, tell each other about your exams, then
read the tapescript on page 172–3 to see if you got everything right.

3 These exercises (or parts of exercises) are taken from the different exams. Do at least two of them with a partner, then compare your answers with a pair who did the same exercises.

Note: Each exam includes a wide range of exercises. These are just a small sample.

1. FCE

Complete the second sentence so that it has a similar meaning to the first, using the word given. Do not change the word given. You must use between two and five words.

1. I don't want to discuss this subject at the moment.

rather

I .... discuss this subject at the moment.

2. Could I stay with you for the weekend?

put

Could you .... for the weekend?

3. People say that Paris is a wonderful city.

supposed

Paris .... a wonderful city.

4. I haven't received a reply from Rachel yet.

still

Rachel .... a reply.

5. I looked quickly through the paper while I was waiting.

look

I had .... through the paper while I was waiting.

6. 'Would you like to go out for a meal?' George asked Olga.

felt

George asked Olga .... out for a meal.

From FCE test

2. CAE

In **most** lines of the following text, there is **one** unnecessary word. It is either grammatically incorrect or does not fit in with the sense of the text. For each numbered line **31–48**, find this word and then write it in the space at the end of the line. Some lines are correct. Indicate these with a tick ✓. The exercise begins with two examples **(0)**.

0 In the early part of this century, Bob Tisdall achieved an extraordinary   ✓

0 feat by winning four events within the only space of two hours in the   *only*

31 Oxford and Cambridge Athletics and Match: the shot, the long jump, the

32 120-yards hurdles and the 440-yards. Because of at that time

33 university athletics made for the front page of the national newspapers

34 and as Tisdall was extremely handsome as well, he became an

35 internationally known. He was offered to parts in films and attractive jobs

36 in business. But he was more interested in seeing the world and he took

37 up a position in India and forgot about the sport for a while. Then

38 someone reminded him about that the Olympics were coming up in four

39 months' time. He decided to have a go and went to Los Angeles

40 where he represented for Ireland in the 400-metres hurdles.

41 Although it was not only his third race ever in this event, he won it with a

42 record-breaking time of 51.7 seconds. His own feat is particularly

43 remarkable in the light of the intense training that all athletes undergo

44 today before them entering the Olympics. Tisdall's 'training' consisted of

45 going to the bed for a week beforehand in the Olympic village. On

46 the day of the race, he felt being wonderfully rested. He got up and went

47 straight from his bed to the track. He did one lap before finishing the race

48 to check how fit he was feeling himself and then took up his position in the starting line.

From CAE exam

3. OXFORD Higher

Answer BOTH tasks in this question.

You have two tickets for a Tina Turner concert next week.

1. You would like to invite your friend Kathy to come with you, but you are not sure if she is free to come. Write the note you send. (About 40 words)

2. Unfortunately, Kathy cannot come with you, so you want to sell the tickets. Write a notice for the noticeboard at your school/workplace. (About 20 words)

CITY ARENA
TINA TURNER in concert
2 December 1996 8pm
Seat B45 Balcony
Price £25

Seat B46 Balcony
Price £25

CITY ARENA
TINA TURNER in concert
2 December 1996 8pm
Seat B45 Balcony

From Oxford Higher November 96, Paper 1

4. ARELS Higher

Listen to the recording and follow the instructions.

Part One

First you'll hear six remarks which might be made to you in various situations when you're using your English. Some are questions and some are comments. After each one reply in a natural way. Here's an example to help you.

   – Sorry to keep you waiting.
   – That's all right. Don't worry.

From ARELS Higher 67

4 What do you think of these exercises? Did you find them easy or difficult? Discuss in groups.

5 In your opinion, what *should* an English test contain? Discuss again in your groups, then tell the class your ideas.

THAT'S A MATTER OF OPINION

Language focus

expressing opinions
agreeing and disagreeing
wedding vocabulary
words with different meanings

military service
conditional sentences:
unreal past and present

DO WE STILL NEED MILITARY SERVICE? opinions; agreeing and disagreeing

1 Switzerland has a unique system of military service. Listen to Daniel describing how it works, and make notes. At the end compare with a partner.

If you have military service in your country, in what ways is it similar to or different from the Swiss system?

2 Mark the stress on the words in the box, as in the examples. Which words would you need to talk about military service?

compulsory	wéapons
to abolish/abolition	self-defence
voluntary	well-equipped
a deterrent/to deter	roots
to provide security	to eradicate
basic training	to go to war

3 Swiss people, mostly from Ticino, were asked for their views on compulsory military service. Read the text, and put the people's names next to the sentences 1–4 below which *most accurately* describe their views. Compare your answers with a partner.

COMPULSORY MILITARY SERVICE:
for or against?

Agnela Carletti, 60, artist: If I had the power, I would abolish compulsory military service everywhere. For Switzerland it's totally pointless having an army at all: who would want to attack Switzerland when they keep all their money here?

Rosalia Albisetti, 80, retired school teacher: I lived through two wars so I understand the importance of having a strong army for self-defence; but things have changed now. I don't think we should have compulsory military service.

Nadia Castelli, 33, office worker: It is ironic that as a neutral country, Switzerland has a more modern and better-equipped army than many other countries which are not neutral. A voluntary, professional army should satisfy most people, whether they are for or against the army.

Paola Laudi, 26, criminologist: I would prefer total abolition, but I honestly don't think we can do without the army. Apart from being a deterrent, it also provides the average Swiss with a sense of security.

Carlo Lorusso, 66, retired businessman: For the Swiss, doing military service has been a part of life for so long that its roots would be very hard to eradicate. Deep down I'm not sure we really want to change this long tradition.

Enrico Giorgetti, 41, journalist: Military service should be abolished. Switzerland is a neutral country and as such it should not be concerned with arms and weapons as if we are about to go to war. Costa Rica in Central America is a neutral country and doesn't have an army; if they can do without one, so can we.

Gianni Quanchi, 34, bank official: I think we should maintain compulsory military service as a means of serving our country. But the army should have a more social role and use its resources to solve environmental and other practical problems.

David Baumann, 26, law student: In basic training I wanted to die, but now that I'm older I think it was worth the experience. I met guys from other classes and other regions of Switzerland whom I would never ordinarily come into contact with, and we all had to get along together in teams.

From *The European*

1. **'I'm in favour** of compulsory military service.'

2. **'I've got mixed feelings about** compulsory military service.'

3. **'I'm against** compulsory military service.'

4. **'I'm strongly opposed to** compulsory military service.' *Agnela*

4 We can express agreement or disagreement with people's opinions on a scale like this:

I completely/totally agree with ...

I tend to agree with ...

I agree to some extent with the person who said ...

I don't really agree with ...

I totally/completely disagree with ...

Compare and discuss your views in small groups, using the language above to comment on the opinions in the text, and add any other arguments you think are relevant.

1   Work with a partner, and write down at least four more sentences using the words
from the wordpool. Each sentence must contain the word *if*.

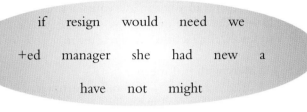

if   resign   would   need   we

+ed   manager   she   had   new   a

have   not   might

Example: *If she resigned, we might need a new manager.*

Compare your sentences with the ones on page 157. Are there different ones? Write
them in your list.

2   With your partner, answer these questions about the eight sentences.

   a. What is the difference in meaning between sentences 1 and 2?
   b. What is the difference in meaning between sentences 2 and 3?
   c. In sentence 3, did the woman resign or not? What about in sentence 5?
   d. What is the difference in meaning between sentences 6 and 7?

3   Read the situation and check any new items of vocabulary.

A middle-aged businessman was driving through the city centre one day, and when he got to
the traffic lights a sports car driven by a young man talking on his mobile phone stopped
beside him. The lights changed to amber and the young man sped away, narrowly missing a
girl who was crossing the road, and hitting a rubbish bin which spilt its contents over the
road. The businessman decided to follow him and try to catch up with him ...

CD The people on the recording were asked these questions:

What would you have done in this situation?
Would you have reacted like the businessman?

Listen and complete the tapescript below, then compare with a partner.

GARETH: I would've just sworn and driven on, I think. I mean you can get yourself into terrible trouble with, you know, people who drive like that. It says something about their personalities, doesn't it? You know, the fact that they're they're capable of behaving like that.

MARCELLA: Yes, but they shouldn't be allowed to get away with it. I mean ....and reported it. I know it seems like a small thing and they'd probably tell me to just go away. What can you do? But ...

IAN: You'd have taken the number.

MARCELLA: I ...., yeah, and reported it. I'd have done that definitely.

IAN: I .... but if ... depending on how I felt, ...

4 Practise saying the sentences you completed, using the contractions. Then, in small groups, give *your* opinion – say what you would or might have done, and why.

5 Read this situation and check you understand the vocabulary.

A housewife shopping in a department store noticed a young couple with a baby in a pushchair who were acting suspiciously. They kept looking around them, watching for store detectives, talking quietly to each other out of the sides of their mouths. They moved round the aisles but kept coming back to a display of silk shirts. The housewife saw the man pick up half a dozen shirts and hide them in the pushchair, under the baby. The housewife went up to the man and told him to put them back.

In your groups, discuss what you would have done, and why. When you have finished, write your most common response on the board (using *would/might have done*) and compare with other groups.

6 CD Listen to the people on the recording discussing the situation. Do you agree with them? Why? Why not?

1 Here are some events that form part of a traditional wedding/marriage in Britain. In what order do they occur, and how long does each one typically last, do you think? Discuss in small groups.

> reception   anniversary   wedding ceremony   honeymoon
> stag/hen night   engagement   proposal

Your teacher can tell you the answers. Is it the same in your country?

2 Put the paragraphs in the first half of the text in order, then compare with a partner.

Why we like a decent proposal

Consider for example the case of Joanne Mills: she was fed up with waiting for her partner, Michael Cordwell, to propose. Four years ago, she took a tin of red paint to the place where he worked, and painted a proposal across the side of his van. 'I was very embarrassed – not because she had asked me, but because the way she did it was so unsubtle,' says Michael. He told her to get down on one knee and ask the permission of his father. She did, and Michael <u>agreed</u> to marry her.

It is perhaps surprising that women are still quite so old-fashioned about this issue of who proposes, <u>given</u> the rise of feminism and the high likelihood of marriage ending in divorce. But although attitudes to marriage have changed a great <u>deal</u> over the past two decades, it seems that most people are still strongly attached to the idea of a traditional proposal, with a few notable exceptions.

It all started with Queen Margaret of Scotland who, in 1288, decreed that in a leap year a woman could <u>propose</u> to any man, as long as he was <u>single</u>. If he refused, he received a £1 <u>fine</u>.

The law was <u>dropped</u>, but the custom remains: 29 February is traditionally the day for women to turn the tables and propose to their partners. It's the once-in-every-1,461-days opportunity.

But, according to a survey by the cosmetics firm *Fabergé*, couples should look before they leap. Only 29% of men would say 'yes' if their girlfriend proposed to them on 29 February. One in three women admit they are too nervous of being <u>turned down</u> and more than half of them believe it is still a job for the boys.

3 Now read the rest of the text and

- put a tick (✔) beside any opinions you agree with;
- put a cross (✗) beside any opinions you disagree with;
- put a question mark (?) beside any statements you find surprising.

But whether the proposal comes from the man or the woman, there is still a large body of opinion which believes that a proposal, particularly a romantic one, remains a vital <u>ingredient</u> in the recipe for a successful marriage. Sandra Boler, editor of *Brides* magazine says that 'people want commitment and to be seen together. Long may it continue, and I'm all for big dresses for the wedding. It's not something to be ashamed of.'

Set against the romantic school, which believes romance to be the <u>foundation</u> of a good marriage, is the modern school, which believes that lengthy thought and consideration are vital. Agony Aunt, Virginia Ironside, argues that the idea of a proposal is rather distasteful. 'It is a cheeky thing to do, because one is under great pressure to say yes. It is terribly humiliating to be turned down. To propose in public really is shocking. As for getting down on one knee, it's an invitation to be kicked in the face.'

Marriage guidance counsellors also recommend that people talk over the idea of marriage at great length before leaping into it. The romantic attraction of popping the question can often lead people, on the spur of the moment, into ill-fated marriages. As one counsellor puts it: 'There are people who propose in the middle of a bungee jump, but in general it is well thought through. It is still the ultimate commitment to make. Living together is one thing, marriage is something else altogether.'

From *The Independent*

Compare and discuss your answers in groups.

4 Many words have more than one meaning or use. In the text above, for example:

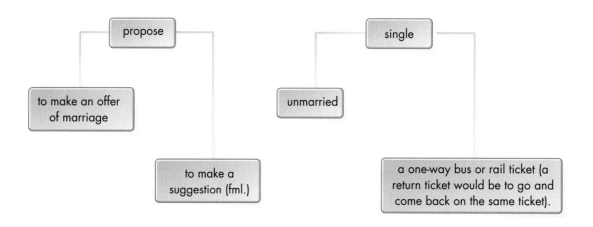

Can you find a suitable synonym/paraphrase from the box for the rest of the underlined words, as they appear in the text?

> reject   part   penalty   abolish/stop   consent/say yes
> when you consider   amount   basis

5 Now can you write sentences to show the underlined words being used with a different meaning? (The part of speech might be different in your examples.) Work with a partner and use a dictionary to help you. When you have finished, compare your sentences with another pair.

6 Imagine you were attracted to the idea of a glamorous proposal. Which of these would you find the most exciting (to make or receive)? Discuss in small groups.

1. Hire a light aircraft and fly a banner from the back with your proposal on it.
2. Take your partner up in a hot air balloon and propose in mid air.
3. Print it out in a firework display.
4. Put it in neon lights in the main square where you live.
5. Send a message via the national football stadium during a match.
6. Propose during a phone-in programme on the radio.

Now think of three new ideas, and tell them to the rest of the class.

PERSONAL STUDY WORKBOOK

In your Personal Study Workbook, you will find more exercises to help you with your learning. For Unit 16, these include:

- an exercise on words with different meanings
- an exercise on figurative meaning
- an exercise on *if* sentences
- pronunciation: sentence rhythm
- a text about military service in different countries
- listening to people expressing opinions

REVIEW AND DEVELOPMENT

REVIEW OF UNIT 14

1 I've smashed a glass | verb + noun collocation |

Match a verb from the green box with an object from the photos and write a sentence to show how they could be used together. Use each verb and object once only, then compare your answers with a partner.

Example: *I tripped over the step as I went into the house.*

bump into   bruise   spill
rip   mislay   trip over
scratch   smash   leap over

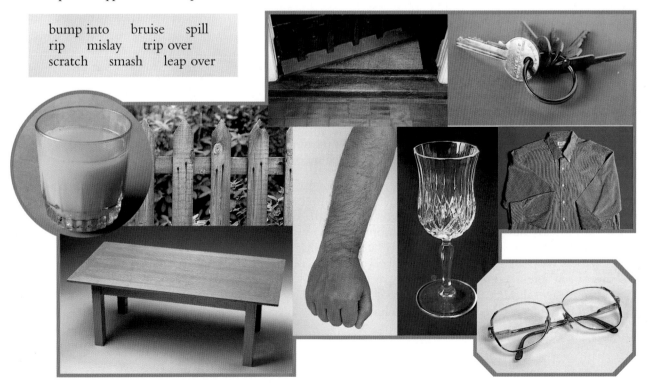

---

2 Why was she sacked? | past continuous + *always*; *keep* + *-ing* |

The people in the sentences all lost their jobs because they were clumsy, absent-minded or not suitable for the job. Complete each sentence with a suitable bad habit using the past continuous + *always*, or *keep* + *-ing*.

1. He lost his job as a waiter because ...
2. She was a hotel receptionist but they dismissed her because ...
3. He worked as a bank cashier but he was given the sack because ...
4. She was a weather forecaster for a while but they had to sack her because ...
5. He was a nightwatchman but they fired him when they discovered that he ...
6. She was a zoo keeper but lost her job because she ...

REVIEW OF UNIT 15

1 Find out what others think | expressing quantity |

Work in small groups. Using the topics in the box or any others you like, complete the sentences below by *guessing* the opinions of the whole class or individual members of the class. When you have finished, find out if you were correct by asking the class.

more money	compulsory military service for women
abortion	a complete ban on smoking in the building
the legalisation of cannabis	a law banning the use of mobile phones in restaurants
extra homework	fewer breaks during lessons
longer prison sentences	vote in a general election
fewer television channels	

Example: *We believe that most people in the class would* **like to have more money.**
or **disagree with compulsory military service for women.**

1. We think the vast majority of the class would ...
2. We feel that very few of us would ...
3. We think there's probably a huge difference between ... and ... on the subject of ...
4. In our opinion, hardly anyone would ...
5. We're confident that nearly everyone would ...
6. We think there's probably a slight difference of opinion between ... and ... on the subject of ...

2 Get rid of it | vocabulary |

We can use *get rid of something/somebody* in place of a number of verbs and in many different contexts. Can you replace it in the sentences below with suitable words or phrases? The first one has been done for you.

1. I'm hoping to *get rid of* my old car this year. (= sell)
2. You can *get rid of* those old newspapers; I don't need them.
3. If we want to have more chairs in the classroom, we'll have to *get rid of* a couple of tables.
4. She *got rid of* him because he was consistently late for work.
5. Sadly the boss will have to *get rid of* at least six workers if business doesn't improve soon.
6. I've never been able to *get rid of* my London accent.
7. It's a dreadful law – I think the government should *get rid of* it.
8. How did the murderer *get rid of* the dead body?

MANNERS

Language focus
functional language: surprise, requests,
enquiries, apologies and excuses
vocabulary: money and manners

describing change
past tenses for distancing
letter writing: style and layout

EXCUSE ME, WOULD YOU MIND ...?

1 Read the social situations in the box and check that you understand the vocabulary. How would you *feel* in each situation? (e.g. embarrassed, upset, relieved) Tell a partner.

1. You park outside a pharmacy and dash in with a prescription for some urgent medication for someone in your family. When you come out, a traffic warden is writing out a parking ticket and about to give you a fine.
2. You are in an area you don't know very well, and you suddenly remember your boss gave you a small package that has to be sent express post this afternoon. Post offices close in half an hour.
3. Your neighbour is a very careful driver who is mad about his car. One day, you meet him in the street and he tells you he was involved in an accident. Although the car is a write-off, he wasn't badly injured.
4. A guest who is staying with you comes home late, after you have gone to bed. In the morning, you discover the front door is wide open – obviously, your guest forgot to shut it securely.

2 What might you *say* in each situation? Discuss with your partner.

3  Listen to the conversations based on the above situations and answer the questions.

Situation 1:
Does the driver have to pay a fine or not?
Situation 2:
Who is able to explain the way – a man or a woman?
What is the way to the post office?
Situation 3:
How did the accident happen?
Did the woman sound sympathetic or not?
Situation 4:
Does the person accept that they left the door open?
Does the person apologise?

Listen again, and complete the tapescript on pages 157–158.

4 The phrases you completed are ways of expressing different functions. Now look at these sentences (which are similar) and decide if they are grammatically correct. If they are wrong, correct them.

REQUESTS FOR INFORMATION
(you aren't sure if the listener knows the answer)

1. Do you happen to know where is the nearest post office?
2. Have you any idea if the box office is still open?

QUESTIONS EMPHASISING SURPRISE

3. What on earth happened?
4. Why on earth do you need a second TV?

APOLOGIES AND EXCUSES

5. Sorry, I didn't realise about the parking restrictions.
6. I'm really sorry – I didn't mean to.

POLITE WAY TO ASK OR TELL SOMEONE TO DO SOMETHING
(usually formal)

7. I'd be really grateful that you could give me a hand.
8. Would you mind to shut the window when you go out?

Compare your answers in small groups.

5 Complete the dialogues below using language from Exercise 4.

1. A. ....?
   B: I think it starts at 8.00, but I'm not absolutely sure.

2. A: We've decided to sell the dishwasher, the washing machine and the microwave.
   B: ....

3. A: Hey, John! You've put the iron down on the carpet and it's burnt a hole.
   B: ....

4. A: ....
   B: Yes, I'll do my best, and I'm sorry there has been a delay.

6 Work with a partner. Choose two of the situations below and act them out, using some of the language you have learnt. Change roles and act them out again.

1. You're lost in a foreign city on your own at night. The underground is closed, and there don't seem to be any buses running. You'd like to find a taxi rank. You see a passer-by.

2. Yesterday you borrowed your classmate's dictionary to look something up, and discovered it in your bag when you got home. In the following lesson you give it back, but your classmate is a bit upset and says he couldn't do his homework properly.

3. A friend is staying in your home for a few weeks. You get on well, but your friend plays music very loudly late at night, and you can't sleep.

4. A friend of yours is a brilliant student, but has just heard that she has failed her final exams at university. You meet her in the street.

THE WAR ON MANNERS

1 Work with a partner and complete the missing adjectives and verbs in the table.

	NO				YES
untidiness (adj = _____untidy_____)	1	2	3	4	5
swearing (verb = _____)	1	2	3	4	5
courtesy (adj = _____)	1	2	3	4	5
rudeness (adj = _____)	1	2	3	4	5
aggression (adj = _____)	1	2	3	4	5
cheating (verb = _____)	1	2	3	4	5
respect for older people (verb = _____ older people)	1	2	3	4	5

Using the scale 1–5, how would you rate yourself on these things?

Example: *I would give myself 3 for untidiness – I'm not really tidy or untidy – but 1 for swearing because I never swear.*

Are you happy with your self-assessment or would you like to be different in any way? Tell your partner.

2 Look at the headline to the text on page 130. What does it mean and what do you think the text will be about? Tell your partner.

---

3 Read the text and answer these questions while you read.

1. Do you agree that these changes are taking place in society in your country? Put *yes* next to the changes you think are happening, and *no* next to the changes you cannot see.
2. Do you agree that these changes (if they are taking place) are a threat to society?

War on manners threatens us all

The collapse of good manners could pose a greater threat to society than crime, a published report said yesterday. Everywhere from doctors' surgeries to sports grounds, courtesy is being replaced by rudeness, untidiness and generally bad behaviour.

Women are more at risk in this war on manners because traditional respect by men has declined as a result of years of feminism, according to the report, *Gentility Recalled*, which has just been published by a think tank* comprising a group of academics. They claim that swearing is now increasing in daily life, and rudeness and aggression have become the norm. Hardly any part of society is exempt from these changes.

Health and sport

It is claimed that doctors are losing the respect of their patients because of the growing trend to call patients by their first name. Doctors who were once highly respected members of the community are no longer seen in this way, and are now subject to the same abuse and aggression that is found elsewhere.

On sport, the report said that the decline in organised games at school was affecting the development of good manners and social skills. Cheating at sport from some of our best-known sportsmen was also becoming more widespread, again setting a poor example for the children who admire and worship them.

The clothes of contempt

Clothes are becoming outwardly aggressive and sexually explicit, said sociologist Athena Leoussi. She added: 'The deliberate neglect of personal appearance, the wearing of work clothes on social occasions, the use of gym clothes in supermarkets, are all signs that a contempt for society and for other people is on the increase. Leather jackets, guerrilla headbands, pierced noses, studded leather boots, aggressive tattoos are all declarations of war.'

Attempts by older people to dress and act young are gradually destroying the respect for elders, the report added.

Respect at home

'The daily routine of polishing shoes, writing thank-you letters and having respect for adults and strangers once encouraged discipline and self-control among children and helped to produce a civilised society,' said Professor Michael Aeschliman. 'Keeping to daily household chores and family routine is of enormous benefit to anyone facing depression and misfortune,' he added. 'And when the family comes under pressure and starts to break down, there is nothing to replace it. The natural outcome of theories which say the family is unimportant could be the collapse of civilisation,' warned Professor Aeschliman.

* A group of specialists, brought together usually by a government, to develop ideas on a particular subject and to make suggestions for action (*Cambridge International Dictionary of English*)

From *The Daily Mail*

Discuss your answers in small groups.

4 Look at these phrases from the text. What do they have in common? Discuss with your partner.

... is being replaced by ...	... has declined ...
... is now increasing ...	... a growing trend ...
... the decline in ...	... is becoming more widespread ...
... is on the increase ...	... are gradually destroying ...

With your partner, make some statements about the topics in the box using the language above to describe a change that is taking place.

Example: *In our country, organic food is becoming more widespread and the use of pesticides is declining.*

pesticides/organic food
crime/unemployment
road building/the countryside
conventional/alternative medicine
handwriting/computers
marriage for life
terrestrial and cable/satellite TV

5 In small groups, choose one of these topics and discuss it.

> A: Can you think of other ways in which people are becoming less polite/more aggressive? Or do you think people are becoming more polite/less aggressive?

> B: When you were a child, what manners were you taught? Do you still observe these manners, and would/do you teach them to your own children?

1 ▭ Follow the instructions on the recording to complete the layout of the letter below in the space provided. (Don't read the letter yet.)

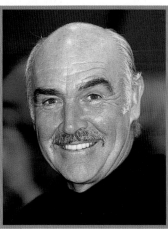

Dear Mr Connery

We are a newly formed charity and our aim is to promote good manners among young children.

Our activities include visiting schools and playgroups, giving lectures and putting on plays, pantomimes and puppet shows. In order to raise funds, we have often organised sponsored walks and swims. We have also received generous donations from organisations and private individuals.

Our most prestigious event is the annual competition to find the boy and girl with the best manners in the country, and this year **we were hoping** to find a celebrity from the world of showbusiness to support us. We appreciate that you are very busy, but **we thought** this cause would appeal to you. **We were** therefore **wondering** whether you would be available to give out the awards at the next prize-giving ceremony in London to be held on 10 April.

I would be grateful if you could give me an answer by the end of the month to allow us time to make the necessary arrangements.

I look forward to hearing from you.

When you have listened to the recording, check your answer with your teacher.

2   What did you learn about other types of letter from the recording? Discuss with a partner.

3   Read the letter and decide the purpose of:
- paragraph 1
- paragraph 2
- paragraph 3
- paragraph 4

4   Look at these sentences from the letter. They don't specifically refer to *past time*, but are used to give a particular effect. What effect do they give?

We *were hoping* to find a celebrity ...
We *thought* this cause would appeal to you.
We *were wondering* whether you would be available ...

5   Make sure you understand the following words/phrases as they may be useful in the letter you are going to write.

a charity
a celebrity
to raise funds
to make/to receive a donation
a sponsored walk/swim/run

to sponsor someone
to hold/organise an event
a competition
to support an organisation/a charity
a ceremony

6   Work in small groups. You are going to form a new organisation or charity – something serious or light-hearted. Decide which famous person you will write to for support, then write the letter together.

When you have finished, give your letter to another group to read. See if they can make any corrections or suggestions.

PERSONAL STUDY WORKBOOK

In your Personal Study Workbook, you will find more exercises to help you with your learning. For Unit 17, these include:

- an exercise to practise making requests
- a word building exercise
- an exercise on emphatic questions
- a text which asks: do we need good manners?
- pronunciation: sounds and spelling
- listening and responding to different questions and situations

---

REVIEW AND DEVELOPMENT

REVIEW OF UNIT 15

1   Carry out your own experiment   speaking

Carry out your own experiment in small groups over the next two/three days, or two/three weeks. You are going to find out how different people respond to a simple situation. You can think up your own situation or use one of these.

1. Put two or three bits of litter on the floor in one of the corridors in your school where people pass by. Put a litter bin quite near the litter. Count the number of people who pass and note down the number who stop, pick up the litter and put it in the bin. If possible, ask people who did not pick up the litter why they didn't.

2. If you have a library, put several books on the floor near one of the shelves. Make a similar note of the people who pick up the books and return them to the correct shelf.

3. Put a notebook near the entrance to your school. As students enter, note down how many pick up the notebook and hand it in at reception.

When you have completed the experiment, report on your findings to the rest of the class.

2 More compensation | passives |

Here is another story of compensation. Complete the text with words from the box, putting each verb in the correct active or passive form.

| pester damages award (2) verdict sue protect hold force |

Last year, two British women (1) .... £3,000 in (2) .... after they (3) .... by the staff at a holiday hotel.

The two women (4) .... the tour operators, Thomson, on their return to Britain, and (5) .... the money by a county court for 'psychological injury', following the unwanted attention they experienced while on their trip abroad.

Lawyers for the women welcomed the (6) ...., saying it would (7) .... holiday operators to be more careful in future in their choice of accommodation.

However, British tour operators are now wondering just how far they can (8) .... responsible for the behaviour of hotel staff, and what they can do to (9) .... themselves.

From *The Independent*

Compare your answers with a partner.

REVIEW OF UNIT 16

What would you have done? | conditionals; pronunciation |

A With a partner, complete these questions in a suitable way, but don't answer them.

1. If your teacher hadn't come to class today, ...?
2. If your school decided to put on a show, ...?
3. Would you have come to class today if ...?
4. If nobody in class had done the last piece of homework, what ...?
5. If you could ask your teacher any question you liked, ...?
6. How would you have felt if, last week, the students in your class ...?

B ▭ Listen to the recording. Note down any questions which are different from yours.

Using the recording, practise the questions, paying attention to the contractions and weak forms.

C Read your own questions again, then shut your book and ask a new partner as many as you can remember. Do you think your partner's answers are correct and truthful?

WHAT ARE THE ODDS?

> **Language focus**
> degrees of possibility and probability   revision of *will* for prediction
> future continuous and future perfect   revision of grammar and vocabulary

THE PROBABILITY FACTORS OF LIFE   expressing degrees of possibility and probability

1   What is your response to this statement? Choose one of the answers a) to d), then discuss it with a partner, giving your reasons.

> More accidents happen in the bathroom than in the living/dining room.

a) That's quite likely to be true, because ...
    (= *probably true*)
b) That could/might be true, because ...
    (= *maybe/possibly true*)
c) I doubt if that's true, because ...
    (= *I don't think it's true*)
d) That sounds highly unlikely, because ...
    (= *I'm almost certain it's not true*)

Your teacher will tell you the answer about Britain.

2   Here are some more statements about Britain. First, check any new words with your partner and a dictionary. Then discuss the sentences using language from Exercise 1. At the end, put *true* or *false* next to each sentence.

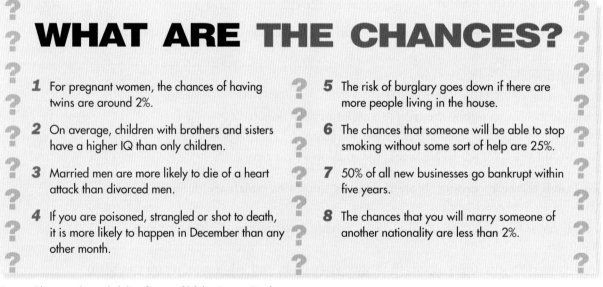

WHAT ARE THE CHANCES?

1 For pregnant women, the chances of having twins are around 2%.

2 On average, children with brothers and sisters have a higher IQ than only children.

3 Married men are more likely to die of a heart attack than divorced men.

4 If you are poisoned, strangled or shot to death, it is more likely to happen in December than any other month.

5 The risk of burglary goes down if there are more people living in the house.

6 The chances that someone will be able to stop smoking without some sort of help are 25%.

7 50% of all new businesses go bankrupt within five years.

8 The chances that you will marry someone of another nationality are less than 2%.

From *Chances: the probability factors of life* by James Burke

Your teacher will tell you the answers about Britain.

Do you think any of these statistics would be different in your country?

3 📼 On the recording you will hear some more facts about some of the statements in Exercise 2. Which statements, and what do you learn? Make notes.

4 Notice these constructions from the statements.

The chances of having twins *are* ... (high/low)
Married men are *more/less likely to* die of a heart attack *than* divorced men.
The risk of successful burglary goes up/down *if* there are more people living in the house.
The chances that you will marry someone of another nationality *are* ...

Work with a partner, and make your own examples using these constructions and the topics in the box.

> becoming rich overnight
> drivers in their forties and fifties
> getting married more than once
> catching a cold
>
> people who work up ladders
> getting caught in a thunderstorm
> people who own pets

Example: *The chances that you will become rich overnight are very low.*

WHAT WILL YOU BE DOING?   revision of *will*; future continuous and future perfect

1 Work with a partner. Match the sentences with the pictures and give a reason for your answer. Can you name the tenses?

When I leave class, I'm sure it will rain.
When I leave class, I'm sure it will be raining.
When I leave class, I'm sure it will have stopped raining.

A   B   C

2 📼 Now listen and complete the dialogues.

1.
A: Oh, Betty, by the way, could .... tonight – just to confirm things for tomorrow?
B: Well, actually my flatmate ...., so can I give you a ring when we've eaten?
A: Yeah, OK then.

2.

C: Do you want me to pop round this evening to pick up those samples?

D: Yes, could you?

C: Yes, sure – what time?

D: Sevenish.

C: Fine.

D: No, actually, could you make it a bit later? My ....
.... and he gets really irritable ....

C: [*giggle*] No problem – I'll come at about 8, then.

D: Great.

3.

E: Oh dear, ... Sue and Mike's tonight – not after the
last time. That meal Sue served up was absolutely dreadful.

F: .... – he was a bit embarrassed about that last
meal and he's not working at the moment.

E: Oh, well, that's a relief.

With your partner, discuss why *will* + verb, *will be* + *-ing* and *will have* + past participle are being used.

3 Remember that some verbs are not usually used in the continuous form.

Example: ~~By next week, I'll be understanding the future continuous.~~
~~We'll be having two cars by the end of the year.~~ (when *have* = *possess*)

Are these sentences correct or incorrect? Discuss with your partner, then check your answers in the Language Reference on page 151–2.

1. By this time tomorrow, I'll be knowing my exam results.
2. In a week's time, I'll be working in Norway.
3. This time next week, we'll be sitting on a beach in Jamaica.
4. I'll never be believing my son committed those terrible crimes.
5. After my baby is born next month, I'll be having three sons.
6. Don't ring me at 8.00 because I'll be having dinner.

4 Complete the questions with a partner using *will (do)*, *will be (doing)*, or *will have (done)*.

In a year's time,	
– do you think you	(still study) English?
– do you think your English	(get) better or worse?
– do you think you	(have) the same hairstyle?
– do you think you	(live) in a different flat/house?
– do you think you	(lose touch with) the other people in your class?
– do you think your country	(have) a different government?
– do you think someone in your family	(work) abroad?
In ten years' time,	
– do you think you	(still have) the same friends?
– do you think you	(change) very much?
– do you think you	(still live) in the same town/village?
– do you think you	(like) the same kinds of music?
– do you think you	(still do) the same things in your spare time?
– do you think you	(be) much better off?

LOOKING INTO THE FUTURE …

Check your answers with your teacher.

Now interview two other people, using the questions in the table. Do any of their answers surprise you?

5 Work with a partner. Write three more questions like the ones in Exercise 4 to ask another pair. If possible, ask them questions using your knowledge of them.

Examples: *Lee, do you think you'll be married to Su Jin in two years' time?*
Gita, do you think your brother will still be working for Texaco next year?
Joao, do you think you'll have passed your driving test by the end of this year?

In the answers, you could use:

yes, definitely	that's quite/very likely	maybe	I doubt it	
that's highly unlikely	no, never in a million years!	you must be joking!		

ODDS AND EVENS

⭐ Play this game in groups of four. You will need a dice, some counters and some question cards which your teacher will give you. Put the pile of cards face down in the middle of the board.

⭐ Each group of four divides into two pairs, A and B. Either pair can land on 'free squares' and doesn't have to answer a question. However, pair A can only land on odd numbered squares, and pair B on even numbered squares.

⭐ If you throw the dice and you can't move to a correct square, you stay where you are.

⭐ If you throw the dice and you can move to a correct square (odd for A, even for B), you must first answer a question correctly. You are allowed to discuss it with your partner. If you don't get it right, you stay where you are.

⭐ The question card should be read aloud by the opposing pair and repeated if necessary, but not shown. You have to complete the second sentence so that it has a similar meaning to the first sentence, but incorporating the new word you are given.

Here are some examples of the questions:

Would you prefer to stay in this evening?

RATHER

(Answer: Would you rather stay in this evening?)

You mustn't smoke in here.

ALLOWED

(Answer: You aren't allowed to smoke in here.)

Unit 18 WHAT ARE THE ODDS?

REVIEW AND DEVELOPMENT

REVIEW OF UNIT 16

I've got mixed feelings – have you?   giving opinions; modifiers; (dis)agreeing

A Look at the sentence beginnings which are ways of expressing opinions. Put the word or phrase on the left in the correct position.

Example: STRONGLY   *I'm* ⟨*strongly*⟩ *opposed to ...*

VERY MUCH	I'm in favour of ...
RATHER	I've got mixed feelings about ...
GENERALLY SPEAKING	I'm against ...
VERY MUCH	I've always been against ...
NOT AT ALL	I'm in favour of ...
ON THE WHOLE	I'm not very keen on the idea of ...
PARTICULARLY	I've got strong views on ...

Check your answers.

B Check that you understand the phrases in the box, then write four or five sentences combining the sentence beginnings above and the topics to express your opinion.

Example: *I'm very much in favour of heavy fines for illegal parking.*

heavy fines for illegal parking	increased spending on arms and defence
abolishing laws on soft drugs	boxing as an Olympic event
tough sentences for young offenders	letting children watch TV whenever they want
capital punishment	raising the school leaving age in my country
national lotteries	laws protecting the privacy of all citizens

C Work in small groups. Tell other people your opinions and see if they agree with you. Discuss your reasons.

You may need to use these expressions:

I completely/totally agree …
I tend to agree …
I agree to some extent … because …
I don't really agree …
I totally/completely disagree …

REVIEW OF UNIT 17

Polite enquiries   embedded questions

You are in a railway station where English is spoken. Which of the these question forms would you use if you were speaking to:

a. someone who works in the information office?
b. a stranger in the station?

Do you happen to know
Could you tell me } if the Brighton train has left yet?
Have you any idea   when the Brighton train leaves?
Do you know

What is the difference in style and grammar between the embedded questions above and these questions?

Has the Brighton train left yet?
When does the Brighton train leave?

With a partner, change these simple questions into embedded ones.

1. What time does the Cambridge train arrive?
2. How much does it cost to leave a suitcase here?
3. Are there any snack bars round here?
4. Where's the ladies'/men's lavatory?
5. How long does it take to get to Dover?
6. When's the next train to Brussels?

Act out dialogues on unsuspecting strangers in your group, like this:

A: Oh, excuse me.
B: Yes?
A: Are you going to Dover?
B: Yes.
A: Good – well, have you any idea how long it takes to get there?
B: I don't know exactly – roughly an hour, I'd say.
A: Right. Thanks.

You may wish to use some of these expressions:

| I haven't a clue | I've no idea | I haven't the faintest idea |
| I'm not absolutely sure but it must be … | | It's probably … |

LANGUAGE REFERENCE

1

DETERMINERS: *BOTH, NEITHER, ALL, NONE, EVERY, EACH*

Both

1. *Both of* + pronoun (+ plural verb)
   Both of them are going to the conference.
2. *Both (of) +* noun
   Both my parents *are still alive.*
   Both of my parents *are still alive.*
3. *Both* + noun + *and* + noun
      + adj   + *and* + adj
      + verb + *and* + verb
   Both my brother and my sister *will be there.*
   They were **both tired and emotional.**
   He **both shoots and rides.**
4. Noun/pronoun + *both* + verb
   We both *enjoyed the film.* (= **Both of us** *enjoyed the film.*)
   They *are* **both** *working tomorrow.* (= **Both of them** ...)
   The children have **both** *spent their money.* (= **Both (of) the children** ...)

Notice the position of *both* with auxiliary verbs in the examples above.

Neither

1. *Neither of* + pronoun/plural noun
   Neither of my sisters *has/have★ a job.*
   Neither of them *has/have a job.*
   ★ In more formal style, a singular verb is used; in more informal style, a plural verb can be used.
2. *Neither ... nor ...*
   Neither my brother nor my sister *has★ got a job.*
   ★ In informal style, a plural verb is also possible.
   This is basically a negative version of the structure *both ... and.*

All

We use *both* to talk about two things, we use *all* to talk about three or more, but the grammatical structures we use with *both* and *all* are similar.
   All (of) the students *were late.*
   All of them *were late.*
   They all *arrived late.*

None

   None of my colleagues *was/were happy.*
   None of them *was/were happy.*
As with *neither*, the verb is singular in a more formal style, but can be plural in a more informal style.

Every/each

   Every/each child *was given a present.*
Note that the verb must be singular.

ELLIPSIS

We often leave out words to avoid repeating ourselves, or in some cases when the meaning can be understood without them. We call this *ellipsis* and it takes many forms in English.

So + auxiliary + pronoun/noun

Ellipsis occurs after *so* and *neither*:
   He's got a sports car and **so have I.**
   They like mountaineering and **so do their children.**
   I can't ride and **neither can the others.**
   He doesn't like it and **neither do I.**

Ellipsis after auxiliary verbs

To avoid repetition we can use an auxiliary verb to replace a complete verb phrase if the meaning is clear.
   He wears leather trousers, **which I never do.** (= *I never wear leather trousers.*)
   I wanted to help them, **but I couldn't.**

2

CONNECTORS: CONCESSION AND CONTRAST

1. *Although, even though, though, in spite of, despite (the fact that)*

When you want to contrast two pieces of information in a *single sentence* and say that the second fact is surprising after the first, you can use these connectors.

I like him	*although* *even though* *though* *despite the fact that* *in spite of the fact that*	*we're very different.*

You can also begin the sentence with the connectors:
   Although *we're very different I like him.*
   In spite of / **Despite** *the cold wind I felt quite hot.*

You can also use the *-ing* form after *in spite of* and *despite*.
   In spite of / **Despite** *los**ing** my wallet, I still enjoyed the trip.*

2. *Whereas* and *while*

When we want to express a clear contrast often between two subjects within *one* sentence, we can use *while* or *whereas*.

> Mary lives in luxury **whereas** her sister lives in poverty.
> Northerners tend to be more outgoing, **while** people from the south are more reserved.

While and *whereas* do not necessarily link surprising contrasts together, unlike *although*, *in spite of*, etc.

3. *However* and *nevertheless*

Both of these connectors link contrasting ideas in *two different sentences* separated by a full stop or a semi-colon.

You can use *however* and *nevertheless* when you are expressing a contrast which is surprising, as with *although*, etc.

> I like him very much. **However**, we are very different.
>   **Nevertheless**,

You can also use *however* in the same way that you use *while* and *whereas*:

> Mary is rich. Her sister, **however**, is poor.
>   **However**, her sister is poor.

You cannot use *nevertheless* in this way.

PRESENT PERFECT SIMPLE and CONTINUOUS

1. When we talk about an activity or situation that began in the past and has continued up to the present moment, we can often use the present perfect simple or continuous with very little difference in meaning.

   I've worked there for three years.
   I've been working there for three years.

3 years ago	now
I started working there.	I still work there.

Note:
As with other continuous verb forms, we don't normally use the present perfect continuous with state verbs such as *know*, *understand* or *seem*.
Certain verbs by definition do not have duration and are therefore rarely used in the continuous form: *finish, start, decide, find, discover.*

2. The present perfect simple is used for a completed activity that happened in a period of time before now. If we use the present perfect continuous, it suggests that the activity is not complete:

   *He **has done** the housework.* (and has finished it)
   *He **has been doing** the housework.* (and has perhaps stopped for the moment but not finished it)

If you state a specific amount or number, you will generally use the simple rather than the continuous form. Compare:

> *I've been writing / I've written some letters this morning.*
> *I've written six letters this morning.*

> *I've been spending / I've spent a lot of money recently.*
> *I've spent over £1000 recently.*

3. We often use the present perfect continuous when we want to emphasise the still evident result of an activity which has recently finished.

> *It's **been snowing**.* (There is snow on the ground, but it isn't actually snowing at this moment.)
> *You've **been making** toast.* (I can smell it.)

PAST   NOW

PAST PARTICIPLES

Past participles can follow directly after nouns as reduced relative clauses:

> *a stocking **worn** by Queen Victoria* (= which was worn by ...)
> *Two letters **sent** by express delivery arrived late.* (= which were sent by ...)
> *The secretary **sent** by the agency was very efficient.* (= who was sent by ...)

3

WISH AND *IF ONLY*

1. *Wish/if only* + past simple

To talk about a situation in the present that we would like to be different:
*I **wish** I **had** a mobile phone. If I did, I could use it anywhere, at any time.*
*I **wish** I **could speak** Japanese, but I can't.*
*I **wish** you **didn't have to** go to work today.*

I *wish* it wasn't★ so cold.
             weren't

Note:
★ *Was* is more informal than *were* and is mostly used in speech.

2. *Wish* + *would*

To express annoyance, regret or impatience when someone or something continues to do something or won't do something.

> *I **wish** you **wouldn't interrupt** me when I'm speaking.*
> *I **wish** the weather **would improve**.*

Note:

Wish + past simple and *wish* + *would* are sometimes very similar in meaning. However, notice the contrast in these examples:

> I **wish** John **spoke** French. (He doesn't know how to speak it.)
> I **wish** John **would speak** French. (He knows how to, but he refuses to do so.)

3. *Wish* + past perfect

To talk about a situation in the past that we regret now or would have liked to be different.

> I **wish** I **hadn't eaten** so much chocolate – I feel sick.
> I **wish** I'd **booked** the hotel earlier.
> I **wish** I'd **been working** there when Don was the manager.

SO AND SUCH

Uses

To emphasise adjectives and nouns, often followed by a result clause.

> It was **so** hot we went to the beach.
> It was **such** a hot day that we went to the beach.

Form

You use *so* with adjectives without nouns:

>   cold
> It was **so**   windy   that we stayed at home.
>   horrible

You can use *so* with adverbs:

> He spoke **so** loudly we had to ask him to be quiet.

You can also use *so* before *much, many, few* and *little*:

> It's **so much** more convenient living near the centre.
> There was **so little** time to do everything.

You use *such* before a noun, or an adjective + noun:

> **such** (a/an) + (adjective) + noun
> **such** a nice day (singular, countable)
> **such** lovely children (plural, countable)
> **such** terrible weather (uncountable)
> **such** fun (uncountable)

FOCUS ADVERBS

These adverbs emphasise or point to one key part of what you are saying.

> This is **just/simply** to thank you for the lovely gift.
> It was a lovely day, but we **particularly** enjoyed the picnic.
> Soup is a great meal, **especially** when you are cold.

Note:

You usually put these immediately in front of the word or clause you want to emphasise.

4

MODALS OF DEDUCTION ABOUT THE PAST

Must've and *can't have* + past participle

When we want to say we are *almost* 100% certain about something in the past, based on the evidence we have, we can use *must've* + past participle in positive statements and *can't have* + past participle in negative statements. Continuous forms are also possible.

> A: *Why is he knocking on the door?*
> B: *He* **must've forgotten** *his key.*

> *The fans look happy so their team* **must've won**.

> A: *Look – she's coming out of the library.*
> B: *Yes – she* **must've been studying**.

> *They* **can't have left** *– the lights are still on.*

Compare:

> *He's forgotten his key.*
> (This is a fact I know is true.)
> *He* **must've forgotten** *his key.*
> (I'm almost sure, but I don't know for certain.)

Could've and *might've* + past participle

When we want to say that it is possible that something happened in the past or we are giving a possible explanation for something, we can use *could've* or *might've* + past participle. Continuous forms are also possible.

> A: *Why isn't he here yet?*
> B: *I don't know. He* **could've missed** *the bus or he* **might've got** *lost.*

> *Where are my glasses? I* **might've left** *them in the kitchen, I suppose.*

5

NOUNS

Uncountable nouns

Some nouns are always uncountable; they don't have a plural form, they are used with a singular verb, and they are not used with the indefinite article *a/an*.

Here are some common uncountable nouns which are often countable in other languages:

luggage	baggage	information	advice
furniture	homework	housework	equipment
weather	progress	traffic	machinery

Some nouns can be countable and uncountable:

home	He lives in an old people's home. [C]
	He's at home today. [U]
experience	She doesn't have much experience in banking. [U]
	Living in Japan was a very interesting experience. [C]

Plural nouns

Plural nouns only have a plural form, i.e. they end in *s*, and they can't be used with an indefinite article. They usually take a plural verb. Here are some examples:

> *premises   surroundings   refreshments   outskirts*
> *headquarters   goods   clothes   scissors   binoculars*
> *sunglasses   trousers   jeans   headphones*

Compound nouns

These are nouns formed from two or more words. Here are some examples:

> *youth hostel   T-shirt   sister-in-law   estate agent*
> *taxi rank   shopping mall   law court   contact lens*
> *alarm clock   air conditioning   credit card   bathroom*
> *baby-sitter   pedestrian   toothpaste   lampshade*
> *precinct★   public lavatory★   central heating★*

Most compound nouns are written as two words, but some can be hyphenated (e.g. baby-sitter) or written as one word (e.g. bathroom). If you aren't sure, check in a dictionary.

Most compounds have the main stress on the first word (e.g. **youth** hostel). The ones marked ★ have the stress on both parts (e.g. central **heating**).

Collective nouns

These are nouns which refer to a group of the same things or people. They can usually take a singular or plural verb. Here are some examples:

> *government   jury   committee   audience   council*
> *public   staff   press   crew   gang   family*
> *army   herd   data   group   flock*

ADJECTIVES AS NOUNS

Certain adjectives can be used with a definite article to describe groups of people in a similar social or physical condition. Here are some examples:

> *the rich   the poor   the blind   the deaf*
> *the elderly   the unemployed   the injured*
> *the French   the Japanese   the disabled*
> *the handicapped   the young*

PAST PERFECT SIMPLE AND CONTINUOUS

When we are talking about the past, we can use the past perfect simple or continuous to refer to an earlier event or state when we want to make it clear that this event happened before another past event.

> *She suddenly remembered she **had left** her hat on the bus.*
> *When I met him, he **had been working** for the company for ten years.*

PAST · NOW

PAST · NOW

Differences between the two forms

The past perfect continuous may be used to emphasise the activity itself and its continuing nature:

> *He **had been looking** for ages, and then one day, he found his ideal home.*

If we use the past perfect continuous, it suggests that the activity is not completed.
Compare:

> *We were angry because they* **had eaten** / **had been eating** *our food.*

In the first example, the food was finished; in the second, it suggests that at least some of the food had gone, but some *may* still remain.

COMPOUND ADJECTIVES

A compound adjective is made of two (or occasionally three) parts, usually written with a hyphen (-). Both parts of the compound are usually stressed.
Here are some examples:

> *air-conditioned   self-contained   semi-detached*
> *built-up   old-fashioned   brand-new*
> *run-down   well-kept   short-sleeved*
> *well-dressed   clean-shaven   high-heeled*
> *tight-fitting   good-looking   easy-going*

If you look back at Unit 1, page 10, you will find more examples.

6

PRESENT CONTINUOUS AND FUTURE CONTINUOUS (FOR ARRANGEMENTS)

Both the present continuous and the future continuous (*will be* + *-ing*) are used to talk about an event arranged or scheduled for the future, and in this use they are often interchangeable:

We're going to Tokyo today – **we're staying** *with friends.*
we'll be staying

In both cases, the arrangement to stay with friends in the future has already been made.

However, speakers sometimes prefer the future continuous when they are giving important information to the listener which may affect or involve them and which they may need to act upon.

The coach party **will be leaving** *at 8.00, so don't be late.*

WOULD

1. *Would* is commonly used in *if* sentences when referring to imaginary or improbable situations about the present or future.

   We **would stay** *longer if we had more time.*
   How **would you feel** *if someone gave you $1,000?*

2. *Would* can be used to express repeated or habitual past actions, and is similar in meaning to *used to*.

   When we were living in the country, we **would** *collect mushrooms from the forest.*

   However, *would* and *used to* are not interchangeable when talking about past **states**.

   When I was younger I **used to have** *long hair.*

   Here, only *used to* can be used and *would* is not possible.

3. In the negative form, *wouldn't* can be used to express a refusal or unwillingness:

   I asked her nicely, but she **wouldn't help.**

   It is also used with inanimate objects:
   The car **wouldn't start** *this morning.*
   I gave it a push but the door still **wouldn't open.**

4. *Would* is used as the past tense of *will* in reported speech.

   She warned us that it **would be** *dangerous.*
   He told her it **would cost** *a lot of money.*

7

PREPOSITIONS OF PLACE

These notes explain the prepositions in the lesson, but obviously do not cover all prepositions of place.

In

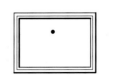

In can be used to describe something inside an area enclosed by boundaries or limits.

> *in*   the top left-hand corner
> the bottom right-hand corner
> the foreground/background
> the middle of the picture

> *in*   the front row
> the High Street

Note:
A common exception to this is *on the left/right* (*-hand side*).

On

On can be used to describe something on the surface of something.
> *The vase is* **on** *the counter.*
> *She rested her arm* **on** *the balcony.*
> *I put my name* **on** *the label.*
> *She's got a gold band* **on** *her arm.*

Note:
With certain parts of the body we often use *round* in preference to *on*.

> *the belt* **round** *her waist*
> *the tie* **round** *his neck*
> *the chain* **round** *her ankle*

With

We can use *with* when describing a particular distinguishing feature:

> *a boy* **with** *big brown eyes*
> *the man* **with** *the tattoo*
> *a girl* **with** *beautiful long hair*

We can also use *with ... on* or *in* to mean *wearing something*:

> *the man wearing the grey suit*
> *the man* **with** *the grey suit* **on**
> *the man* **in** *the grey suit*

Down and across

We can use these to indicate particular positions/directions:

> *The dotted line runs* **down** *the middle of the picture.*
> *The wavy line runs* **across** *it.*

LOOK = SEEM

Look + adjective

We do not use adverbs after *look* when it means *seem*. Compare:

> He **looked** happy. = He seemed happy.
> (**not** He looked ~~happily~~.)

Look like + noun

> The building **looked like** a church.
> The man at the door **looked like** an insurance salesman.

Look as if/as though + clause

We use this to say something is likely or possible.
> It **looks as if** it's going to rain.
> He **looks as though** he's been in the sun.

MODAL VERBS – HYPOTHESISING

We use modal verbs *would*, *could*, *might* to talk about improbable or imaginary situations in the present or future.
Imagine you couldn't hear for a day. How would it affect you?

> I **wouldn't be able to/couldn't** use the phone.
> I **would have to** ask people to write messages down.
> I **couldn't/wouldn't be able to** listen to the radio.
> It **might** help me be more understanding about deafness.
> (i.e. it is possible that it would help me)

8

IT'S TIME + PAST TENSE

We use the structure *it's time* + past tense or *it's about time/it's high time* + past tense for added emphasis when we want to say that something should happen now or should already have happened.

> It's **time** we left – it's getting dark.
> It's **about time** you bought a decent car.
> It's **high time** this law was changed.

9

DEFINING AND NON-DEFINING RELATIVE CLAUSES

Look at these examples:
> He's the man **who gave me the money**.
> The place **where they work** is beautiful.
> Have you seen the books **(that/which) I bought today**?

The parts in bold type above are called 'defining (or identifying) relative clauses' because they define or identify the noun they follow. For example, in the first sentence, we learn *which* man the speaker means – the man who gave me the money. (If the sentence was just

He's the man, our response would be to ask, 'Which man?')
Now look at these examples:

> The man, **who already had a criminal record**, was sent to prison for two years.
> The escape, **which surprised everyone**, had obviously been very carefully planned.
> The police officer, **whose arm was broken in the fight**, was given an award for bravery.
> He was taken to Paddington Green police station, **where most of the demonstrators were being held**.

The parts in bold type in these sentences, called 'non-defining (non-identifying) relative clauses' do not identify the nouns in each example, but give extra information. For instance, in the first sentence, the main information is that the man was sent to prison for two years; the fact that he had a criminal record is extra information. We show this by putting the extra information between commas.

Look at these contrasting examples:

> 1. My brother who is in the army has got a Porsche.
> 2. My brother, who is in the army, has got a Porsche.

In the first sentence, the speaker is identifying which brother he means – we assume he has more than one brother. He might go on to say: *but my brother who works in a bank rides a bicycle.*
In the second sentence, the speaker may only have one brother, and is simply giving extra information about his Porsche-driving brother.
Non-defining relative clauses are more common in writing than in speech.

10

PURPOSE CLAUSES

If you want to talk about the purpose or reason for doing something, you can use a number of connectors.

Infinitive clauses

> He went to Australia **in order to★** see his family.
> *to* / *in order to★* / *so as to★*

You can also make the last two infinitive structures negative; notice the word order.

> She turned the TV down **in order not to★** / **so as not to★** disturb them.

In informal speech, you would be more likely to use *so that* + modal verb:

> She turned the TV down **so that** she wouldn't disturb them.

So that

This structure is usually followed by modal verbs, such as *can, could, would*, etc.

> *I bought the house **so that** my children would have security.*
> *I want to finish this **so that** I can send it tonight.*

Note:
* All structures marked with an asterisk are more common in formal language.

ATTITUDE ADVERBS AND PHRASES

We use a wide range of adverbs and phrases to show our reactions and opinions on what we are talking about. These adverbs and phrases also link our ideas together coherently within sentences and between sentences. Here are some common ones used when showing your feelings:

fortunately	*unfortunately*	*surprisingly*	*naturally*
luckily	*ideally*	*interestingly*	*sadly*	*strangely*
unbelievably	*incredibly*	*ironically*	

> *I lost my keys. **Luckily**, my neighbour had a spare set.*
> *She arrived late, so **unfortunately** we went without her.*

These are some more common linking words and phrases used in spoken English:

> *We thought it would be hard but **actually** / **in fact**, it wasn't.*
> (= contrary to expectation)

> *It's a long story, but **eventually** / **in the end**, we got there.*
> (= after a long time and a lot of problems)

> *There are many ways of losing weight: **for instance** / **for example**, dieting and exercise. But …*
> (used when giving examples)

> *It was a horrible room, but **to be honest** we didn't care that much.*
> (used when showing one's attitude)

> *She didn't seem very pleased to see us. **Anyway** / **anyhow**, we went in and told her why we had come.*
> (used when moving on to the main point or the next stage of what you are saying)

See also ADVERBS AND ADVERBIAL PHRASES in Unit 12.

11

VERB PATTERNS

Here are some common examples of four of the basic verb patterns. You will also find that some verbs can take additional patterns to the ones below. Use a dictionary to check if you are unsure which pattern to use.

Verb + infinitive

offer	*promise*	*refuse*	*threaten*	*decide*	*forget*
manage	*want*	*seem*	*hope*	*choose*	*agree*
mean (= intend)	*expect*				

Verb + -ing

avoid	*admit*	*deny*	*suggest*	*imagine*	*enjoy*
finish	*can't stand*	*don't mind*	*give up*	*keep*	

Verb + object + infinitive

persuade	*beg*	*encourage*	*advise*	*ask*	*tell*
permit	*want*	*warn*	*expect*	*remind*	*force*
allow	*invite*	*teach*			

Verb + object + preposition

accuse somebody of noun/+ *-ing*
thank somebody for noun/+ *-ing*
prevent somebody from + *-ing*
blame somebody for noun/+ *-ing*
praise somebody for noun/+ *-ing*
introduce somebody to noun
congratulate somebody on noun/+ *-ing*
apologise (to somebody) for noun/+ *-ing*

12

QUESTIONS

Ellipsis in questions

We often omit words in questions in informal speech when the context makes it clear what we mean. In these questions, the intonation rises.

> *You seen my tie?* (= have you seen)
> *Having a rest?* (= are you having)
> *Want a cigarette?* (= do you want)
> *Busy?* (= are you busy)

Question tags

1. We use question tags to check when we aren't sure about something; in this case, the intonation on the tag rises.

    You're Bill, aren't you? (I'm not sure.)
    No, actually, I'm David – I'm Bill's brother.

2. We also use question tags to ask for agreement; in a sense these are not 'real' questions. In this case, the intonation on the tag falls.

    A: *She's lovely, isn't she?* (I think so and I expect you to agree.)
    B: *Hm, delightful.*

Form

You **can** drive, **can't** you?   It **isn't** raining, **is it**?
  + auxiliary   – auxiliary   – auxiliary   + auxiliary

If the main sentence doesn't have an auxiliary, you need to use the appropriate form of *do* in the question tag.

*She **drives** a Porsche, **doesn't** she?*
*You often **get** colds, **don't** you?*
*They **arrived** late, **didn't** they?*
*He **used to** work here, **didn't** he?*

Negative questions

We often ask negative questions to get confirmation for something we believe to be true.

Haven't you got enough money? Let me lend you £1.
The speaker can see that the person hasn't enough money.
Can't you open that? I'll do it.
The speaker can see that the other person can't open it.

We also use them as a polite or tentative way of suggesting a course of action.

A: *Let's go.*
B: *Don't you think we should wait a bit longer?* (= I think we probably should wait.)

Dangling prepositions

In everyday speech, if a question word is the object of a preposition, then the preposition often comes at the end of the clause.

*What do you want that box **for**?*
(We don't usually say *For what do you want that box?* It sounds very formal.)
*Who are you looking **at**?*
*Which hotel will you be staying **in**?*
*How long are you going **for**?*
*What are you so worried **about**?*

Statements as questions

These are also used as confirmation of what the speaker believes to be true or has just learnt. The intonation usually rises.

You've got three sons? That must be fun.
You're leaving already? But it's only 7 o'clock.
They missed the train? How annoying!

See also EMBEDDED QUESTIONS in Unit 17.

ADVERBS AND ADVERBIAL PHRASES

Form

Many adverbs of manner are formed by adding *-ly* to a related adjective:

sad/sadly, nervous/nervously, quiet/quietly

There are also several spelling variations:

1. adjectives ending with *-y* change to *-ily*, e.g. *happy/happily*

2. adjectives ending with *-ic* change to *-ally*, e.g. *tragic/tragically*

3. some omit the final *-e*, e.g. *gentle/gently, irritable/irritably*

Some adverbs have the same form and meaning as the related adjective, e.g. *fast, straight, hard, late*:

He drives very fast.   *Go straight ahead.*
She works hard.   *We got there late.*

Some adjectives cannot be made into adverbs:

1. adjectives already ending *-ly*, e.g. *silly, friendly*

2. some adjectives ending *-ed*, e.g. *surprised, puzzled*

3. some common adjectives, e.g. *difficult, afraid*

With the first two groups we can often express more information about an action or event using a phrase with a general noun. For example:

*'Please sit down', he said **in a friendly manner**.*
*She looked at me **in a very puzzled way**.*

With the last group we can sometimes use a prepositional phrase:

*He spoke **with difficulty**.*

Note:

Many adverbs of manner have the same meaning as the adjective:

*A **nervous** laugh*   *He laughed **nervously**.*
*An **anxious** look*   *She looked at me **anxiously**.*

Some adverbs ending *-ly* have a different meaning from the related adjective: *hardly* (= almost not at all) doesn't mean the same as *hard*; *lately* (= recently) doesn't mean the same as *late*.

See also ATTITUDE ADVERBS AND PHRASES in Unit 10.

13

OBLIGATION, PERMISSION AND ENTITLEMENT

There are a number of ways of expressing obligation in English:

Have (got) to/must + verb

> We **have to**
> We **have got to** get there before 7.00, or it will be too late.
> We **must**

Note:

Have (got) to tends to be used for obligations imposed by an external authority (laws, regulations, etc.). *Must* tends to be used more for obligations we impose on ourselves.

> You **have to** wear a helmet on a motor bike. (This is a law.)
> I **must** get my hair cut before I go on holiday. (No one is telling me to do it.)

However, there are *many* occasions when the forms are interchangeable. It is also important to remember that *have (got) to* is much more frequent than *must* in spoken English.

Be forced to + verb

> At school we **were forced to** eat everything on our plates.
> People should not **be forced to** retire at 65.

We use *be forced to* to talk about something we are obliged to do by others against our will; in other words, we don't want to do it.

MORAL OBLIGATION

Ought to/should + verb

We can use both forms to give our opinions about what is right and fair:

> People who earn the most **should** **ought to** pay the most tax.

Should is more common than *ought to*.

PERMISSION

> You **aren't allowed to** **can't** sit here without a ticket.

Note:
We say *you aren't allowed to*, not *it isn't allowed to*.

ENTITLEMENT

> You **have the right to** **are entitled to** see your medical records.

This not only means you are allowed to see your records, but also gives you the authority to see them. This suggests you are in a more powerful position.

IF ... EVER/IF EVER ..., WHENEVER

These connectors can mean *every time that (something happens)*.

> **If ever I**
> **If I ever** get lost in town, I ask someone the way.
> **Whenever I**

> The cat hides under the bed **whenever we** **if ever we** have a storm. **if we ever**

Whenever has the idea of something which occurs relatively frequently; *if ever* suggests that something may happen occasionally and is more hypothetical.

Whenever can also be used to mean *any time that*.
> You can come **whenever** you like.

EXPRESSING DEGREES OF POSSIBILITY AND PROBABILITY

There are a number of ways of expressing possibility and probability in English. The scale below shows some of the common ways, and these are arranged in order of probability.

> It's **definitely** true.
> It's **highly likely** to be true.
> It's **probably** true.
> or It's **likely** to be true.
> It **might** be true.
> or It **may** be true.
> It's **unlikely** to be true.
> or **I doubt if** it's true.
> It's **highly unlikely** to be true.
> It **definitely** isn't true.

PRESENT AND PAST HABITS

Simple and continuous tenses

The present simple and past simple (often with frequency adverbs/adverbial phrases) can be used in English to describe habits:

> They **leave** the house at 9.00 **every morning**.
> One of my friends **often goes** to that restaurant.
> We **never drove** to the centre of town – it was too busy.

We can also use the present continuous/past continuous (often with *always, forever* and *continually*) to talk about habitual actions which are often not planned, and often cause irritation.

> I'm **always losing** my keys. (I don't intend to do it and it irritates me.)
> She's **forever telling** me about all the money she earns.
> He **was always falling** asleep at his desk, so he got the sack.

Some characteristic habits are pleasant, however:

*He's **always buying** me flowers.*

Compare:

*He **always leaves** the door open, so that latecomers can get in.* (This might be a deliberate, planned action of his.)
*He's **always leaving** the door open and the room gets really cold.* (He may not even think about shutting it.)

Keep + -ing

We can use *keep doing* to talk about repeated actions/activities:

*I **keep getting** headaches.*
*He **keeps telling** me he's leaving, but he never does.*

Would and used to do

See Unit 6, 'Would' point 2.

Participle clauses

See also Unit 2, past participles.
Here are some of the ways in which present participles can be used in clauses:

1. To give more information about nouns, often replacing a relative clause:
   *The man **pushing** the wheelchair looked like a guard.* (who was pushing ...)

2. To show that events happened simultaneously, replacing *when*:
   ***Opening** the door, she gave a sudden cry.* (When she opened the door ...)

3. To show that one event is the result of the other, or explains the cause/reason for the other (often formal):
   ***Knowing** it was too late, I turned back and went home.* (Because I knew it was too late ...)

15

PASSIVES

The passive is often used when we want to focus on the person or thing affected by an action, rather than the agent (responsible for the action).

1. *The prisoners **were taken** into the exercise yard.*
2. *The magazines **are** always **delivered** on a Monday.*
3. *The survivors **have been taken** to hospital for treatment.*
4. *Several messages **had been left** on his answerphone.*

The agent responsible:

– may be known but too obvious to mention (as in Example 1);
– may be known but not important (as in Examples 2 and 3);
– may be unknown (as in Example 4).

Sometimes, the agent is important and is mentioned at the end of the phrase for emphasis:

*The exhibition is full of work which was done **by disabled people**.*
*Didn't Bach write this concerto? No, it was written **by Vivaldi**.*

WHETHER

Whether is normally used when we are talking about choices or alternatives. It is used in particular structures and patterns and is sometimes interchangeable with *if*; for instance, to introduce indirect 'yes/no' questions.

*I don't know **whether/if** they'll be able to come or not.*
*He wanted to know **whether/if** the flight was full.*

We only use *whether* (not *if*) in the following cases:

1. before *to* infinitives:
   *I can't decide **whether** to leave school or stay on.*

2. after prepositions:
   *It depends **on whether** we want to stay the night.*

3. where the phrase *whether ... or not* means *it doesn't matter if*:
   ***Whether you do it or not**, the result will be the same.* (It doesn't matter if you do it or not, because the result will be the same.)

EXPRESSING QUANTITY

There are a number of ways in which we can describe quantity.
Example: describing the number of people:

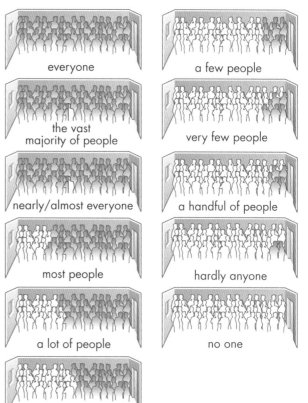

everyone

a few people

the vast majority of people

very few people

nearly/almost everyone

a handful of people

most people

hardly anyone

a lot of people

no one

quite a lot of people

Note:

A few and *few* may refer to the same number of people but have a different emphasis; *a few* may be a small number, but a satisfactory one, *few* suggests a small number which is unsatisfactory or insufficient.

> *A few people came to the meeting.* (not many, but enough)
> *Few people came to the meeting.* (not as many as we wanted or expected)

CONDITIONAL SENTENCES

We often use *if* sentences when talking about 'unreal' situations – in other words, where we are imagining the consequences of present events that are unlikely to happen (improbable) or past events that didn't happen.

> *If she **had** a car, she **wouldn't cycle** to work.*★
> (= She doesn't have a car, so she does cycle.)
> *If I **had left** earlier, I **would've got** there on time.*★★
> (= The fact is, I left late, and so I didn't get there on time.)

We can modify the consequence by using modal verbs.

> *If she **had** a car, she **might not cycle** to work.*★
> (= It is possible that she wouldn't cycle.)
> *If I **had left** earlier, I **could've got** there on time.*★★
> (= I would have been able to get there on time.)
> *If I **had left** earlier, I **might have got** there on time.*★★
> (= It is possible that I would have got there on time.)

★ often called 'second conditional'
★★ often called 'third or past conditional'

It is also possible to refer to present or future situations and say how these would have been affected by imagined changes in the past. These are often called 'mixed conditionals'.

> *If she **hadn't lost** her job, she **wouldn't be** in debt now.*
> (= She lost her job, and now she is in debt.)
> *If we **had won** that American contract, **I would still have my job** today.*
> (= We didn't get the contract then, so I don't have a job now.)

17

PAST TENSES USED FOR DISTANCING

We can sometimes use past tenses (past simple and past continuous) to create a distancing effect when making certain requests and suggestions and asking questions. We do this to sound more polite in more formal relationships; or to sound more tentative – we do not want to assume people will do what we want them to do.

> *I **was wondering** if you might be free tomorrow – I might need your help.*
> *Did you want to see the room before you decide, sir?*
> *We **were hoping** you could do this before Thursday.*
> *I **was really looking** for something a little cheaper, in fact.*
> *I **wondered** if you might be interested in this job.*

EMBEDDED QUESTIONS

We use questions of this type to be more polite, often when we want to show the listener that we do not assume that they know the answer.

> ***Do you happen to know** where the Tate Gallery is?*
> ***Have you any idea** when the last bus leaves?*
> ***Do you know** if there is a post office near here?*

Compare the word order in direct and embedded questions:

> ***Where is** the Tate Gallery?*
> *Do you happen to know **where** the Tate Gallery **is**?*
> ***When does** the last bus **leave**?*
> *Have you any idea **when** the last bus **leaves**?*

You can also use this form to be more polite when you think the listener can answer the question:

> ***Could you tell me** how to get there?*

See also QUESTIONS in Unit 12.

18

DEGREES OF POSSIBILITY AND PROBABILITY

See Unit 13.

FUTURE SIMPLE, CONTINUOUS AND PERFECT

We use *will* + base verb to make predictions about the future based on our opinions, beliefs or guesses.

> *I think he **will probably be** late; he often is on Fridays.*
> *You don't think it **will rain**, do you?*
> *I'm pretty sure she **won't fail** her test.*

Compare:

> *It's **going to** rain – look at those clouds.* (future prediction based on present evidence)
> *I think it'**ll rain** later.* (future prediction based on opinion, rather than present evidence)

We use *will + be doing* to talk about actions already in progress at a particular moment in the future.

> *Don't ring at 8.00 – I'll **be having** my dinner.* (Dinner will be in progress at that time.)
> *I'll take my umbrella – it'll **probably be raining** when I come out of the cinema.*

We also use the future continuous to talk about predicting or guessing what is in progress at the moment.

> *Don't bother him now; I expect he'll **be having** lunch.*

Some verbs are not usually used in the continuous form: for example, *have* meaning possess, *know, understand, believe, seem, be,* etc.

We use *will* + perfect infinitive to talk about things which will have been completed or achieved no later than a certain point in the future.

NOW   REPORT FINISHED   PERSON LEAVES

> *I'll **have finished** this report by the time you leave.*
> (We don't know when the person will finish it, but we know it will happen between now and the time in the future when the other person leaves.)
> *Martin thinks he **will have done** the living room by the end of the week.*

The future perfect is often used with *by* + time expression (*by six o'clock, by the end of the year*). We can also use this tense to talk about something now that we think or guess has happened in another place:

> *We can't contact him there – he'll **have left by now**.*

See also Unit 6.

ADDITIONAL MATERIAL

Unit 2 A GOOD NIGHT'S SLEEP Exercise 3

ANSWERS TO QUIZ

1 c Different people need varying amounts of sleep. Healthy adults usually need between 6 and 8 hours a night. However, a small minority can get by on less than 4 and a half hours or need more than 10 hours. *nevertheless/although*

2 b More isn t always better. Having a lie-in to catch up on sleep can make you feel sluggish. Quality is more important than quantity, and it helps if you can get the same amount of sleep at the same times each night.

3 b Avoid caffeine after 2 o clock in the afternoon. Its effects last longer than we imagine. Excessive drinking of alcohol can also disrupt sleep. Nevertheless, a single glass of wine shouldn t create sleeping problems. *but/however*

4 a Surroundings are very important to good sleep. Bedrooms shouldn t be too hot, too cold nor too noisy. Exercising during the day will not necessarily help you sleep at night, as the adrenalin and drive will stay in your system.

5 c Getting out of bed may help. Do something you find relaxing such as reading, watching TV or listening to music.

6 c We sleep in different ways at different times during the night. During REM sleep the brain is very active, our eyes move quickly from side to side and we dream.

7 c Although it is difficult to identify a single cause of nightmares, stressful situations definitely increase their likelihood. *in spite of/even though*

8 b According to laboratory research, most recalled dreams retain some colour. The more vivid the recollection, the stronger the memory of colour.

9 a Even though most sleepwalking is harmless, extreme cases may involve potentially dangerous behaviour, such as driving cars, loading shotguns and mistaking a bed partner. *despite the fact that/despite*

Unit 2 SLEEP AND OTHER PROBLEMS, Exercise 3

1. ... for ages now, so I thought I'd just have to live with it, but recently I(*'ve gone/'ve been going*) to an osteopath, and the sessions with her, along with the exercises she gets me to do on my own, really seem to be helping. Of course, it could be ...

2. ... and it can take quite a while. At the moment, I mean, it's a real nuisance, because for the last few days I(*'ve woken up/'ve been waking up*) at five in the morning and then of course, by the afternoon I'm exhausted, but I've forced myself to stay awake and I'm just starting to get used to the change ...

3. Well, I used to get them a lot, so whenever I did, I avoided certain types of food and just put up with them, but I(*'ve just discovered/'ve just been discovering*) this fantastic ointment which clears them up in no time. I wish someone had told me about it ten years ago ...

4. Almost everyone I know has been to all sorts of different doctors. Well, me, I (*'ve seen/'ve been seeing*) three specialists, and all of them have said that living in a big city is making it worse. So, I just have to make do with my inhaler and get on with it ...

5. ... three or four hours. I should have known better, but you just forget, you know, and it's really ruined my holiday because since the second day, I(*'ve sat/'ve been sitting*) in the shade all the time and I(*'ve spent/'ve been spending*) at least £30 on lotions and creams to relieve the pain, not to mention making Paul's life a misery ...

Unit 3 DON'T JUST SIT THERE – DO SOMETHING! Exercise 6

Scene 1: reactions and explanations

There are about six people near the man and woman. They soon become aware that the man is pestering her. Some look at him for a moment; others try to ignore them. Eventually one man in his mid-twenties speaks up. 'Leave her alone,' he says quietly. The man does so. When the others were asked why they had not intervened, one man said, 'You have to be careful. People like him can be mentally disturbed. He might have started to threaten me, and there aren't enough guards on these trains, that's the problem.' Another woman in her mid-twenties said, 'I wanted to tell her to get off the train with me, just to get rid of him, but the other man spoke up first.'

Scene 2: reactions and explanations

Nobody does anything. Later, Sarah Radcliffe, 44, a secretary, said, 'I just wanted him to stop talking. It was preventing me from reading my paper.' Another man, a 24-year-old electronics engineer, said, 'I thought they were together.' Then he added, 'Something like this happened the other night. I intervened but the situation just escalated, making it worse.'

Scene 3: reactions and explanations

A young couple nearby said nothing. In fact, they started smiling; they thought it was funny. But when the man asked the woman for a kiss, another man, Raymond Turner, 27, took action. He put his hand on the man's shoulder and said, 'I think you should leave her alone.' Afterwards, he said that he decided to stick up for her because it was obvious she couldn't really protect herself. When questioned later, the couple said, 'In London, you often get pestered. She should have got off the train, or told him to go away. There was no reason for us to do anything about it.'

Unit 4 PLEASE LEAVE A MESSAGE ... Exercise 4

Situation 1
You are Alice receiving Sally's return call. Be careful – Sally may still be a bit sensitive about what happened. If she's a bit reluctant to go out with you, try to persuade her.

Situation 2
You are Sally, returning Derek's call. You had completely forgotten about babysitting tomorrow, and you've already agreed to do something important. (Decide what it is.) You're really embarrassed about letting Derek and his wife down, especially as it's not the first time.

Situation 3
You are Patience, receiving Sally's return call. You're worse than ever and need to tell someone what has happened. Try to persuade Sally to pop round and see you.

Situation 4
You are Sally, returning Martin Bellingham's call. You ring at 11.00 (you've only just got in). Paula has told you all about her friend Martin – he's nice, but terribly unreliable, so double-check all the arrangements. Give him clear instructions to avoid the one-way system. 10.00 is too late – try to make it a bit earlier.

Unit 8 Scandal Exercise 1

Case Study 2

A story has just appeared in the national newspapers that a respected high court judge has been charged with a drink-driving offence. It appears the judge was initially stopped for speeding in a built-up area, but when the police carried out a routine breathalyser test, the judge was found to be significantly over the legal limit of alcohol. No accident occurred during the incident.

Unit 8 Political issues Exercise 1

Other factors may include:
- the leader's spouse or family
- specific regional issues, e.g. road building
- the past record of the party
- the character of the leader
- the way your friends/colleagues vote
- the state and credibility of other parties
- specific events such as political scandals

Unit 8 Political issues Exercise 4

Lynn: Well, I've always voted for the same party in Britain, not because I agree with all their policies, necessarily, but because when you look at all the parties, they're the least of all the evils. And the issues that concern me .... to do with, well, telling the truth. I don't think it's a crime to say you're sorry when you've got something wrong. Erm, I think it would be nice if people just had ...., and so I look for people with the integrity and who are prepared to tell the truth, even if it's not what we all want to hear. Erm, I'm not looking for ...., because I think that actually lets other people off the hook; it means that they don't have to be responsible for what happens ...., so I'm looking for people who motivate me and others to take action for themselves, and I'm very concerned about education because I think it's the one thing that can help people move from one social class to another, and I think that the worst thing that dogs our country at the moment is ....

Trude: Well, back in Germany, I have voted for different parties, because it's actually different from here, from England because we have quite a few parties that are middling, and so it always depends on who the politicians are, of the moment, really – what their outlook is, so that can change, so I always was flexible about this. For me the main issue is, erm, the .... problems, and if a party shows that they are really concerned and they are, you know, about to do things that I think are very important, then, erm, I'm ....

Jeff: Erm, I was brought up in the States by a family that always voted Republican. It was always party politics, we didn't even speak to Democrats. Erm, but then when I was growing up, the Vietnam War happened. I think people my age

.... ; the vote came down to a younger age, and I started voting – mostly Democrat – I think they care more about people. Certainly, Clinton now has tried very hard to introduce national health – which would be awfully nice. It makes sense in England; I don't know why it can't in the States. Erm, better education and er ...., I think. Under the Republicans, the poor really suffer, and, erm, maybe we can finish with party politics and try to make ....

Unit 8 Review and development Review of Unit 7 Exercise 3

The Fortune Teller
by Georges de la Tour (1593–1652)

Project: GROUP MAGAZINE Exercise 3

... so she went to Spain, determined to become successful and return home in triumph. But it didn't work out like that, and she couldn't get a job or a flat, and ended up sleeping on a friend's floor. It all seemed rather depressing and her dreams began to fade.

Then she saw a job advertised in the paper; although it didn't look very interesting she felt she should make an effort and phone the number. Not wanting to take further advantage of her host's phone bill, she went out to find a call box. She wandered around aimlessly for hours before finally deciding to phone. She only had one large note worth about $10 and needed some change, so she went and sat in a posh café with tables outside – the kind of place you think of sitting in with a glass of wine, having a wonderful time.

The waiter brought her a drink and came back with a huge bundle of notes. He hadn't looked properly – he must have thought it was worth $50. It was a huge amount of money to her and she sat there staring at it. In the end, ...

Unit 13 Is it right? Is it fair? Exercise 5

Version 1

JACQUI: Should people be forced to retire at 60 or 65, or should they have the right to carry on working if they wish? What do you think?

LINFORD: Well, I think if they're fit and healthy, I don't see any reason why they ....
.... retire. I mean, I think .... is just a bit harsh,
really, I think it ....

JACQUI: Really? Why?

LINFORD: Well, you know, especially mature people are very experienced; they've got a lot to offer young people, you know, they've learnt a lot, they've had a lot of invaluable experience, and for them to have to go, I just think is too hard.

JACQUI: But if they stay on working until they're much, much older, what about the young people? There are far too many young people unemployed, and they need the chance to start work. I think basically people should be forced to retire at 60 or 65, whatever age, in order that young people can take over the jobs.

LINFORD: Yes, but I mean, to be forced to go, I think that's just too hard, you know, these people have been working all their lives and sometimes they ....
work because their pensions are so low.

JACQUI: Oh, but I mean fixed age retirement ....
They have to think about the young people. I mean, if not, some people are going to carry on far too long, and then, you know, they're going to become less competent physically and mentally. I think .... young people, they ought to think about their retirement, what they can do when they stop working, you know, all the fun things they can do ...

Version 2

KATHERINE: When workers are made redundant, do you agree with the principle 'last in, first out'?

PAUL: Hmm, it's a difficult one (it is) particularly in the 90s when, you know, redundancy is so common. (hmm) I think if, if you have to have a policy, erm, then 'last in first out' is a clear one, (hmm) and it would work the same for everybody.

KATHERINE: I don't like it as a policy myself because it's so clear cut. I think the clarity of the policy is not necessarily in its favour. I think redundancy ....
...., and then I suppose if you don't get
enough voluntary redundancies and .... a company decision,
then maybe the company .... people's
individual circumstances.

PAUL: Hmm. Don't you think that people also ....
for loyalty to a company? I mean how would you feel if you'd been working for somewhere for 40 years; somebody joined, six months, and redundancies came along and you were on the list and he wasn't?

KATHERINE: Well, that is a good point, and I think that's what I mean about taking into concern the individual, erm, so maybe that would come into your argument.

PAUL: That's why people say they ...., and why 'last in, first out' works.

KATHERINE: But that's only one side of it. I think in that case you may end up, the company .... who are doing a very good job, they've just started, brought fresh blood into a company and you're having to get rid of them and keep on somebody who really is maybe past it, and only out of loyalty (hmm) you're, you're having to keep them on.

PAUL: So you'd like to see ...

Unit 16 So what would *you* have done? Exercise 1

1. If she resigned, we might need a new manager.
2. If she resigned, we would need a new manager.
3. If she had resigned, we would've needed a new manager.
4. If she had resigned, we might have needed a new manager.
5. If she hadn't resigned, we wouldn't have needed a new manager.
6. If she hadn't resigned, we might not have needed a new manager.
7. If she had resigned, we would need a new manager.
8. If she had resigned, we might need a new manager.

Unit 17 Excuse me, would you mind ...? Exercise 3

1.

DRIVER: Oh, excuse me, no, er, is it too late? I ...

TRAFFIC WARDEN: Yes, it is too late, I'm sorry.

DRIVER: I'm really sorry, I .... I had to go to the pharmacy. I've got some urgent medication that I needed to get, and I was literally there for two minutes. Is there any chance of just letting me off? I mean it was a ...

TRAFFIC WARDEN: It doesn't actually make any difference. I'm sorry, you were parking on the double yellow line, you've got a ticket.

DRIVER: I .... I didn't see the line.

TRAFFIC WARDEN: Well, it says very clearly up on the lamppost here that er ...

DRIVER: Yeah, but have some heart! I mean, I had to go into the pharmacy. I mean it was a ...

TRAFFIC WARDEN: I'm terribly sorry, but it's a dangerous place to park. There are many accidents that occur because you've parked right on the corner here on the double yellow line.

DRIVER: Where on earth am I supposed to park, then?

TRAFFIC WARDEN: I've got to, er, I've got to move on.

DRIVER: No, excuse me, look, my explanation is quite valid, and I think that you, the least you can do is let me off this. I mean, it doesn't take much to ...

TRAFFIC WARDEN: Well, if you want to put it down in writing and complain to the, er ...

DRIVER: No, I don't want to put it down in writing, I want to sort it out right here! I think you just ...

TRAFFIC WARDEN: I'm terribly sorry, there's nothing I can do.

DRIVER: Oh, that's ridiculous!

TRAFFIC WARDEN: Yes, if you pay it within 21 days, thank you.

DRIVER: You're enjoying this, aren't you!

2.

WOMAN 1: Oh, excuse me, er, ... ?

MAN: Oh, yeah, I think, erm, I think there's one on Palmerston Road. That's ...

WOMAN 1: Yeah?

MAN: Well, let's ... just get my bearings straight, OK. Right over here, that's Queens Road, right over here on the left. (yeah) OK, you go down Queens Road, and you go two blocks down, right and you'll turn left on, I think it's Berwick Avenue (yes) turn left there and ...

WOMAN 1: It sounds far!

MAN: Well, it's not that ... no, it's not really that far. Darn! No, I'm not really sure if that's really the right way ... You're asking an American!

WOMAN 1: I know!

MAN: Oh, wait, wait! Excuse me, ...
            ....

WOMAN 2:   Oh, yeah, erm, let me think. There used to be one on Palmerston Road, but that
            one's closed down. They built another one, though, on Jones Street, yeah, Jones
            Street. If you just go straight down here, take a left at the lights, and second on the
            right. That's Jones Street.

WOMAN 1:   Yes, I think I remember now. OK, thanks very much.

MAN: OK, bye. Thanks!

3.

WOMAN: Sam, hi! You're walking to work – I don't believe it! Getting some exercise at long
            last!

SAM: Yeah, right. No, my car, you must have heard about my car.

WOMAN: No.

SAM: Oh, last week. I had an accident, just over by the pub.

WOMAN: Oh! Oh, my God. ....

SAM: Oh, it's a complete write-off now. I was just going, going to the pub. You know the
            intersection just before it?

WOMAN: Yeah.

SAM: Well, I put the brake on, there was some black ice on the road, and just, the car
            went straight through the intersection.

WOMAN: Oh, no, and smashed into that fence?

SAM: No, no I didn't ... a car was coming from the left going through the intersection and
            hit me on the side, through the passenger side so luckily it was, I was OK, well, a bit
            of whiplash ...

WOMAN: Oh, ...?

SAM: Yes, well, I mean as I said, it hit the passenger's door, so I was OK. Yeah.

WOMAN: Wow!

SAM: But it's, er, I can't believe it, you know. Just had the car done up.

WOMAN: Such a beautiful car as well, oh, I'm really sorry to hear that, Sam.

SAM: Yes, well, that's what happens ...

4.

NEEMA: Hi, Michèle.

MICHELE: Oh, hi, good morning. Slept OK?

NEEMA: Yeah, yeah, fine. Um, I was wondering if I could have a bit of a word with you ...

MICHELE: Oh, yes, yes, certainly.

NEEMA: Last night when you came in, I think you left the door open.

MICHELE: Did I?

NEEMA: The front door, yes. Anyone could have, you know, come in and stolen whatever
            they liked.

MICHELE: Oh, I was sure I closed it behind me.

NEEMA: Oh, yes, I know, but it was open this morning. ....
            .... when you come in at night?

MICHELE: Yeah, I'm often ... you know, I'm going out a lot and I always check behind me,
            because obviously I know it's important to close doors behind you, specially not in
            your house ... you know, is your lock working OK?

NEEMA: Yes, the lock is working fine. ....
            ....
            when you come in, because it was only you that came in last night. I locked it
            behind me.

MICHELE: Are you sure? There's nobody who came after me or anything like that?

NEEMA: No, Michèle ... it was only you.

MICHELE: Well, I really don't understand.

NEEMA: Well, the door was open – how do you explain that, then?

MICHELE: Well, I don't – maybe there is something wrong with your door, because I took the
            handle, I pulled it, I heard the click, and I thought, 'right, I'm in.'

NEEMA: Well, the door was open this morning, Michèle, so if you could just check it when
            you come in at night, then maybe this won't happen again, yeah?

MICHELE: Well, I will double check but you know, I was pretty sure I closed it.

NEEMA: Right, OK, well, I'll see you later.

ADDITIONAL MATERIAL

TAPESCRIPTS

UNIT 1 WHAT HAVE WE GOT IN COMMON?

Common features

Exercise 3

A: OK, yeah, yeah, we've thought of, we've got something, yeah.

B: Ah, right then. Um, I've got a bit of a feeling actually about this.

C: Have you?

B: Yeah. Does it have anything to do with sport?

A: Yes. (*laughter*)

C: Is it, er, in any way connected to the team that you support?

A AND D: No.

B: Ah, that's that theory, then.

D: Stumped. That's two questions.

B: That's two questions.

C: Was that a clue? Is it anything to do with cricket?

A: No, that's three questions.

B: Is it anything to do with football?

D: It is, yeah.

B: So, it's to do with football, so, and it's not connected with the team you support. Is it, erm, to do with the fact that you both play?

D: Sort of ...

A: Yeah, sort of.

C: Is it to do with an injury that may have occurred during playing?

A: Yes, yes, you're on the right track.

B: Is it that you've both broken your leg playing football?

A: No. But you're quite warm.

C: Has it got anything to do with the fact that you have broken a bone of any sort during football?

D: Very very close.

A: So close it's unbelievable, but no.

D: But no.

B: Is it ... is it that while playing football you've each been injured in some way that you couldn't play for a long time, so you might've broken something or sprained something – you've been laid off?

A: Yes.

C: Is that it?

A: Well done. Eight, wasn't it, eight questions?

D: Yes, we've both been hospitalised with football injuries.

B AND C: Ahh.

Dictogloss

Exercise 3

When you are listening to a foreign language, you probably won't worry if there are a *few* new words, but a *lot* of new vocabulary will almost certainly be a major problem. Sometimes though, a speaker may use familiar words and you still don't understand. This may be because they are speaking quickly, or they have an unfamiliar accent. It's also true that it's harder to understand two or three people than just one person, mainly because there are lots of interruptions and people speak over each other. Finally, if you don't know much about the topic of conversation, it's more difficult to follow.

Exercise 5

JACQUI: I don't know about you two, but I find it almost impossible, when I'm speaking on my mobile phone, to understand what the other person is saying to me if they're speaking a foreign language. For instance, I live in France, and when I'm phoning someone to ask for the train times or if I'm anywhere but in a room on my own, so if I'm in a café, if I'm on the street, I just can't understand, I can't understand what they're saying, it's so difficult.

LINFORD: Yeah, I know what you mean. I mean, I find it really difficult to understand people on the phone because you can't see their movements, their gestures or their expressions, so if you're not quite sure of what they're saying, it's just that much harder to, to take on board, because you can't see anything. (Hm ... very difficult) But, erm, yeah, it's ... but ... and also speakers that don't speak clearly – you know, mumble or just speak very quietly. It's so frustrating because you want to ask them to speak up.

KATHERINE: Yes, and they have to repeat it so many times ... and I have a problem, when someone's telling a story, but they don't start at the beginning and go on to the end, they keep going backwards and forwards. (yeah) That's very difficult.

JACQUI: Yes, so you don't know whether they're saying it *has* happened, it *might* happen, it *will* happen. (Hmm) And also when people, when someone's telling you a story, and you're really interested, and then suddenly, they go off the point and they start talking about something else, and you think, 'Is it me? You know, have I misunderstood?' I think when you're having to concentrate like that, it's very, very difficult when they start talking about something else.

KATHERINE: I think it's difficult to concentrate for a long time. I can only really manage a short burst of listening, and then my mind wanders. (Yeah.)

JACQUI: Yes, I think it's very tiring listening to a foreign language for a long time. (Yeah.)

UNIT 2 SLEEPING IT OFF

Sleeping Beauty

Exercise 3

KAREN: What I really liked, I don't know if it happened to you, was when, when she actually sort of moved and turned over ...

NIGEL: Yes ...

KAREN: All the group of people went round to the other side so they could be where her face was, so ... that was actually what they were interested in, not the whole thing ... they were sort of moving like a, like an audience ... it was odd ...

NIGEL: Weird ...

KAREN: Strange ...

NIGEL: I saw someone come in and just burst out laughing ...

KAREN: Yeah, well ...

NIGEL: They did, they just burst out laughing, and I thought she was going to laugh as well, actually.

KAREN: Yeah ...

NIGEL: I'm sure her face twitched.

KAREN: Yeah?

NIGEL: I'm sure she couldn't have been taking it seriously.

KAREN: Yeah, and the children, I thought the children's reactions were, were funny as well. There, there were a couple of little ones there and they just burst out crying ...

NIGEL: I know. I saw them; they were very upset – they didn't know if she was alive or dead, did they?

KAREN: No – just wanted to get out.

NIGEL: It's an extraordinary thing to take children to see, anyway, really, isn't it? Extraordinary thing for *us* to go and see!

KAREN: Did you see those people as well that were just sort of waiting, waiting ... 'She's not going to move, she's not going to move ... yes, she is, no, she's not ...' Of course she's going to move! sort of ... almost scoring the number of times she twitched.

NIGEL: I know. And one chap was just staring at her for about half an hour; I mean, why?

KAREN: Yes, I saw him – I avoided him! Yeah – do you think people go day after day?

NIGEL: Well, a huge amount of people did go.

KAREN: Yeah, and you'd sort of hear people ... I was just amazed that it would attract so many people, yet they were so sort of sceptical about it – but they'd gone.

NIGEL: Yes. It was funny seeing people's reactions though, I mean a few people were just like us – they just actually went, the main reason they went was to see what other people's reactions would be.

KAREN: Yeah, well, yeah, I agree with you, I mean, that was really interesting actually watching them ...

Sleep and other problems

Exercise 2

See page 153.

UNIT 3   HOW DO WE BEHAVE?

DON'T JUST SIT THERE – DO SOMETHING!

Exercise 2

WILLIE: I think they probably know each other, because although he's giving her a bit of a hard time (at least it looks that way), I've just got this feeling they might be brother and sister, 'cos they look quite like each other.

NICK: I don't agree, actually ...

WILLIE: No?

NICK: No, I think, I think he's drunk or something, and, er, being quite threatening. I mean, he's pestering her, definitely, and she's just decided, 'Look, the way out of this is just to ignore him,' you know ...

WILLIE: You don't think she's just seen something out the window?

NICK: No, no, I don't.

CECILIA: No ... I actually think that she's had enough of him annoying her, and she's got up, and she's about to leave, and he's trying to ...

WILLIE: Oh, really?

CECILIA: Yeah, and he's trying to say a final word to make her stay. I think that he's noticed her and he's been chatting her up for ages, and she's had enough, and she's about to leave, and he's having a last ...

WILLIE: So they didn't know each other before, you think?

CECILIA: No.

NICK: No, not at all, no, I think she was standing there, and he's actually, he's maybe been talking to other people, and they've all been ignoring him, and then he's come down to try his luck with her, and she's just, you know, praying for the next station to come up.

CECILIA: Mm.

WILLIE: Mm.

Thanks for everything

Exercise 2

1.

Dear Auntie Carole and Uncle Charles,

I'm writing to thank you very much for the generous cheque you sent me for my birthday. As you know, I have been hoping to get a car for ages as it would simply be so much more convenient, and now I'll be able to afford one. When I've bought it, I'll come and visit you.

I hope you're both well and have a lovely holiday in France.

Love,

David

2.

Thanks for a lovely evening on Saturday. The meal was wonderful and it was great to see you both in such good form. We particularly enjoyed meeting your crazy neighbours and look forward to seeing you here after we get back from our holidays.

Best wishes

Jan and Terry

3.

Dear Dieter,

This is just to thank you for looking after me so well last week. I really appreciated the help you gave me; without it, the trip wouldn't have been such a great success.

It was very kind of you to put me up in your own home and I felt I got to know a bit more about life in a German family. I particularly enjoyed the trip to the mountains; we were lucky to have such beautiful weather.

Professionally, I was delighted that we had such fruitful discussions and feel that we can now proceed to the next stage of the project without delay.

Please give my regards to Bettina, and I look forward to seeing you in Milton Keynes in September. Until then, with kind regards,

Marion

I was really embarrassed

Exercise 2

PAUL: I think, er, the most embarrassing thing that ever happened to me was when I met my in-laws for the, must have been the first time, (mmm) and, er, Sally and I had been going out for about a year before we decided to get married, and, er, I didn't know anything about her family, hardly anything, so I was rather nervous, and, er, she suggested that we went down to their house, because they used to live in the country, (Yeah) and we went down there for the weekend. Er, so anyway, I agreed to go. And, er, the whole thing started really badly because I turned up wearing my suit, you know, wanted to look smart (Mm) and, erm, I looked really out of place because everyone else was wearing jeans or T-shirts and stuff. (Hm, hmm) And Sal's mother came, er, to meet us at the station – we went by train – and she kissed Sal, and she sort of came towards me in a very friendly way and so without really thinking about it, I, I kissed her on the cheek, and she just leapt back, you know, um, completely shocked and outraged, (laughter) it seemed and I realised straightaway I'd got things wrong there. But, um, anyway, in the evening we had dinner, which was a total nightmare. Sal's dad wanted to know what I did for a living, right. Well, when he found out that I was a policeman, he started asking me what I thought about sentencing for, er, you know, criminals, burglars, whatever, and I kind of, I reckoned just by looking at him that he was the kind of, kind of guy who would, who would like to see thieves put away for life, you know, (Mm) so I suppose I took a rather strong line on it and I said I really hated burglars, I thought they were awful and I felt so bad about the victims, and, you know, all that kind of thing. And then I noticed there was this terrible silence. No one said a word and Sally suddenly got up and said that we had to go. I never even got the chance to thank them for the meal or anything; and, er, you know, I found myself more or less running out of the door. And it wasn't till we got home that Sally actually told me that her dad had spent three years in prison for housebreaking. (laughter, no!) I couldn't believe it. I just, I wished, you know, the whole thing had never happened. (Oh dear!)

Exercise 4

Version 1

NICK: This is something that happened when I was about 16, and I had a Saturday job, which was working in a, a small restaurant that was attached to a pub, er, in Yorkshire, and, erm, my duties were to, erm, really serve the wine, er, open the bottle, er, present the bottle first, then open it and serve the wine. I was a wine waiter, erm, but, erm, one, er, one day, they were understaffed and they asked if I'd do some serving as well, and they'd been promising to, to teach me how to do silver service, which is like, serving the food with a spoon and a fork, erm, and so I started to do that. And, er, obviously I wanted to be as good as the other waiters and waitresses, but I wasn't; and, um, this ... a table of, er, it was a party of four, and it was a woman's birthday, 50th birthday or something, and she ordered, er, four glasses of iced water. And I thought I'd be able to carry that on a tray, but, er, it was beyond, beyond me, I'm afraid. And as I walked up to the table, I sort of tripped and it went all over her, all the water, and it was terribly, terribly embarrassing .. um, but she was really nice and, er, she gave me a huge tip at the end and I just felt terrible.

Version 2

CECILIA: Yeah, I remember when I was at college, a couple of years ago, that something that I'll never forget happened to me, and I always check because of this thing that happened. Um, on a Friday we all used to go out, it was like a ritual, we'd go to the disco, we'd go to the pub first, and then go to a club or a disco, and, um, this time we decided to like, go to the pub first. So we went to the pub, and there was like, some people from another college that we didn't really like or that didn't like us, we don't know, but there was a kind of 'vibe' there. And we were kind of, um, sussing each other out the whole night, and my friends decided that it was so awkward that they wanted to leave now, and just said, 'Come on, let's skip this bit and get on with the evening.' So I thought, OK, then, but I was really dying to go to the toilet, so I insisted that I went, and they were saying, 'No, you can go, you know, when we get there,' and I said, 'No, I have to go now,' and so I went, and I went very quickly, you know, and did everything quite quickly, I did wash my hands in fact, I did everything quickly. And, um, then when I came out, my friends were really pointing at me, and there was this, it was, like, a huge pool table in the middle of this room and the pub, the sort of bar was on one end and I had to walk from the toilets right to the other end where my friends were, and these other people from this other college, and erm, I noticed that they were staring and pointing, and some were laughing and some were kind of, telling me to hurry up. So I walked over as dignified as I could, and, um, they pointed to me, told me that I'd actually tucked my skirt into my tights at the back (Oh, no!) and everybody was staring at me, it wasn't in admiration; they were thinking I was looking really stupid, and I just quickly sort of pulled my skirt out and left quickly ...

REVIEW AND DEVELOPMENT
Review of Unit 1

Exercise 1B

1. flu 2. missed 3. rows 4. fare 5. flour 6. weak 7. allowed
8. peace

UNIT 4 GETTING YOUR MESSAGE ACROSS

What on earth do you mean?

Exercise 5

Version 1

1. Gareth

I was working in the southern states of America, and, er, and I was asked to a reception, so I put on a suit and tie, and, you know, tried to look smart, and, er, a woman picked me up, er, and drove me to the reception, and we had a very nice chat on the way, and we got to the reception and I got out of the car, and of course American cars are a little bit different from, from ours in England, so I said, er, I said to

her, 'How do I lock?' and she said, 'Why, you look fine.' (That's wonderful!)

2. Marcella

Well, one night this friend of mine rang me up and asked me to do him a favour, that when I went into work the next day, to tell our boss that he wasn't coming back to work. Well, you know, I really don't know why I actually agreed to do it, but I said yes. I didn't really want to, but however, I said yes; went into work the next day, saw the boss, said to her that he wasn't coming back to work – she was raging, of course – erm, but I really couldn't give her any more explanation than that, and, er, so worked away, then the next day, there I am at my desk, and in he comes! (What?) As cool as a cucumber! And I said to him, 'I thought you weren't coming back! You told me to tell the boss that you weren't coming back!' and he said that I was wrong, that what he meant was that he wasn't coming back the next day. (Oh) So he gave me the impression that I had completely got the wrong end of the stick, but actually I didn't; I'm convinced that he totally misled me, so, I mean, it was a really embarrassing situation, and, er, I've never spoken to him since. (I'm not surprised!)

Version 2

1. Marcella

There was a few of us out one night in a restaurant, about six of us altogether, and, er, there were some visitors in from the southern states [of America], and one of them had a very strong accent, and she was talking about a friend of hers who was really quite zany, and she went on to describe all the things she said and did, and she said she was 'a doorbell'. And I said, 'God!' You know, a doorbell? And she said, 'Yes, she was, she was a doorbell,' and I said, 'I've never heard that expression before, it's wild, you know, a doorbell – what does "a doorbell" mean?" She looked at me blankly and went 'a doorbell.' (laughter) So this exchange took place where she was saying 'a doorbell and I was saying 'a doorbell', and everybody looking completely blank round the table ... (Adorable!) it was 'adorable'! So since then, all my friends whenever we're describing somebody say, 'Oh, she's a doorbell!'

2. Lynne

Well, I experienced a couple of misunderstandings when I was in China; (Hmm) the first time that comes to mind was when I was in a tea house, and I went into the tea house and I had a bit of Chinese, I'd learnt a few words. I went up to the counter and I said, erm, 'I'd like a tea, please,' politely, and they have a phrase in China which means, 'we don't have it,' and you hear it quite a lot, and so the woman at the counter said, 'we don't have it,' and I was looking around, and everyone was drinking tea, it was a tea house, so I said. 'no, no, no, I'd like a cup of *tea*, please,' and she just kept saying, 'we don't have it,' like she couldn't seem to grasp what I was getting at or maybe she didn't *want* to grasp what I was getting at, so I stood there and I didn't have any means of telling her what I wanted, of communicating with her, and so I just had to leave. I just felt really pathetic. And then on another occasion I remember I was asking for the People's Hotel, but because of the tonal thing in the Chinese language, it turned out that I was asking for the People's Prawn (laughter) and I think they were pointing to the river in Guang Jo and saying, 'it's in there,' and laughing a lot. (Right)

Please leave a message ...

Exercise 2

Hiya, this is Sally. Sorry I can't take your call right now, but if you'd like to leave a message and your name and number, I'll get back to you as soon as I can. Please speak after the tone. Thanks for calling. Bye!

Sally – this is Alice. Listen, I'm so sorry for not turning up the other night. I'm sorry I let you down. Um, listen, I'd like to invite you to Sunday lunch, right? We're going to the Waterfront Restaurant. I want to make up for it. Um, I hope you can call me back before the weekend – 886 9430, that's 0171 886 9430. I'd really like to see you there – hope you can make it. OK, speak to you soon ...

Oh, hello, Sally, erm, is it working? Yeah, it's Derek here, Sally, next door. Look, I'm phoning up, it's about the babysitting tomorrow you said you'd do for us. I want to double-check everything is OK. Erm, oh what ... yeah, I'm working late at the office tonight, what's new, so, er, you can ring me here, er, 0987 498087 or, er, maybe, well, could you pop round later? Just put a note through the door or something. Er, thanks very much. Did I – it's Derek – did I say that? Yeah. Bye!

Oh, Sally, you're not there. Hi, it's, it's Patience. Erm, I really need to talk to you. Erm, listen, Jonathan and I have split up. We've split up and the wedding's off. Oh God, I'm in such a mess, it's a disaster! Erm, I've got to cancel all these arrangements. Look, I'm really desperate to talk to you. Can you, can you ring me at my sister's this evening? What's the num ... oh yeah, the number's, er, 456 9920 just, any time, doesn't matter how late, as soon as you get in. All right, speak to you soon. Bye!

Hi, Sally – my name's Martin Bellingham. I'm the poor bloke that, er, Paula's asked to help move her stuff from your place into, er, Dave's. Um, if you can give me a call back, er, later on this evening, because unfortunately, I won't be able to make it tonight as arranged, erm, I need to know if you'll be in tomorrow at about 10 a.m. Erm, I also need to know how to get to your place, I know it's near the church, but there's a one-way system which I'm not sure about, and I don't want to get stuck in the traffic. So if you could give me a call on my mobile number which is 08954 88023, before 11.00 tonight, that would be great. Thanks.

UNIT 5 BUILDINGS

Nouns are building blocks

Exercise 1
1. The factory was too small, so the company has decided to move to new premises on the outskirts of town where the surroundings are also more pleasant.
2. The facilities in the sports centre include not only an outdoor swimming pool and gym, but also an attractive seating area near the squash courts where you can get refreshments.
3. Our company has branches all over the country, but the most important decisions are taken at our headquarters in New York.

Design your own school

Exercise 3
Version 1

CUSTOMER: What can you tell me about this first one, erm, Amora House?

ESTATE AGENT: Ah, Amora House, well, I think you'll like this. It's very conveniently situated. There are quite a few buses that stop outside and the underground is only a minute's walk.

CUSTOMER: Oh!

ESTATE AGENT: Erm, it is in a built-up area, as you can see from the picture. It's this modern office block, it's the whole of the third floor, so it's quite spacious, (yes) and you needn't worry about running up and down the stairs – there is a small lift, it's not big but, erm, you know, there is a lift. Erm, it's also, it's also centrally heated, er, and it's in very good condition, really. Erm, the plumbing and the electrics are recently renewed, so that's good. Erm, oh, there's no air conditioning ...

CUSTOMER: Ah, right.

ESTATE AGENT: ... forgot to tell you that. And, er, just really needs a little bit of renovation, a bit of paint, that's all really.

CUSTOMER: OK, it's in a built-up area. Is there a problem with noise, traffic?

ESTATE AGENT: Oh, no, no, no, none at all, it's very well insulated and it's double glazed, so there's no problem at all.

CUSTOMER: Double glazed? That's excellent. And this second one, Dado Court, what can you tell me about that?

ESTATE AGENT: Ah, Dado Court, yes, it's in a very quiet area, erm, it's a residential area, almost in the country, really. It's been very, very well built and as you can see from the picture, it has lovely grounds. It's, er, it's even got a tennis court, which should please the students!

CUSTOMER: Excellent.

ESTATE AGENT: It's completely self-contained. Erm, it is on a bus route, there's only one bus, I'm afraid, and also it's about a 15-minute walk to the bus stop, but, er, it is accessible. Erm, the building itself is a little run-down. It does need some renovation, a little more than just a bit of paint, er, but the central heating system is absolutely brand new, so I can guarantee that that works.

CUSTOMER: Right. And air conditioning?

ESTATE AGENT: No. No, no air conditioning. Erm, so I think that might, oh, and also, there are, just up the road, erm, a few, I think there are two or three coffee bars, and there's a pub, so plenty of places for the students to eat in.

CUSTOMER: Good.

Version 2

ESTATE AGENT: Well, we've got two properties which would be suitable for the language school; the first one here, you see the picture, it's Amora House. It's very conveniently situated to bus and underground routes, in a built-up area ...

CUSTOMER: Right.

ESTATE AGENT: Erm, as you can see, it's, it's quite a tall building, and the vacant space is on the third floor.

CUSTOMER: Ah, so is there, is there a lift, or ...

ESTATE AGENT: Oh, yes, there's a lift.

CUSTOMER: Oh, good, what's that like?

ESTATE AGENT: It's a good lift, I mean, it's a pretty new building. Erm, it takes three people at a time, so I don't know what the class sizes are, obviously there's stairs, so ...

CUSTOMER: You mentioned that it's, it's a built-up area. Now is it a very noisy area?

ESTATE AGENT: No, no, not too noisy, I mean obviously, it's quite a new building, so there's double glazing and everything ...

CUSTOMER: No, but we will need to ... I mean, for instance, in the summer, we will need to open the windows, if the weather's hot, and get some air in the classrooms.

ESTATE AGENT: Oh, right.

CUSTOMER: I'm thinking of the noise element for concentration.

ESTATE AGENT: Right, well it's not air conditioned, um, but other floors do have air conditioning, so it's not impossible to install it if you wanted to.

CUSTOMER: Right.

ESTATE AGENT: Um, the building itself is in good condition; the plumbing and the electrics are OK. Um, obviously in the winter it's OK because it's centrally heated. One of the problems is the entrance is shared with the other companies, so I don't know if there's a problem with, you know, some of the students ...

CUSTOMER: I shouldn't think that should be too much of a problem.

ESTATE AGENT: Right. Well, I think it's a, I think it's a good property. The other one here is Dado Court which is an older building; it's in a quiet, residential area, beautiful building, as you can see ...

CUSTOMER: Lovely, yes, yeah.

ESTATE AGENT: ... very well built, lovely grounds; there's a tennis court in the back ...

CUSTOMER: Hmmm!

ESTATE AGENT: ... parking facilities, no problem there; you've got the whole building to yourselves, it's completely self-contained.

CUSTOMER: Right. Whereabouts is it situated? It's not in the city centre, is it?

ESTATE AGENT: No, it's not, I mean, it's a bus, bus ride away, (ah, ah) it's on a bus route. It is a bit of a walk to the bus stop, but, you know, if people can drive or ...

CUSTOMER: Yeah, just thinking about the students needing, you know, facilities such as, you know, café, bars, restaurants. I mean, what's in the surrounding area?

ESTATE AGENT: It's not a problem because there are two or three snack bars in the area, so that's, that's OK.

CUSTOMER: Right.

ESTATE AGENT: The building itself is a little bit run down. It needs a bit of renovation.

CUSTOMER: I see. Well, that would explain the price, which is quite reasonable.

ESTATE AGENT: Yeah, but I mean certain aspects are, you know, brand new, the central heating is brand new.

CUSTOMER: Oh, well, that's something.

ESTATE AGENT: There's no air conditioning, unfortunately, but, you know, with big windows like that, it would be fine in the summer.

CUSTOMER: Yes. Lovely and quiet. Well, gosh, it's a difficult decision ...

REVIEW AND DEVELOPMENT
Review of Unit 3

Exercise 2

1. I wish I could speak French really well because I love France.
2. I wish I had loads of money – that would be nice.
3. I wish I was more patient. I have no patience whatsoever.
4. I wish my brother wouldn't come in late at night and start banging around – [it] really annoys me.
5. I wish I hadn't cheated in my driving test – I might have passed.
6. I wish I had gone to university because I think education's really important.

Review of Unit 4

I beg your pardon?
Pardon?
What did you say?
Hmmm?
What?
Could you repeat that?
Could you speak up a bit, please?
Sorry, can you slow down a bit?
I didn't get that.
I didn't follow that.
I didn't quite catch that.
I can't make out what you're saying.
Sorry – I must have misheard you.

UNIT 6 TRAVELLING CAN BE HARD WORK

Seat hog!

Exercise 2
Version 1
1.
SHEILA: The thing that annoys me is people using headphones. I'm sitting there, trying to read my book, and this insistent 'ttittittittitti' goes on and you just can't concentrate.

2.
IAN: The thing I find most irritating is people eating on train and bus journeys. Why is it that they have to chomp their way through two hamburgers and two cups of coffee and then throw their discarded wrappings all over the floor? It's not necessary and it smells and it's disgusting.

3.
NIGEL: The thing that really annoys me is when you're going on a long coach or train journey, and somebody comes along, and perches themselves down beside you and tries to strike up a conversation; and it usually goes something like, 'Hello, let me tell you about me,' and you spend the next three hours being talked at by this person. It annoys me so much because I don't like travelling anyway, and I'd rather just sort of sit quietly on my own and, you know, try and go to sleep or something.

4.
CECILIA: The thing that really gets to me is when I'm travelling, and there is somebody who is near me, or opposite me or anywhere around me that's picking their nose, as if I can't see them, or scratching. It just makes me feel really ... I want to say to them, 'Can you stop doing that, please, or wait till you get off?'

DENICA: Yeah, I know what you mean.

CECILIA: It's horrible, disgusting!

DENICA: I know – disgusting! Yeah! (laughter)

Version 2
1.
KAREN: The thing that gets me is when you get on a long distance train that's absolutely packed and you haven't reserved a seat and there's one seat left and someone's spread all of their belongings and possessions right across it, and you stand there and say, 'Is that seat taken?' and then very disgruntled, they will just about move you a tiny space. And you've paid for your ticket just as much as they have, and you have to squeeze yourself in. It's, it's just dreadful, really selfish.

2.
NICK: I think the thing that really annoys me on a train is people who use mobile phones.

DENICA: Oh, yeah ...

NICK: But I mean, 'cos, I have a mobile phone, and if I use it I'm quite discreet, but they seem to ... some people seem to feel they've got to talk at four times the normal volume, and so they're shouting away. Usually they're just saying, 'I'm on the 8.47' you know, and it's like they're just wanting to share their life with you, and I don't want it, and it just annoys me because I don't want to be hearing what other people are thinking.

DENICA: No, I know.

3.
DENICA: I mean, the thing that I find irritating as well is when people's kids just won't shut up, when you're trying to, you know, sleep or relax on the train, and these kids are running up and down the corridors, and you know, you don't want to have to be involved in other people's lives to that extent.

4.
WILLIE: Yeah, well, what really annoys me, though, is, um, when you're on the train and someone gets on, and they're wearing those, like, headphones, 'cos they've got ...

DENICA: Oh, yeah ...

WILLIE: ... a Walkman or a portable cassette, and you can hear the music's up really loud, but you can't hear the music, all you hear is the kind of squeaking noise from their headphones ...

CECILIA: Tstststst ...

WILLIE: ... that's right, and they're making noises too. And it just goes on and on and on...

CECILIA: I hate that!

WILLIE: You either want to switch it off, or you want to listen to it yourself, preferably switch it off!

DENICA: Yeah, so irritating.

I'll be arriving at eleven

Exercise 3
1.
MARGOT: Hi.

DEREK: Hello, Margot, it's Derek here.

MARGOT: Oh, Derek, hi! Hi, sweetie, how are you?

DEREK: I ... I'm fine. Er, a slight change of plan ...

MARGOT: Mm hm ...

DEREK: I was meant to be meeting Bob and Jean, and, um, getting a plane in the evening ...

MARGOT: Yeah, sure.

DEREK: ... and they're actually, they've got a meeting or something, so I can come earlier. I've actually managed to get ...

MARGOT: Oh, great!

DEREK: ... an earlier flight so ...

MARGOT: Oh, what time?

DEREK: Well, I'll be getting into JFK at 7.00 p.m. now.

MARGOT: OK, OK, now let's think. Now, I can't meet you at seven, because I, I've got to pick up Shelley from her class. I can get to JFK by eight o'clock ...

DEREK: Um, well, er, that's OK, I tell you what I'll do, I'll get the airport bus.

MARGOT: Oh, no, no, no, no, no, you're going to have all this, all this luggage, you've got all your stuff with you, no, no, no, I'll pick you up, don't worry about it, don't get a taxi or anything, just meet me at the information desk, OK ...

DEREK: Yeah ...

MARGOT: ... there's a coffee shop right there, and I'll be there at eight o'clock.

DEREK: OK, yeah, OK, that's what I'll do, I'll get a coffee and I'll just wait for you.

MARGOT: Have a great flight.

DEREK: Thank you. All right – see you!

MARGOT: Bye!

2.

JACKSON LOMAX: Hello, could I speak to Mr Lea, please?

MR LEA: Mr Lea speaking.

JACKSON LOMAX: Mr Lea, it's Jackson Lomax here of Merson Electronics.

MR LEA: Ah, Mr Lomax – nice to talk to you. How are you?

JACKSON LOMAX: I'm very well – how are you?

MR LEA: Very well indeed. What can I do for you?

JACKSON LOMAX: Did you get my letter of the 10th of June?

MR LEA: Yes, I did.

JACKSON LOMAX: About Dr Robinson's visit?

MR LEA: That's correct, yes.

JACKSON LOMAX: Right, well, now, there have been a couple of changes, I'm afraid, so I'm just calling you to tell you about those ...

MR LEA: Uh, hm.

JACKSON LOMAX: Er, Dr Robinson's visit to KJP Trading ...

MR LEA: Hmm?

JACKSON LOMAX: ... unfortunately has had to be cancelled.

MR LEA: I see.

JACKSON LOMAX: So Dr Robinson would like to spend the whole time at Pansing International with you. Would that be all right?

MR LEA: That's an extra two days, yes, yes, that would be possible, yes.

JACKSON LOMAX: That's great. So could you possibly extend the booking at the Raffles Hotel for an extra two nights?

MR LEA: Another two nights for Dr Robinson. Yes, I'll get my secretary onto that at once, yes.

JACKSON LOMAX: And if you could make some appointments for her to see a few more people while she's there ... as this part of the visit has now been cancelled, that would be good as well.

MR LEA: Yes, I think that will be possible.

JACKSON LOMAX: Well, do what you can, anyway.

MR LEA: I certainly will.

JACKSON LOMAX: Now there's just one other thing. Could you, um, be responsible for making sure Dr Robinson can get her return flight?

MR LEA: Yes, yes.

JACKSON LOMAX: It just simply means getting, getting her a car to the airport, er, on July the 14th.

MR LEA: Yes, that'll be the 14th, and what time is her flight?

JACKSON LOMAX: The flight is 15.00.

MR LEA: 15.00, so if I arrange for a car to deliver her at the airport for check-in at about 14.00, that would be ...

JACKSON LOMAX: At the latest, I would have thought ...

MR LEA: Yes, yes.

JACKSON LOMAX: So that's July 14th at 15.00.

MR LEA: July 14th, 15.00 is the flight. Yes, I think so, Mr Lomax, that shouldn't be a problem. Anything else?

JACKSON LOMAX: No, I think that's it. You are aware that Dr Robinson is a strict vegetarian; I put that in the letter, did I?

MR LEA: Yes, yes, you mentioned that in your letter, yes.

JACKSON LOMAX: Good, well, thank you very much, Mr Lea.

MR LEA: Thank you, Mr Lomax.

JACKSON LOMAX: I'll be in touch again soon.

MR LEA: Pleasure speaking to you.

JACKSON LOMAX: Bye bye.

MR LEA: Bye bye.

UNIT 7 HOW DOES IT LOOK?

Colour blind

Exercise 4

INTERVIEWER: Dr Smith, what exactly is 'colour blindness' and how many people does it affect?

DR SMITH: Well, essentially it's the inability to distinguish one colour from another, although the most common form of the condition usually involves difficulty with the colours red and green. And it's an interesting fact that the condition affects men far more than women.

INTERVIEWER: Really?

DR SMITH: Hmm, about one in 12 boys is affected, but only one in 100 girls. And also it's much more common amongst white people than black or Asian people.

INTERVIEWER: Right. But what exactly is colour blindness?

DR SMITH: Colour blindness means that the light-sensitive structures at the back of the eye don't work well. As I said, most people have difficulty with red and green. For some of them, reds look dull, almost grey. Others have problems with green, which looks grey, and they also find it hard to distinguish oranges and browns.

INTERVIEWER: So it's just those colours.

DR SMITH: Well, there is a more unusual condition which may develop as a result of poisoning from chemicals or drugs, and that affects blue. Complete colour blindness where the victim sees the world in black and white is fortunately extremely rare.

INTERVIEWER: OK. Is colour blindness something you can inherit from your parents, and is there a cure?

DR SMITH: It is hereditary, yes, apart from the cases of poisoning I mentioned. A lot of people with colour blindness in fact don't even realise there's anything wrong with them, though nowadays children are tested for the condition using coloured dots and plates.

INTERVIEWER: Right. And the cure?

DR SMITH: I'm afraid there is no cure. The only thing people can do is recognise they have the defect, and then use this knowledge in their choice of career – for example, you can't become a sailor, or a pilot or an engine driver if you suffer from colour blindness.

INTERVIEWER: Really?

DR SMITH: Yes, and, and when you're doing certain tasks, however simple they may seem, you do need that ability to distinguish colour; for example, changing an electric plug.

INTERVIEWER: OK, well, thank you very much, Dr Smith.

That really suits you

Exercise 5

Version 1

JACQUI: You know, I really, really like going to weddings; not, not just because they're happy occasions, or normally happy occasions, but because you can watch everybody and watch what they're wearing (Hmm) and nowadays, I think it's quite different from in our parents' day, when you always, well, women always wore very smart hat, gloves, suit – nowadays you see all sorts of fashions on women, you see very flowing dresses, trouser suits. I even saw someone wear shorts! (Hmm) I mean, they were quite smart shorts, and not, really, not everyone wears hats any more, and hardly anyone wears gloves.

LINFORD: Yeah. Well, I like going to weddings, 'cos it's one of the very few times you actually get a chance to dress up (Hmm) because most of the time I find myself wearing jeans or sweatshirts, or casual things, so it's really nice to actually be able to put on a suit and a tie for me, personally, so I really enjoy the occasion and the event because you get to dress up and play the role of, you know, being at a wedding.

JACQUI: Have you ever worn a top hat? Because men wear top hats sometimes.

LINFORD: Not really, but, erm, I'm sure I'll get to wear one if I ever get to be someone's best man or maybe even my own wedding! (Hmm)

Version 2

KATHERINE: I think it's much easier for men going to weddings, because you just have to put on your suit and your tie, and you look smart. (Hmm) Women have a whole rigmarole of deciding what to wear – should I wear a hat? And should I wear gloves? And ... it's very difficult for a woman to look, look the part, I think.

PAUL: Well, I'm not sure I agree with you there, I mean, speaking from my personal experience, I was an usher at my sister's wedding, a few years ago, and she wanted us all in morning suit (Yes) so it was the full thing, you know, the trousers, the long jacket, the long waistcoat ...

KATHERINE: Very smart ...

PAUL: ... very, very smart, and it was in August, (Oh!) and it was boiling hot, and I found it very, very restricting and didn't really enjoy wearing it at all. (Hmm) I was really, really happy to be at the reception in slightly more casual clothes.

KATHERINE: Yes, well, I once went to a very informal wedding, where the bride and the bridesmaids were wearing denim dresses and bare feet, and everybody was wearing garlands of flowers, and it was all set in a garden (Oh, brilliant!) so it was rather lovely.

PAUL: Hmm. What did you wear?

KATHERINE: Erm, well, I wore, um, I was probably one of the smartest people there, because I didn't realise that it was so informal, so I quickly took my jacket off and, um, took my shoes off eventually as well, so that I fitted in more.

PAUL: Brilliant. I've worn a kilt!

KATHERINE: Have you?

PAUL: Yes. Unfortunately, at this particular wedding, it was freezing and I froze. (laughter) I did have something on underneath.

KATHERINE: I wasn't going to ask. Are you Scottish?

PAUL: No, no, but the friend who was marrying was.

KATHERINE: Right.

REVIEW AND DEVELOPMENT
Review of Unit 5

Exercise 2

I'd been staying with some friends in Madrid and it was the last night of the holiday. We decided to go and see a thriller which had been filmed in a ruined castle in Scotland. It wasn't a terribly interesting film, but the building and surroundings were spectacular.

When I got back to London the following day, there was a postcard from my brother who'd been on holiday in Scotland. The photo on the card looked really familiar. Later on, I realised where I'd seen it before. It was the same ruined castle they'd used in the film in Madrid.

UNIT 8 ADDRESSING THE ISSUES
Political issues

Exercise 3
See page 155.

REVIEW AND DEVELOPMENT
Review of Unit 7

Exercise 2

1. Can you make a jacket out of marble?
2. Is purple lighter than mauve?
3. Is beige a yellowish-brown?
4. Can you tell the difference between cotton and velvet just by looking at it?
5. If you're colour blind, can you tell the difference between red and green?
6. Would bright red, purple and pale lemon look nice together?
7. Would black and grey clash?
8. Is tartan the same as striped?
9. Is silk more fashionable than nylon?
10. If something fits you, does it mean you like it?
11. If you go window shopping, does it cost a lot?
12. If something doesn't suit you, should you try another size?

UNIT 9 MAKING THE MOST OF YOUR TIME
Time management

Exercise 1

Version 1

AISHA: My problem is that I really can't, I can't seem to get down to a decent day's work.

NEIL: Right.

AISHA: The phone goes constantly, (Hmm) I have people queuing at my desk, asking for information, bits of advice, and I actually can't achieve a proper day's work, I mean, do the big work that I really have to do.

NEIL: Right. Erm, I suggest that you get your secretary to filter all the calls; make sure she only lets through the most important ones, the most urgent ones. That way, you find your time is ... you'll have much, much more time to do things, er, on your own. The other thing I suggest is, er, I think you should delegate responsibility. I mean, don't do it all yourself. You have other people there to do things for you. Make sure that they do it! OK?

AISHA: Yes, you're right. It's easier said than done.

Version 2

LAUREN: I'm having some, er, problems with my meeting technique; the meetings that I, that I am conducting seem to go on too long, which I wouldn't mind if we were actually getting something done, (Hmm) but they go on a long time, and also I, I have trouble controlling the people attending the meeting. Everything seems to get out of hand, and everyone seems to have something to say, and I wondered if you had any feedback for me.

SION: Yes, I do know that these things can get out of hand, so my first suggestion would be that you set a very firm time limit for these meetings: absolutely specific, it will start at two o'clock, and it will finish at 2.45; don't let it run over any longer than that. And furthermore, I don't know how many people attend the meetings, but if it's possible for you to whittle the numbers down, have senior members of staff only, who can then relay to more junior personnel what has been discussed at the meeting, because the more people you have at a meeting, the more people will want to speak, and that's how these things get out of control.

LAUREN: Hmm. Thank you very much.

Meeting a deadline

Exercise 2

Late last night, Customs officials at Dover seized drugs – all of it thought to be cocaine – with an estimated street value of more than one and a half million pounds.

This comes at a time when Customs officials have been particularly vigilant following the seizure in Rotterdam just six weeks ago of cocaine said to be worth over two million pounds, and there have been subsequent rumours of a large shipment of cocaine entering this country.

Today's discovery resulted from a routine search on a van travelling from Ostend, containing mostly Belgian chocolate. Customs were suspicious because the van was unmarked, and at first they thought they had uncovered a shipment of stolen chocolates. However, they soon realised that they had made a much more significant and valuable discovery.

So far, the driver's identity hasn't been disclosed, but he was travelling alone and is thought to be in his twenties. He is now helping police and Customs officials with their enquiries.

This is the third major drugs haul by Customs officials this year and they believe they may have destroyed one of the largest drug smuggling rings operating in Europe.

This is Pat Harman in Dover, and now back to the studio.

UNIT 10 TELLING STORIES IN ENGLISH

You'll never guess who I met ...

Exercise 3

A: Hi, Sue, how are you?

B: Oh, great; I've just come back from South Africa, actually.

A: No! What were you doing there?

B: I'm working on a project to do with primary schools, but I must tell you ...

A: What? Something happened to you?

B: Oh, yes. Actually, I met Nelson Mandela!

A: You're joking!

B: No, really.

A: Well, go on ...

B: Well, I was staying in a hotel in Johannesburg and I got friendly with a woman in the restaurant, and I saw her several mornings, so anyway ... one morning she said she was going to a big ceremony, and Nelson Mandela was going to be there, (Yeah) oh, and she'd got special seats in an enclosure with famous people, so of course I said 'Can I come?' (Yeah, I bet) and to be honest, ... I didn't expect her to say yes, but in fact ... surprisingly she did, so anyhow ... we went and eventually ... Mandela turned up, and I said hello to him. I just felt really privileged to have met him. (Yeah) He looked exactly as I expected.

A: Wow! That's amazing! Talking of famous people ... I was in my local coffee bar the other day and Mel Gibson and Tom Cruise walked in ...

Exercise 5

Version 1

1. Gareth

A friend of mine had just been offered a really wonderful job, and she rang me up and she said I'd like you to come and celebrate with me. I'm going to take you out for a terrific meal. And she'd chosen this restaurant in the west end of London, really smart restaurant where lots of, you know, starry people go. And we turned up and there were plenty of faces that you recognised and, er, we were being very cool about it, and then suddenly we saw over in the corner at a very discreet table was Mick Jagger. Well, of course we both stopped and stared at him, the thing that struck me I think was that, of course he's a man over 50 now and in my head I still see him as a, you know, a young rocker. Anyway, we sat down at the table and had this wonderful meal but I was furious with her because instead of looking at me throughout the meal, she was staring at Mick Jagger.

2. Lynne

Well, I was a student at Bath University at the end of the seventies and I had to write an interview for our student newspaper about Dustin Hoffman, (Right) because he was making a film in Bath or something. And so I had to go down and meet him, er, near the baths (Really?) and he was supposed to get out of his taxi and there were lots of TV people around, and when he did get out it was quite lovely 'cos he pushed all the TV people out of the way and came and talked to me and it was quite extraordinary really; he was much shorter than me, much shorter than I expected, and he had like a mug of tea with a dirty old tea bag in the bottom and he sort of gave that to his minder and then he had, he took out a razor and started shaving and just being incredibly silly and my impression of him was well ... he was ... I think I was giggling a lot as well 'cos I was quite young, but I think he was trying to wind me up really and I was just slightly disappointed.

Version 2

1. Marcella

It was about two years ago, and I was on holidays in the very far south of Ireland, down in Kerry, and I was driving back up to Dublin through the midlands, which is not at all particularly interesting, it's not touristy or anything, and I wanted to have some lunch, 'cos I was starving, so I was passing through this very ordinary little village, and I saw a pub, and, just an ordinary, small little pub, and I went in, and, er, I was standing at the counter and then I spotted a friend of mine who I hadn't seen for ages, guy called Michael, over, er, at the window, and, er, he'd been made redundant from his job, and I hadn't seen him for ages, but I'd heard that he'd actually taken up chauffeuring as part of, well, a new change of career, and so I went flying over to him, 'cos we used to be such good friends, and then we'd lost contact, and he was sitting with this huge, large man. I couldn't believe it. When he turned round, it was Marlon Brando. (Good Lord!) And I have adored Marlon Brando since I've been a kid. I mean, I was completely dumbstruck, and I'm sure it was written all over me, you could see it, I, just standing there, open mouthed, and I couldn't say anything, and he was so nice, 'cos I'd say that that happens to him all the time, and he was just so sweet and charming. It turned out that he was looking for locations for some film or other that he was going to do, but I was just, I couldn't believe it ...

2. Jeff

My wife and I were invited to my cousin's wedding, my cousin's daughter's wedding, and we arrived there and we were a little bit surprised at the size of the house and how many guests there were, but anyway we just carried on – lovely reception, lots of Pimms, everybody was feeling very convivial. And I got chatting to this guy, and we had a perfectly normal sort of conversation, about fifteen minutes. And I walked away and my wife pulled me to one side, 'Do you know who that is?' I said 'No'. 'That's Winston Churchill's son.' I went, 'I was telling him about, like, dogs and how I hate kids and he was being very polite'. Anyway, I didn't talk to him again for the rest of the wedding. (laughter)

A tale of poison

Exercise 4
HOBBYIST
by Fredric Brown

'I heard a rumour,' Sangstrom said, 'to the effect that you ...' He turned his head and looked about him to make absolutely sure that he and the druggist were alone in the tiny prescription pharmacy. The druggist was a gnomelike, gnarled little man who could have been any age from fifty to a hundred. They were alone, but Sangstrom dropped his voice just the same. '... to the effect that you have a completely undetectable poison.'

The druggist nodded. He came around the counter and locked the front door of the shop, then walked toward a doorway behind the counter. 'I was about to take a coffee break,' he said. 'Come with me and have a cup.'

Sangstrom followed him around the counter and through the doorway to a back room ringed by shelves of bottles from floor to ceiling. The druggist plugged in an electric percolator, found two cups and put them on a table that had a chair on either side of it. He motioned Sangstrom to one of the chairs and took the other one himself. 'Now,' he said. 'Tell me. Whom do you want to kill, and why?'

'Does it matter?' Sangstrom asked. 'Isn't it enough that I pay for ...' The druggist interrupted him with an upraised hand. 'Yes, it matters. I must be convinced that you deserve what I can give you. Otherwise ...' He shrugged.

'All right,' Sangstrom said. 'The *whom* is my wife. The *why* ...' He started the long story. Before he had quite finished, the percolator had finished its task and the druggist briefly interrupted to get the coffee for them. Sangstrom finished his story.

The little druggist nodded. 'Yes, I occasionally dispense an undetectable poison. I do so freely; I do not charge for it, if I think the case is deserving. I have helped many murderers.'

'Fine,' Sangstrom said. 'Please give it to me, then.'
The druggist smiled at him. 'I already have.'

Exercise 5
The druggist smiled at him. 'I already have. By the time the coffee was ready, I had decided that you deserved it. It was, as I said, free. But there is a price to pay for the antidote.'

Sangstrom turned pale. But he had anticipated – not this, but the possibility of a double-cross or some form of blackmail. He pulled a pistol from his pocket.

The little druggist chuckled. 'You daren't use that. Can you find the antidote' – he waved at the shelves – 'among those thousands of bottles? Or would you find a faster, more virulent poison? Or if you think I'm bluffing, go ahead and shoot. You'll know the answer within three hours when the poison starts to work.'

'How much for the antidote?' Sangstrom growled.

'Quite reasonable. A thousand dollars. After all, a man must live. Even if his hobby is preventing murders, there's no reason why he shouldn't make money at it, is there?'

Sangstrom growled and put the pistol down, but within reach, and took out his wallet. Maybe after he had the antidote, he'd still use that pistol. He counted out a thousand dollars in hundred-dollar bills and put it on the table.

The druggist made no immediate move to pick it up. He said, 'And one other thing – for your wife's safety and mine. You will write a confession of your intention – your former intention, I trust – to murder your wife. Then you will wait till I go out and mail it to a friend of mine on the homicide detail. He'll keep it as evidence in case you ever *do* decide to kill your wife. Or me, for that matter. When that is in the mail, it will be safe for me to return here and give you the antidote. I'll get you paper and pen ...'

'Oh, one other thing – although I do not absolutely insist on it. Please help spread the word about my undetectable poison, will you? One never knows, Mr Sangstrom. The life you save, if you have any enemies, just might be your own.'

UNIT 11 EATING OUT
Food quiz

Exercise 2
1. What's the name of the white stuff used to make bread?
2. What do you call the dressing made from oil and vinegar that you put on salad?
3. What do you call food when it isn't cooked?
4. What's the name of the condition you may experience the morning after you have drunk too much alcohol?
5. What do you call the yellow part of an egg?
6. What is another word for dessert?
7. What is another word or expression meaning *vomit*?
8. What's the general word for a drink you have before a meal?

Who refused to do what?

Exercise 2
1.
IAN: Oh dear, clumsy of me. Another dribble.
SHEILA: Filthy.
IAN: Pardon?
SHEILA: You're filthy.
IAN: No, no, no it's only a dribble. It won't notice in a minute. I suppose I'll have to have it cleaned if we're going to this wretched wedding, though.
SHEILA: You can't go to the wedding in that suit.
IAN: Why, what's wrong with this suit?
SHEILA: You've had it for years and it's absolutely filthy.
IAN: Well, if I have it cleaned it'll be as good as new.
SHEILA: No, no, no. You've absolutely got to buy a new one.
IAN: Buy one? Don't be so stupid!
SHEILA: What do you mean, stupid?
IAN: I'm not buying a new suit – it'd be a total waste of money.
SHEILA: Well, there'll be plenty of other opportunities for you to wear it.
IAN: When?
SHEILA: Well, we'll be invited to other weddings for one thing, and funerals I expect.
IAN: Well, I can have this one cleaned again, can't I?
SHEILA: No you can't. I mean, honestly, if you just see yourself. Have you looked in a mirror recently?
IAN: Well ... no, not particularly.
SHEILA: Well then do. Next time you go home, you have a look and see how shabby it looks. I mean is it fair on me?
IAN: Well, I mean, if it's cleaned, it'll be pressed, it'll be very very smart.
SHEILA: No it won't. It's gone, it's worn, you can see.
IAN: Oh for goodness sake, I wish I'd never mentioned your wretched wedding.

2.
NIGEL: I had a word with George about, erm, getting next week off ...
KAREN: Yes?
NIGEL: Unfortunately, no can do.
KAREN: Oh!
NIGEL: I'm really sorry, a couple of days, he said, you know, Thursday and Friday, take a long weekend, but the whole week, no way. We've just got too much on at the moment at the office.
KAREN: Oh, but you know how much I've been looking forward to this week. I put the whole week aside.
NIGEL: I know. I'm really sorry. I thought, I thought he'd let me ... but just not possible.
KAREN: Well, couldn't you go down with the plague or something? Flu?
NIGEL: I can't, I can't.
KAREN: Chicken pox?
NIGEL: No, I really can't!
KAREN: Mumps.

NIGEL: You must understand. We've got to get this order finished by the end of February.

KAREN: Oh well, I'm terribly disappointed, you know. I really am.

NIGEL: Look. This will be all over in a couple of weeks. How about we go skiing in March?

KAREN: Yes, I could do that.

NIGEL: Come on!

KAREN: Oh, all right. I mean, I'll have to check it all out. Yes, all right.

3.

NICK: That was nice.

CAROL: Gorgeous.

NICK: Would you like a cappuccino?

CAROL: Love one.

NICK: I'll get the waiter's eye if I ... Oh, Carol, come on, that's the third this evening.

CAROL: What, you're counting now?

NICK: I thought you were giving up.

CAROL: I didn't say I was going to give up, I said I was going to cut down and try and save money for the flat.

NICK: So, that's cutting down, is it?

CAROL: Well I am trying to.

NICK: Well I think you're gonna have to cut down a bit more if you're gonna save any money.

CAROL: Oh, well you talk about me cutting down a bit more. What about you?

NICK: What?

CAROL: Well, I think you could make a bit of an effort at saving some money.

NICK: I thought I was.

CAROL: What! What with that new shirt you've bought?

NICK: This isn't a new shirt. What are you talking about? I don't spend money on clothes.

CAROL: Well, OK not clothes, then. What about the car?

NICK: Uh, uh, I've been promising myself that car.

CAROL: I let you have that car because I know, I knew you wanted it. Can't you let me do a few of the things that I'd like to do?

NICK: I admit the car is a luxury, and, er, you know, maybe I'll just keep it for the year, OK, and we'll talk about maybe getting something cheaper, but I don't spend money on clothes and I think that what you're doing, is, is ... if you added it up through the year it would be far more costly than a new wardrobe.

CAROL: Well, look I'm really trying, and as long as ... look, as long as we both try to save money, then, you know, I think that's, that's all we can do really, but we can't just cut everything out completely.

NICK: Well ...

CAROL: I'll try if you try.

NICK: Yeah, well, that's what I was going to say; a bit more effort on both sides, maybe.

CAROL: All right then.

REVIEW AND DEVELOPMENT
Review of Unit 10

Exercise 1

Barry glanced out of his office window at the car park below. Two police officers were getting out of a car, making their way towards reception. Barry froze.

'... and I've had a lot of trouble with the computer this morning, so I'll type those letters later,' Gemma was saying.

'Pardon? Oh, fine, don't worry, Gemma,' Barry stuttered, trying to concentrate and think what to do.

The phone rang, screaming to be answered. Barry heard the receptionist's voice in his ear.

'Mr Gordon? There are two policemen at reception. They want to ask you about the computer.'

'Could you tell them I'm in a meeting and I'll be out in five minutes, please?'

Barry's blood ran cold.

UNIT 12 THEATRICAL INTERLUDE
A NIGHT OUT

Exercise 3

She goes over to the gas stove, examines the vegetables, opens the oven and looks into it.

MOTHER: (*gently*) Well, your dinner'll be ready soon. You can look for it afterwards. Lay the table, there's a good boy.

ALBERT: Why should I look for it afterwards? You know where it is now.

MOTHER: You've got five minutes. Go down to the cellar, Albert, get a bulb and put it in Grandma's room, go on.

ALBERT: (*irritably*) I don't know why you keep calling that room Grandma's room, she's been dead ten years.

MOTHER: Albert!

ALBERT: I mean, it's just a junk room, that's all it is.

MOTHER: Albert, that's no way to speak about your Grandma, you know that as well as I do.

ALBERT: I'm not saying a word against Grandma ...

MOTHER: You'll upset me in a minute, you go on like that.

ALBERT: I'm not going on about anything.

MOTHER: Yes, you are. Now why don't you go and put a bulb in Grandma's room and by the time you come down I'll have your dinner on the table.

ALBERT: I can't go down to the cellar, I've got my best trousers on, I've got a white shirt on.

MOTHER: You're dressing up tonight, aren't you? Dressing up, cleaning your shoes, anyone would think you were going to the Ritz.

ALBERT: I'm not going to the Ritz.

MOTHER: (*suspiciously*) What do you mean, you're not going to the Ritz?

ALBERT: What do you mean?

MOTHER: The way you said you're not going to the Ritz, it sounded like you were going somewhere else.

ALBERT: (*wearily*) I am.

MOTHER: (*shocked surprise*) You're going out?

ALBERT: You know I'm going out. I told you I was going out. I told you last week. I told you this morning. Look, where's my tie? I've got to have my tie. I'm late already. Come on, Mum, where'd you put it?

MOTHER: What about your dinner?

ALBERT: (*searching*) Look ... I told you ... I haven't got the ... wait a minute ... ah, here it is.

MOTHER: You can't wear that tie. I haven't pressed it.

ALBERT: You have. Look at it. Of course you have. It's beautifully pressed. It's fine.

He ties the tie.

MOTHER: Where are you going?

ALBERT: Mum, I've told you, honestly, three times. Honestly, I've told you three times I had to go out tonight.

MOTHER: No, you didn't. (*Albert exclaims and knots the tie*) I thought you were joking.

ALBERT: I'm not going ... I'm just going to Mr King's. I've told you. You don't believe me.

MOTHER: You're going to Mr King's?

ALBERT: Mr Ryan's leaving. You know Ryan. He's leaving the firm. He's been there for years. So Mr King's giving a sort of party for him at his house ... well, not exactly a party, not a party, just a few ... you know ... anyway, we're all invited. I've got to go. Everyone else is going. I don't want to go, but I've got to.

MOTHER: (*bewildered, sitting*) Well, I don't know ...

ALBERT: (*with his arm round her*) I won't be late. I don't want to go. I'd much rather stay with you.

MOTHER: Would you?

ALBERT: You know I would. Who wants to go to Mr King's party?

MOTHER: We were going to have our game of cards.

ALBERT: Well, we can't have our game of cards.

(Pause)

MOTHER: Put the bulb in Grandma's room, Albert.

ALBERT: I've told you, I'm not going down to the cellar in my white shirt. There's no light in the cellar either. I'll be pitch black in five minutes, looking for those bulbs.

MOTHER: I told you to put a light in the cellar. I told you yesterday.

ALBERT: Well, I can't do it now.

MOTHER: If we had a light in the cellar, you'd be able to see where those bulbs were. You don't expect me to go down to the cellar?

ALBERT: I don't know why we keep bulbs in the cellar!

MOTHER: Your father would turn in his grave if he heard you raise your voice to me. You're all I've got, Albert. I want you to remember that. I haven't got anyone else. I want you ... I want you to bear that in mind.

ALBERT: I'm sorry ... I raised my voice. *(He goes to the door)* *(mumbling)* I've got to go.

MOTHER: *(following)* Albert!

ALBERT: What?

MOTHER: I want to ask you a question.

ALBERT: What?

MOTHER: Are you leading a clean life?

ALBERT: A clean life?

MOTHER: You're not leading an unclean life, are you?

ALBERT: What are you talking about?

MOTHER: You're not messing about with girls, are you? You're not going to go messing about with girls tonight?

ALBERT: Don't be so ridiculous.

MOTHER: Answer me, Albert. I'm your mother.

ALBERT: I don't know any girls.

MOTHER: If you're going to the firm's party, there'll be girls, there, won't there? Girls from the office?

ALBERT: I don't like them, any of them.

MOTHER: You promise?

ALBERT: Promise what?

MOTHER: That ... that you won't upset your father.

ALBERT: My father? How can I upset my father? You're always talking about upsetting people who are dead!

MOTHER: Oh, Albert, you don't know how you hurt me, you don't know the hurtful way you've got, speaking of your poor father like that.

ALBERT: But he is dead.

MOTHER: He's not! He's living! *(touching her breast)* In here! And this is his house!

(Pause)

ALBERT: Look, Mum, I won't be late ... and I won't ...

MOTHER: But what about your dinner? It's nearly ready.

ALBERT: Seeley and Kedge are waiting for me. I told you not to cook dinner this morning. *(He goes to the stairs.)* Just because you never listen ...

(He runs up the stairs and disappears. She calls after him from the hall.)

MOTHER: Well, what am I going to do while you're out? I can't go into Grandma's room because there's no light. I can't go down to the cellar in the dark; we were going to have a game of cards, it's Friday night, what about our game of rummy?

Exercise 4

Version 1

1. Ralph

RALPH: One of the most, um, difficult experiences as far as learning a new accent, er, was when I had to play an English-speaking Dutchman.

DENICA: Oh, gosh. That sounds difficult.

RALPH: Yeah, well, they speak very good English, as you know, but their accents are quite distinctive, and, er, one of the clues as to how to copy them was when I found out that they actually learn a lot of their English through American television, erm ...

DENICA: Right, yes.

RALPH: The older school learn it from sort of American tapes and things as well, so when they do speak English, they often have 'a slight American accent, you know,' you know, a lot of the sounds come through. Another thing about the Dutch is that the 's's are very strong (Oh?) The 's' is actually with an 'esch' ...

DENICA: Really? Is it?

RALPH: ... so that when they do speak, they sort of talk with American accents but a very strong 'esch' sound, (Aha) so it's quite, it's quite a weird combination, and, er, it's only through sort of finding out actually how they learn to speak English that I managed to copy, copy them.

DENICA: Cor, that's interesting.

2. James

Well, I once had to do a two-person play, erm, and this was in New York, a few years ago, erm, set in South Africa, and, er, luckily for me, I mean, I'd never done a South African accent before at all and, luckily for me, the guy who I was playing opposite was a genuine South African, living in New York, and he hadn't lost any, a trace of his accent, he was really strong South African. And, er, so I just attached myself to him, you know, everywhere he went, I went, and I just listened to him, which was quite difficult because he was a shy guy, but I got him talking, and, erm, I suppose the thing I tried to latch onto most of all, because we had very little time to rehearse, was the rhythm, because certainly African countries the rhythm when they speak is, is a very sort of strong characteristic, so, and I also listened to Nelson Mandela whenever he was on the television, which luckily at the time was quite often. So I suppose the things I would ... I got, I got a silly little phrase like, um, that he would come up with, like, 'the reason is this', and I would listen to, er, the rhythm of his speech and sometimes, and specially in South Africa, there's a kind of a strong, um, rhythm which is very often not an English smooth rhythm (Uhuh) but it sort of has its ... it's like a sort of wave-like rhythm, so it, for example, let me think of a line, like 'You look hot. What on earth have you been doing?' so it would, er ... I don't know, I suppose that you'd listen to a particular, you'd latch onto one thing like the rhythm, and you'd go with that.

Version 2

1. DeNica

Well, erm, I had to, er, play the part of a woman who had been 'inside', in prison for 17 years, and had come from a very poor area in London, and, er, living in London myself, I thought, 'Well, that's going to be pretty easy, I'll just listen to the accents around me,' but actually, there's so many different dialects of a London accent itself: you've got the north London accent, south London, west and east, (Oh, yes, yes) so having listened to all sorts of different London accents which I taped on my cassette player and then played back, I was getting very confused, so I actually enlisted the help of one of the voice coaches, erm, teachers that had taught me at drama school, (Right) and phoned her up and said, 'I want to make this character south London. What are the vowel sounds, and can you give them to me?' and she phonetically gave me the different vowel sounds, and that was really useful to me, and in fact then I worked on specific sounds, but oddly enough, I do find the London accent itself, and all the sort of 'Thames Estuary' quite difficult, just because there is so much variation in them, (Right) erm, and so, you know, the sounds that I was having to teach myself were, well, for instance to be less, erm, aware of the cons..., my consonants, so you know, 'dustbin' became 'dusbin', and glottal stops, 'glo'l stops', actually it's quite an ugly sound if you sort of, lose the consonants, and sort of start putting in these 'glo'l stops', like 'bottle' becomes 'bo'ul', um, and also stretching and bending the vowel sounds, so that you get, you know, 'I was going deaauun the pub' instead of 'I was going down, ' I was going deaauun there', erm, 'eaut' instead of 'out', erm ...

2. Federay

Yeah, I came to England eight years ago from Australia to train as an actor, and had my full Australian accent when I came over, and I had to make a decision quite early on to learn to speak English, (Oh, right) with an English accent, which meant a change in vocabulary, in some cases as well as a new concentration on, on consonants and vowels I'd never paid any attention to before, because the normal Australian accent is really quite lazy, (Yeah) and we speak quite slowly, and it's quite kind of flat, and you don't use the mouth very much, (Hmm) and also have the tendency to go up at the end of sentences, so you make everything into a question, (Question, yeah) and, er, and that's not the English way at all: in fact they're quite the opposite, and they tend to fall off the end of sentences, (Hmm) and, um, so I had to learn really a new musicality, (Oh, right) and basically I had to become a whole lot more fit in the, in the mouth region, so that I could make the sounds that the English make and that Australians don't, and I suppose the mistakes I still make are in diphthong vowels, /aʊ/ and əʊ/ and /aɪ/, and specially on tiny little words like 'it' and 'is' 'cos the English will pronounce them /ɪt/, and I'll say ət/ (Yeah) and completely ignore it altogether, but it's been, it's been a very interesting experience, kind of learning a new way of speaking, yes, and I had to, to really take it on board in my everyday life, not just reserve it as a special voice for the stage. (Hm! Oh, right!)

REVIEW AND DEVELOPMENT
Review of Unit 11

Exercise 1
1. Can you peel bananas?
2. Can you peel strawberries?
3. Can water simmer?
4. Is broccoli fattening?
5. Is an aubergine a vegetable?
6. Can you carve water?
7. Can you carve meat?
8. Do cookery books have recipes?
9. Do recipes include ingredients?
10. Does scrambled egg contain caffeine?
11. Can milk be grated?
12. Do raspberries taste salty?
13. Has a raw egg got a yolk?
14. Can lettuce be sliced?
15. Does fizzy water have a different flavour to still water?

UNIT 13 ON THE JOB

Is it right? Is it fair?

Exercise 4
(See page 156.)

Looking at the downside

Exercise 3
1. A nanny
Well, I find the most difficult things really, the things that are most likely to cause friction are money (Oh, yeah) and, um, well, time-keeping. If you never get a pay rise, or you don't get the baby-sitting money you're owed, then you begin to lose respect, you know, for the people you're working for. And, er, well, it's the same if they're always late back, oh, they always have some excuse, you know, about the traffic or they forgot something or whatever. (Yes, yes, I know what you mean)
And you can also find yourself in very embarrassing situations. If ever I walk in on a row, I just sing loudly, 'cos it can be awful, you know, so I sing so that they know I'm there. (That's a good idea!) Do you know, at one job I had, the phone rang and this woman at the other end, well, she thought I was the children's mother. So she said, 'I'm going to tell you everything. I'm having an affair with your husband (Oh, my God!) and he's too scared to tell you. And I've got some photos to prove it.' (Did she?) And she wouldn't listen to me, I tried to say you know, you're not talking to her, but she just said that and put the phone down. I didn't know what to say to her.

2. A public relations officer for a large travel agent
A: I handle customer relations at head office and I'd say, on average, I receive, oh, about 300 letters or calls a week. (Goodness!) The worst occasions are when people swear at you, abuse you or threaten you with newspapers and lawyers before you've even had time to speak. Inside you think, 'Well, go off and do it then', but, well, I mean, you have to maintain your calm. (Yes, of course) Having said that though, I do draw the line at abusive language. If someone comes on the line saying, 'I don't want to talk to a stupid little woman,' or won't stop swearing at me, then I hang up.
B: Does that often happen?
A: Uh, I guess that's happened to me on two or three occasions since I've been in the job. Oh, and the other thing that can be difficult is insurance claims, because, well it's funny how most people buy their clothes from very ordinary shops, (yes) but when a suitcase goes missing, they will say it was full of Armani suits and Vivienne Westwood dresses or stuff like that, you know. I mean, I suppose it's human nature, but it does make it very difficult for us to deal with those claims, When we know that people aren't actually telling the truth. (Hmm, of course)

3. A head teacher in a poor inner city area
A: Well, the stress starts first thing in the morning with the worry over whether I'm going to have a full complement of staff, I mean, because quite a lot ring in sick quite a lot of the time. And those phone calls start about, about 7 in the morning so I have to find teachers to deputise then at short notice; I do that over breakfast. (Not good for the digestion!) Not very good for the digestion! So I get to school, I'm usually, it's usually about 8.00 and the caretaker and I clean the playground because most of the area seems to use it as a rubbish dump. One morning I arrived to find £10,000-worth of computer equipment just gone. (God!) Completely gone. Then the kids start to arrive about 5 to 9, and I check and see if they're all settled and starting to work. We have a number of pupils from deprived backgrounds, but our school's got a pretty good reputation and generally the kids are very well-behaved, but we do have a growing minority of students whose disruptive behaviour can be a real problem. (In the classroom?) In the classroom, yes. I have to deal with physical violence quite a lot in the classroom (Against teachers or against each other?) against each other and against teachers, yes. There's no difference these days. I mean, quite a lot of the kids just deliberately ignore the teachers, sit with their backs facing them, and there's nothing they can do.

UNIT 14 ACCIDENTS WILL HAPPEN

Are you clumsy or absent-minded?

Exercise 3
My problem is, I'm always mislaying things, important things, such as my front door key or my credit cards – that sort of stuff. And it's really irritating because I know they're important but I keep putting them down in different places in the house – I don't have one place you see where I keep these things – and within hours, minutes even, I can't remember where they are. My wife used to spend half her life looking for things I'd mislaid, but now she refuses to lift a finger to help me.

I remember as a teenager I used to be incredibly clumsy and my body was covered in bruises all the time where I kept bumping into things and falling over. And at home I was forever dropping plates and smashing glasses – my mother would never let me do the washing-up or anything like that, and for a while it got so bad that she would actually hide anything of value so that I couldn't get my hands on it and break it.

Exercise 6
Version 1
1.
DENICA: Well, more and more recently, erm, I keep forgetting where I've put something in my flat. (Right) It's just a habit that seems to be happening more and more, I used to know exactly where I kept everything and be very kind of tidy and what have you. But I keep losing things and ... (Why?) I don't know – perhaps because my life is, is ... I'm so busy these days, um, and I literally don't have time to, you know, tidy

tidy my desk or, you know, really keep things as much in order as, as I used to. And also I tend to, um, go into rooms, um, looking for something and then I've forgotten what I'm looking for because my mind is on all sorts of other things, um, and so I stand in the room and look around and think 'oh no, now what was I looking for?' (Yeah) have to go back out.

2.

LORELEI: When I was younger, I used to be very clumsy, I was always breaking things. Whenever I'd handle anything, it would break, and the worst thing that ever happened because of this clumsiness was I broke an egg of my grandfather's. It was a blown-out egg that had been painted, that he had brought, his mother had given it to him when he was a little boy, he'd brought it from Yugoslavia. He'd had it his whole life – he was 80, and I dropped it, and I broke it. (Ooh, no!) I still choke up when I think about it. He forgave me.

Version 2

1.

WILLIE: I'm not very absent-minded now but when I was younger I think I was very absent-minded and it used to drive my mum and dad mad, I think. And I used to do that thing where in the middle of the day you go into a room, and like, I used to go into the bedroom and I'd suddenly find myself getting undressed, and I'd be in my pyjamas.

DENICA: Oh, really. Why?

WILLIE: Well, to ... 'cos I associated going into the bedroom with getting ready for bed.

DENICA: Of course, I see that.

WILLIE: I'd actually gone in for a different reason.

DENICA: Mmm.

WILLIE: But somehow the act of walking into the bedroom made me think, 'Oh, I must go to bed.' And I'd put on my pyjamas, and halfway through I'd suddenly realise that I'd got it wrong.

DENICA: It was in the middle of the day or whatever.

WILLIE: That's right, and you'd snap back into doing whatever it was you were doing.

DENICA: Sounds very absent-minded to me. Are you better now?

WILLIE: Yeah. Yes, I am, thanks.

2.

NICK: I'm always tripping up. I don't know why, but, er, I used to do it when I was little, um, and my mum used to say I was lazy-footed. And, er, I'd be walking along and I'd catch one foot on the back of the other usually and trip up. And I tend to do it now, not as often, but what I've found myself doing is doing it as a joke, ha ha, so, um, I like doing it, um, if I'm on a walk and there's a lot of people coming the other way, and just as I'm getting up to them, er, I sort of pretend to trip and they all go 'Oh, oh, careful', and it's a very silly joke really, but the people that I'm with know that I'm going to do it, and they hold, hang their heads in despair really.

Drama at 9,000 metres

Exercise 3

So, the thing was, once they took off, Paula's arm was bandaged, and she was given pain killers. She settled back and listened to music on her Walkman and felt a lot better. Anyway, sometime later, she decided to take her shoes off, but when she bent down, she felt a terrible pain under her ribs. She was in agony and called for a steward. So, once again, the doctor came back. At first, apparently, he thought she may have fractured some ribs, but he soon saw that she was deteriorating fast. She was having breathing difficulties and turning blue. He suddenly realised that her lung must have collapsed! So, there was only one thing to do – they had to operate immediately – otherwise, she would die.

And with the help of, er, Tom Wong, Dr Wallace constructed this emergency operating theatre using the back seats of the plane. Apparently, there was some anaesthetic in the first aid kit that they

used, but apart from that, they used the, some very basic instruments. They used a pair of scissors, a little water bottle, a coat hanger, a piece of plastic tubing, and a bottle of brandy that they used as disinfectant to clean the instruments. And with just those basic things, Dr Wallace carried out the life-saving operation. Unbelievably enough, Paula began to feel better almost immediately, and by the time they landed at Heathrow, she was cheerful and quite relaxed.

When they got off the plane she gave the doctor a very grateful kiss, and he received an award later for his work and (the doctor, this is, Dr Wallace) and he gave the money, £32,000, to his university medical school.

REVIEW AND DEVELOPMENT
Review of Unit 13

Exercise 1

1. It's when you take time off work to have a baby.
2. It's when a husband takes time off work to look after his wife and baby.
3. It means to lose your job because there isn't enough work.
4. It's when you lose your job because you're no good at it or you've done something wrong.
5. It's when you finally stop working, often at the age of 60 or 65.
6. It's when you get a better position in your company with more money and responsibility.
7. It's when you officially decide to leave a job.
8. It's to write formally for a job that you have probably seen advertised in a newspaper.
9. It's a phrasal verb, meaning to employ someone.
10. It's when you stop working for a time to protest about something, such as your pay or working conditions.

UNIT 15 WAYS OF BEING BETTER OFF

How honest are we?

Exercise 4

In Britain 52 out of the 80 wallets were returned – that's 65% overall. Now, in America and Europe the figures were a little bit different, but the difference wasn't really very significant. In America the return rate was 67%, which puts them a little bit above the UK. In Europe the figure was lower – 58% overall, although there were some really interesting fluctuations here, much more than in America and Britain. Two Scandinavian cities, for example, Odense and Oslo, recorded an astonishing 100% return rate, while Lausanne in Switzerland and Weimar in Germany recorded only a 20% return rate.

Women were more likely to return the wallet than men: 72% compared with 60%; and people in medium-sized towns were slightly more honest than people in the cities: 67.5% against 62.5%. Now, maybe that's not as much of a difference as some people would've predicted.

The response to the reward was interesting. One man refused it outright and most people were reluctant to accept it.

Exercise 5

Version 1

Why did people return the wallets? Here are the findings:

Several said they came from a religious background, and that it wouldn't be right, they would've felt guilty if they kept it.

Some returned it because, because they knew how, how it would feel if it happened to them.

One person returned it not because the wallet contained money but because he was afraid it might contain something of sentimental value to the owner.

And a number of people said they thought the wallet might belong to someone such as a pensioner or, or an unemployed person – in other words, someone who was worse off than themselves, someone who really needed the money.

But the most common reason people returned the wallet was that they said they had been brought up to be honest and it never even crossed their minds to keep it. They just returned the wallet instinctively.

Version 2

The reasons people gave for returning the wallets were, were numerous. Several people said that they came from a religious background. It would've been wrong to keep it, it would've been sinful and they, they would feel guilty if they'd kept it.

Several returned it because, um, they were empathetic; they knew they would've been very upset if it had happened to them. Er, one person returned it not because of the money but because maybe it would, would've contained something of sentimental value to the owner, something irreplaceable.

Er, one man returned the wallet to the nearest police station without even bothering to look inside. He said it never even crossed his mind to do anything else.

Another man was, was very touched by a photograph in the wallet, er, when he saw the picture of the woman and the two children he said he couldn't possibly have kept the wallet and the money – it would have been on his conscience for the rest of his life.

Some people said that they thought the wallet might belong to someone such as an older person, a pensioner or, or an unemployed person – in other words, someone who was worse off than themselves who might really need that money.

One woman said she was sure the wallet belonged to a workmate and that's why she returned it.

But the most common reason why people returned the wallet was that they had been brought up to be honest and, and it never even occurred to them to keep it. They just returned the wallet instinctively.

Join the rush to sue

Exercise 2
1. Does a verdict give you an answer?
2. If you sue someone, will they be angry?
3. If you receive damages, do you have to pay the money back?
4. Does compensation make you better off?
5. If you settle a dispute, have you solved a problem?
6. If you ruin someone's life, will they thank you for it?
7. If you are awarded damages, will you be happy?
8. If you appeal against a decision, are you satisfied with it?

What's your best price?

Exercise 4
CUSTOMER: Hello!

SHOP OWNER: Hi.

CUSTOMER: Um, I just think this shop's so lovely; I've come past here so many times ...

SHOP OWNER: Thank you!

CUSTOMER: You've got lovely, really lovely things in the window, and, um, I just wonder, I'm looking for a present for my mother, um, and it's her 50th birthday, so it has to be something really, really special (Hmmm) and you've got a pair of earrings in the window, erm, they're sort of, I think they might be garnets or rubies?

SHOP OWNER: Oh, yeah, yeah, they just went in this week.

CUSTOMER: Hmm. I wondered if I could have a look at them.

SHOP OWNER: Yes, of course, of course. Well, there you are.

CUSTOMER: Oh, they really ... you've got really lovely taste. They're beautiful!

SHOP OWNER: Well, actually, my wife does most of the buying, she got them at an auction last week. They've come in from France, in fact.

CUSTOMER: Oh, really?

SHOP OWNER: Yes, a clearance on an old, er, um, estate there, and they are rubies, encrusted in diamonds.

CUSTOMER: Could you, er, tell me the price?

SHOP OWNER: Well, these are quite old and in very, very good condition. The price is £150.

CUSTOMER: Oh, mm. That's just a bit more than, than I was thinking of.

SHOP OWNER: Oh, I see.

CUSTOMER: What a shame. They're so pretty. And, erm, that's, that's your final price?

SHOP OWNER: Well, I mean, I think you'll find that for what they are, they are quite reasonably priced. I mean, would you be interested in telling me what you would be prepared to pay for them?

CUSTOMER: Well, I'm sort of, I was really thinking about, you know, £130, about £20 less? I mean, if you look here, there's a sort of, it looks like they've been mended at some point. You wouldn't sort of ...

SHOP OWNER: Really? Could you ...?

CUSTOMER: Just here, look.

SHOP OWNER: Yes, well, obviously, I mean, they're quite old, and I'm sure, my wife priced it actually, I didn't do that so I'm sure she, that's reflected in the price already, but are you thinking of paying cash?

CUSTOMER: Er, yeah. Yes, I would pay cash.

SHOP OWNER: OK. Well how about a compromise of £135?

CUSTOMER: Well, I think that's great! Yes, thank you, I'll take them.

SHOP OWNER: OK.

REVIEW AND DEVELOPMENT
Review of Unit 14

Exercise 2
1. Is disinfectant used in surgery?
2. Can you get a bruise by breathing?
3. Can a pedestrian collide with a vehicle?
4. If you injure yourself, might a bandage be useful?
5. If you deteriorate, is it a good sign?
6. Do you need an anaesthetic for surgery?
7. If you're in agony, will you definitely collapse?
8. Can you fracture your skull?
9. Do symptoms show that you have an illness?

PROJECT: EDUCATION IN THE ADULT WORLD

English exams

Exercise 2
The First Certificate in English – it's often known as FCE – is the most widely taken of the Cambridge examinations. Candidates for the exam come from a wide range of ages and backgrounds, although the majority are in their teens or early twenties, and perhaps surprisingly about two-thirds are female.

The exam was first introduced in 1939, but it's regularly updated and changes are made. But the basic aim of the exam remains the same – that is to assess general proficiency in English through a series of tests. There are five of these: three written papers which test extended writing, reading comprehension, vocabulary and grammar, then another test on listening, and finally a 15-minute interview to assess spoken English.

The Cambridge Advanced Exam in English – CAE for short – is the next exam up in terms of difficulty. It also has five papers like the FCE and each paper has the same sort of focus. But some of the exercises are a bit different, and of course, they're harder.

Some of the tasks in the Oxford Higher are similar to CAE, but the Oxford exam concentrates solely on reading and writing skills and there are just two papers. One important feature of the Oxford exam is that candidates have to read and write a lot in the time allowed for the two exams, and under such time pressure there is perhaps not quite the same emphasis on accuracy as in the Cambridge exams, and the main consideration is the successful completion of the task within the time limit. For example, in the reading tasks you need to understand the key information in the texts, select relevant information for the completion of the tasks, and be able to cope with difficult vocabulary. In the writing tasks you have to include relevant information and express it in a way that is appropriate for the person who will be reading it.

The fourth exam, the ARELS Higher, only tests the skills of speaking and listening. The exam takes place in a language laboratory and there are six different sections: you have to speak on a topic for two minutes, you have to tell a story from pictures – you have a few minutes to prepare both of these; you have to say how you would respond in a range of everyday social situations; there is also a little grammar test; you also have to read a passage in English as a test of pronunciation; and answer questions about various passages in English.

Exercise 3
The ARELS Higher exam
Part one
First you'll hear six remarks which might be made to you in various situations when you're using your English. Some are questions and some are comments. After each one, reply in a natural way. Here's an example to help you.
- Sorry to keep you waiting.
- That's all right. Don't worry.
Now are you ready? Here's the first.
1. We had a marvellous day on Saturday. What a pity you couldn't make it.
2. Is there anywhere round here where I can get my hair cut, do you know?
3. I'm sorry but I'm afraid I can't come with you tonight. I've got to go and visit my granddad. He's 84 and he's just had a stroke.
4. We've got half an hour before the next meeting. Fancy a quick drink?
5. Oh bother! I've left my money in my other coat.
6. I'm not sure I could eat horse meat. I mean, I know a lot of people do, but I don't think I'd fancy it somehow.

Part two
Now you'll hear some situations in which you might find yourself. Say what it seems natural to say in each situation. Ready?
7. You arrive at a hotel where you would like to stay the night. You haven't reserved a room in advance. What do you say to the receptionist?
8. You're out shopping with a friend and are trying on a coat. You think it's rather smart but you're not sure. What do you say to your friend?
9. You're on holiday with a friend. She wants to go sightseeing today, but you have a terrible headache. What do you say to her?
10. In the middle of the morning your headache is no better and you decide to go to the pharmacy to get something for it. What do you say to the assistant?
11. While sitting on a beach, you get some oil on a pair of trousers. You don't really think it'll be possible to clean them, but you take them to a dry cleaner's just in case. What do you say to the assistant?
12. You're in a restaurant. You ordered chicken and salad fifteen minutes ago, but nothing has arrived yet. What do you say to the waiter?

UNIT 16   THAT'S A MATTER OF OPINION

Do we still need military service?

Exercise 1
INTERVIEWER: OK, Daniel, then, could you just tell me a little bit about military service in Switzerland?
DANIEL: Yes, of course. I would like to start with the length of the military service we have in Switzerland. Er, usually, or it used to be that the basic training was about 17 weeks but now two years ago we had a kind of, er, military reform and it's now 15 weeks. And then you have to go every, or every year or every second year

once to a, we call it a 'repetition' course, and this kind of course takes about, er, 2 or 3 weeks; that depends on the troop. And all in all now at the moment you have to do at least 300 days.
INTERVIEWER: Right. So at what age do you actually finish?
DANIEL: Yeah, it's difficult to say. About 40.
INTERVIEWER: About 40?
DANIEL: Yeah, but then you have to go to the civil protection, but it's just one or two days a year.
INTERVIEWER: Women don't do it, do they?
DANIEL: For them it's voluntary. They can do it, but it's not compulsory for them.
INTERVIEWER: OK. And what about for men? Do you have to do it? Does everyone have to do it?
DANIEL: Yeah, if you're Swiss, you have to do it. Of course there are exceptions. If you are not able for medical reasons, you don't have to do it, but usually everybody has to do it.
INTERVIEWER: OK. And people don't all start at the same level, then. People go in at different levels.
DANIEL: Everybody starts with the basic ... with this kind of basic education, so you can start a career as an officer. You have to do the same thing at the beginning, everybody is equal, and then after a while you or your officers have to decide whether you have to continue or not.
INTERVIEWER: Right. And do you have to spend more time doing military service if you are an officer?
DANIEL: Yeah, absolutely, then you have to go every year. And they start usually 3 or 4 days earlier than, than the normal soldiers. And they have also some kind of instruction courses, technical courses during the year.
INTERVIEWER: Yeah?
DANIEL: Yeah.

So what would *you* have done?

Exercise 3
GARETH: I would've just sworn and driven on, I think. I mean you can get yourself into terrible trouble with, you know, people who drive like that. It says something about their personalities, doesn't it? You know, the fact that they're, they're capable of behaving like that.
MARCELLA: Yes, but they shouldn't be allowed to get away with it. I mean I'd have gone to the police station and reported it. I know it seems like a small thing and they'd probably tell me to just go away. What can you do? But ...
IAN: You'd have taken the number.
MARCELLA: I would've taken his number, yeah, and reported it. I'd have done that definitely.
IAN: I wouldn't have wanted to go after him but if ... depending on how I felt, I would've probably said something.

Exercise 6
IAN: I wouldn't have done just what she did, would you? I mean ...
MARCELLA: No, I wouldn't have.
IAN: I'd've gone to find somebody from the store. I mean, it's not my responsibility. I mean, I would've found a store detective or failing that an assistant.
MARCELLA: That's exactly what I would've done. I think it's very risky to do what she did. I think I would've ... well, it's hard to spot a store detective, so I'd have probably gone to a cashier or somebody else in uniform who looked like they were part of ...
GARETH: It's difficult to know when to act, isn't it? I think I would've, perhaps once I'd seen them behaving suspiciously alerted somebody in the store, you know, I would've said, erm, 'There's a couple over there behaving rather strangely' ...
IAN: A pre-emptive strike, sort of thing?
GARETH: Yeah.

UNIT 17 MANNERS

Excuse me, would you mind ...?

Exercise 3

See pages 157–158.

Letters

Exercise 1

OK, now the letter in front of you has been typed by an individual, not a company, and it's quite formal. But as we go through, I'm going to tell you a few things about informal letters as well – you might want to note this information down on a separate piece of paper. OK, the first thing is to write the sender's address in the top right-hand corner, OK. This has a set order with the number of the house or flat followed by the name of the street; and then underneath that, perhaps the district if it's a big town, then under that the name of the town or city, with the postcode. And it's now common, quite acceptable, to write all this without any punctuation at all. And the address – please write it now in the top right-hand corner – is 12 Barley Avenue (that's B-A-R-L-E-Y) Barley Avenue.
And the next line is West Ealing (that's E-A-L-I-N-G).
Next line: London W5 – then a small gap – 6RJ. London W5 6RJ. Now leave a line, and then write the date directly underneath the address. Now you can do this in several different ways. You can put 10 August, or August 10, or just 10 dot 8 dot 98. So use one of these methods and put today's date in the correct place.
And now, if you want, you could write the address of the person you are writing to. If you do that, you put it on the left-hand side of the paper, and you would usually start the address at roughly about the, the same level as the date which is on the right-hand side. For this letter though, we're not going to do that. Our letter is to Sean Connery, and we begin Dear Mr Connery – please note exactly where it goes.
Now, if you don't know the person's name you just put Dear Sir, or Dear Madam, or Dear Sir or Madam. In an informal letter you still use 'Dear' but you start with the person's first name – for example, Dear Maria or Dear Stephen or whatever.
And at the end of the letter you sign off 'Yours sincerely' – capital Y, but small 's'. So could you write that now at the end of the letter, leaving a line first? The spelling of 'sincerely' is S-I-N-C-E-R-E-L-Y. Now, we put 'sincerely' if we know the name of the person that we are writing to. But if you don't know the name, the traditional ending is 'Yours faithfully'. Now, this is the custom in Britain, although it is true to say that not everyone keeps to it, and I think in America they use different endings – for example, they may finish a letter 'Truly yours'. OK, if you are writing to a friend, then it's usually something like 'best wishes', or often 'love' if it's a member of your family or a very close friend, but not so common between two friends who are men. After the ending, in this case 'Yours sincerely', leave a line, and then put your signature directly underneath. So do that now – write your signature at the end of the letter. And that's it.

REVIEW AND DEVELOPMENT

Review of Unit 16

1. If your teacher hadn't come to class today, would you have had a lesson?
2. If your school decided to put on a show, would you be prepared to take part?
3. Would you have come to class today if you hadn't felt very well?
4. If nobody in class had done the last piece of homework, what would've happened?
5. If you could ask your teacher any question you liked, what would it be?
6. How would you have felt if, last week, the students in your class had gone out for dinner without inviting you?

UNIT 18 WHAT ARE THE ODDS?

The probability factors of life

Exercise 3

A: Hm, that was interesting that, er, for pregnant women, the chances of having twins was, er ...
B: 2%! 2% is incredible, isn't it?
A: I know. I thought it was higher.
B: Did you?
A: But apparently, er, for triplets it's, it's actually lower than 2%.
B: Is it much lower? What is it?
A: Hm. It's one in 3,360. And that's going to change in the future with all the fertility treatment going on ...
B: The statistics go up and up, yeah.
A: So it'll be much more likely for people to have multiple births.
B: Yeah, yeah.
A: What else did we do here? Oh, yes, this was interesting, um, it was the likelihood of getting strangled, or shot or poisoned.
B: And it being in December, which I thought was interesting, at that time of year, when, you know, one thinks of things, as you say, like Christmas or New Year and festivities, parties and things ...
A: Yeah, I know.
B: Strange, isn't it?
A: And also apparently, it's got here that, er, it's, er, really quite likely that you will know the person who murders you.
B: Really? I mean, what, statistically ...
A: 65% of victims know the person who ...
B: 65%?
A: Yeah, knew the person who shot them, strangled them or poisoned them.
B: ... poisoned them, whatever. And as I say, it's likely to happen in December too. How strange. What was the other one? Burglary. I thought this was, this was really quite strange, that for some reason, the risk of, er, the risk of burglary goes up if there are more people living in a house.
A: Well, that's strange too. I thought because with more people coming in and out, you'd have thought a burglar would be put off, but apparently, no, because, you know, they're more likely to leave windows, doors open, etc., (Oh, right) thinking that somebody else has closed them ...
B: ... is going to be coming in later or whatever.
A: Yeah, or yes.
B: And so consequently, they get in, more chances of getting burgled. That's remarkable.

What will you be doing?

Exercise 2

1.
A: Oh, Betty, by the way, could you give me a ring as soon as you get home tonight – just to confirm things for tomorrow?
B: Well, actually my flatmate will have made the dinner by the time I get in, so can I give you a ring when we've eaten?
A: Yeah, OK then.

2.
C: Do want me to pop round this evening to pick up those samples?
D: Yes, could you?
C: Yes, sure – what time?
D: Sevenish.
C: Fine.
D: No, actually, could you make it a bit later? My husband will be making dinner and he gets really irritable if people turn up when he's in the middle of cooking.
C: (giggle) No problem – I'll come at about 8, then.
D: Great.

3.
E: Oh dear, I don't really want to go round to Sue and Mike's tonight – not after the last time. That meal Sue served up was absolutely dreadful.
F: Don't worry, I bet Mike'll make the dinner – he was a bit embarrassed about that last meal and he's not working at the moment.
E: Oh, well, that's a relief.

IRREGULAR VERBS AND PHONETIC SYMBOLS

Irregular verbs

Infinitive	Simple past	Past participle
be	was/were	been
become	became	become
begin	began	begun
bend	bent	bent
bite	bit	bitten
blow	blew	blown
break	broke	broken
bring	brought	brought
build	built	built
buy	bought	bought
can	could	(been able)
catch	caught	caught
choose	chose	chosen
come	came	come
cost	cost	cost
cut	cut	cut
do	did	done
draw	drew	drawn
dream	dreamt	dreamt
drink	drank	drunk
drive	drove	driven
eat	ate	eaten
fall	fell	fallen
feel	felt	felt
fight	fought	fought
find	found	found
fly	flew	flown
forget	forgot	forgotten
get	got	got
give	gave	given
go	went	gone (been)
have	had	had
hear	heard	heard
hit	hit	hit
hold	held	held
hurt	hurt	hurt
keep	kept	kept
know	knew	known
learn	learnt	learnt
leave	left	left
lend	lent	lent
let	let	let
lie	lay	lain
lose	lost	lost
make	made	made
mean	meant	meant
meet	met	met
pay	paid	paid
put	put	put
read /riːd/	read /red/	read /red/
ride	rode	ridden
ring	rang	rung
rise	rose	risen
run	ran	run
say	said	said
see	saw	seen
sell	sold	sold
send	sent	sent
set	set	set
shake	shook	shaken
shine	shone	shone
shoot	shot	shot
show	showed	shown
shut	shut	shut
sing	sang	sung
sit	sat	sat
sleep	slept	slept
speak	spoke	spoken
spell	spelt	spelt
spend	spent	spent
spread	spread	spread
stand	stood	stood
steal	stole	stolen
swim	swam	swum
take	took	taken
teach	taught	taught
tell	told	told
think	thought	thought
throw	threw	thrown
understand	understood	understood
wake	woke	woken
wear	wore	worn
win	won	won
write	wrote	written

Phonetic symbols

Vowels

Symbol	Example
/iː/	see
/i/	happy
/ɪ/	big
/e/	bed
/æ/	sad
/ʌ/	sun
/ɑː/	car
/ɒ/	pot
/ɔː/	taught
/ʊ/	pull
/uː/	boot
/ɜː/	bird
/ə/	among
	produce
/eɪ/	date
/aɪ/	time
/ɔɪ/	boy
/əʊ/	note
/aʊ/	town
/ɪə/	ear
/eə/	there
/ʊə/	tour

Consonants

Symbol	Example
/b/	back
/d/	dog
/ð/	then
/dʒ/	joke
/f/	far
/g/	go
/h/	hot
/j/	young
/k/	key
/l/	learn
/m/	make
/n/	note
/ŋ/	sing
/p/	pan
/r/	ran
/s/	soon
/ʃ/	fish
/tʃ/	top
/ð/	chart
/θ/	thin
/v/	view
/w/	went
/z/	zone
/ʒ/	pleasure

Stress

Stress is indicated by a small box above the stressed syllable.
Example: advertisement

ACKNOWLEDGEMENTS

Authors' acknowledgements
We would like to thank Joanne Collie and Stephen Slater for their original inspiration in the development of *True to Life*.

We are genuinely indebted to our friends and colleagues at International House, London, and the London School of English for their support and encouragement; and for specific feedback, ideas and activities we would like to thank: Frances Eales, Kristina Teasdale, Robin Wileman, Jane Hann, Mark Hind and Lin Coleman.

There are numerous authors whose work has influenced and inspired us, among them Michael Swan, Ros Aitken, Jill Hadfield, Andrew Littlejohn, Penny Ur, Mike McCarthy and Ruth Wajnryb.

At Cambridge University Press we would like to express our very sincere thanks to Kate Boyce for her immense commitment and excellent management of the project. We also wish to thank Helena Gomm, a consummate professional with a great sense of humour. We would also like to thank all those, past and present, who contributed to the design and production of the work.

Particular thanks go to Martin Williamson, who produced and shaped the listening material, and Andy Tayler, the staff at AVP and all the actors who shared their stories with us.

Finally, our thanks go to the commissioning editor, Peter Donovan, who set the project in motion, and to all the staff at CUP.

The authors and publishers would like to thank the following individuals and institutions for their help in testing the material and for the invaluable feedback which they provided:

Mary Anne Ansell; Tess Goodliffe; Gillian Lazar; Liz Munro; Silvia Rettaroli; Julia Sawyer, Australian International College of Language, Southport, Australia; Andrew Thomas, Sydney English Language Centre, Bondi Junction, Australia; Anikó Szilágyi, London Studio, Budapest, Hungary; Zsuzsa Vidra, Globus 2000, Budapest, Hungary; Maggie Baigent, British Council, Bologna, Italy; Carmel Fullam, Buckingham School, Rome, Italy; Ann Travers, Oxford institutes italiani, Vicenza, Italy; Guy Perring and Andrew Hill, Language Education Center, Hiroshima, Japan; James Boyd, ECC Gaigo Gakuin, Osaka, Japan; Jackie Halsal, Karya Yabanci Dil Kursu, Istanbul, Turkey; Bahar Darn, Dokuz Eylül University, Izmir, Turkey; Christopher Hart, Saxoncourt, London, UK; Robin Wileman, International House, London, UK.

The authors and publishers are grateful to the following copyright holders for permission to reproduce copyright material. While every endeavour has been made, it has not been possible to identify the sources of all material used and in such cases the publishers would welcome information from copyright sources. Apologies are expressed for any omissions.

p. 9: The European Ltd for an extract from the article 'Do Europeans share common ideals?' by Birna Helgadottir (*The European*, 26 Oct – 1 Nov 1995); p. 15: Paula Burroughs for extracts from her article 'The simple sleep quiz' in BUPA's *Upbeat* magazine; p. 16: Newspaper Publishing plc for an extract from the article 'The big sleep' (*Independent Weekend*, 9 Sept 1995); pp. 20–21: Solo Syndication Ltd for the extract from the *Evening Standard*; pp. 29–30: Addison Wesley Longman Ltd for definition of *unrequited* from the *Longman Dictionary of Contemporary English*, Cambridge University Press for the definition of *unrequited* from *Cambridge International Dictionary of English*, Mrs John Haycraft for extracts from *Babel in London* by John Haycraft; pp. 37–38: Solo Syndication Ltd for an extract from the *Daily Mail Weekend*; p. 41: Newspaper Publishing plc for an extract from the article 'Virginia Ironside: dilemma' (*The Independent*, 25 Jan 1996); p. 49: Newspaper Publishing plc for an extract from the article 'My first day as a tour rep was a nightmare' (*The Independent on Sunday*, 30 July 1995); p. 53: Ed Victor Ltd on behalf of Robert Cumming for extracts from *Annotated Art* published by Dorling Kindersley Adult; p. 54: Newspaper Publishing plc for the recording based on the article 'Colour blindness' (*The Independent on Sunday*, 18 July 1993); pp. 56–57: Solo Syndication Ltd for extracts from the *Daily Mail Weekend*; p. 60: Addison Wesley Longman Ltd for the definition of *leader* from the *Longman Dictionary of Contemporary English*; p. 60 Cambridge University Press for definitions of *issue* and *policy* from *Cambridge International Dictionary of English*; p. 61 Cobuild Ltd for the explanation of the expressions *it's time* and *it's high time* from *Collins Cobuild English Dictionary*; p 62: Bruce Gyngell for an extract from his article 'It's about time we said "No" to TV sleaze' in *Reader's Digest*; pp. 65–66: Oxford University Press for an extract from *Manage Your Mind* by Gillian Butler and Tony Hope (1995); pp. 74–75: Writers News Ltd for an adapted extract from 'Writing stories that sell' by Mike Wakefield in *Writing Magazine*, 1994; pp. 76–77: Scott Meredith Literary Agency, New York, on behalf of Fred Brown for the story 'Hobbyist' published in *Playboy Magazine*, 1961. Copyright © by HMH Publishing Corporation; p. 79: Guardian News Service Ltd for an extract from the article 'The difference a day made' interview by Annie Taylor (*The Guardian*, Aug 1995); p. 83: Rogers, Coleridge and White Ltd on behalf of John Wells for an extract from the article 'A hum of quiet enjoyment', published in *The Independent on Sunday*, 28 Jan 1996; pp. 89–90: Faber and Faber Ltd

and Grove/Atlantic Inc for an extract from the play *A Night Out* by Harold Pinter, and Judy Daish Associates Ltd for the recording of Act 1, Scene 1 from the play; pp. 98–99: Newspaper Publishing plc for extracts from the article 'What to wear to get that job' (*The Independent on Sunday*, 10 Mar 1996); p. 100: Newspaper Publishing plc for the recording based on the article 'Enough, Already' (*The Independent Magazine*, April 1996); p. 103: Addison Wesley Longman Ltd for the definition of *absent-minded* from the *Longman Dictionary of Contemporary English*, Cobuild Ltd for the definition of *clumsy* from *Collins Cobuild English Dictionary*, Cambridge University Press for the definition of *clumsy* from *Cambridge International Dictionary of English*; p. 105: Bloomsbury Publishing plc for an extract from the *Bloomsbury Guide to Letter Writing* by Nigel Rees, 1994; p. 107: Cambridge University Press for an extract from *From Page to Performance* by Don Shiach (1987); p. 111: Newspaper Publishing plc for extracts from the article 'Mouth burnt on a pie? Join the rush to sue' (*The Independent*, 2 July 1996; pp. 116–18: University of Cambridge Local Examinations Syndicate for questions from past examination papers; p. 120: The European Ltd for an extract from 'Learning about life in the army' by David Baumann (*The European Magazine*, 11–17 Jan 1996); pp. 123–24: Newspaper Publishing plc for extracts from the article 'Why we like a decent proposal' (*The Independent*, 29 Feb 1996); p. 130: Solo Syndication Ltd for an extract from the *Daily Mail*; p. 134: Virgin Publishing Ltd for an extract from *Chances, The Probability Factors of Life* by James Burke.

The authors and publishers are grateful to the following illustrators and photographic sources:
Illustrators: Kathy Baxendale: pp. 22, 29, 43, 44, 46, 79, 80; Lucy Bristow: pp. 67, 68, 106, 128; Linda Combi: p. 58; Lee Ebrell: pp. 31, 82, 84, 88, 91; Max Ellis: pp. 26, 103; Phil Healey: pp. 28, 75, 114, 129, 142, 144, 152; Rob Hefferan: p. 89; Belle Mellor: pp. 25, 102, 134; David Mitcheson: pp. 121, 122; Pantelis Palios: pp. 27, 45, 108; Tracy Rich: pp. 6, 138; Jamie Sneddon: pp. 8, 22, 29, 38, 40, 43, 44, 46, 79, 80, 105, 111, 118, 120, 124, 145, 150; John Storey: pp. 23, 64, 85; Michael Terry: pp. 24, 135; Sean Victory: pp. 56, 57, 76, 77; Kath Walker: pp. 71, 97, 104, 127; Rosemary Woods: pp. 100, 115.

Photographic sources: Action-Plus Photographic: p. 139 *l* (Glyn Kirk); Peter Adams: p. 101 (nurse); Mark Azevedo: pp. 39 *r*, 46 *l*, 101 (publican, lifeguard); Copyright © BBC: p. 93; Anthony Baggett: pp. 54 *c*, 55 *tl* + shirt on line, 83 *c*; Steve Bavister: pp. 54 *r*, 101 *r*, 113 (computer, car, table & chairs, dishes), 125 (fence, step, shirt); Paul Beard: pp. 19 (bald), 34 (diary, brooch, cufflinks, jokes, ornament), 83 *cr*, 125 (glasses, arm); Lyndon Beddoe: p. 109; Bridgeman Art Library, London: pp. 14 (detail, The Maas Gallery, London), 33 *l* (Musée d'Orsay, Paris, France/Peter Willi), 33 *c* (Victoria & Albert Museum, London), 33 *r* (Estonian Art Museum, Tallinn), 51 *tl* (detail, Musée d'Orsay, Paris, France/Giraudon), 51 *bl* (detail, Private Collection), 51 *br* (detail, Private Collection), 51 *tr* (detail, Private Collection); Ryan Bowler: p. 125 (keys, wine glass, juice); Camelot Group plc: p. 139 *r*; Comstock: pp. 65, 69 *bl*; Courtauld Gallery, London: p. 52 (plus 3 details); Edifice: p. 39 *l* (Ryle-Hodges); © The Guardian: p. 16 (E.H. West); Roger Howard: pp. 19 (cowgirl), 24 *l*, 31 *c*, 36 *cr*, 48 *tl*, 101 *l*, 123; Hulton Getty : p. 17 *cr*, *br*; The Independent: p. 98 (David Sandison); The Kobal Collection: p. 29 (Paramount / photo courtesy of Kobal Collection); Melvyn P. Lawes: p. 36 *d*; Life File: pp. 36 *l* (Emma Lee), 47 *t* (Mark Hibbert), 47 *b* (Andrew Ward), 48 *tr*, *br* (Jeremy Hoare), 131 *c* (Nicola Sutton), 131 *b* (Gina Green); Link Picture Library: p. 73 (Roderick Johnson/Images of India); Lookat Photos: p. 119 (Felix von Muralt); Nigel Luckhurst: p. 69 *tr*; The Metropolitan Museum of Art: p. 155 (Rogers Fund, 1960 (60.30), photograph ©1982 The Metropolitan Museum of Art); Richard Mildenhall: p. 16; PA News: pp. 70 *l*, *c* (David Giles), 70 *r* (Barry Batchelor); Popperfoto: pp. 17 *l*, *cl*, *tr*, 34 *bl*, *bc*, *br*, 72 *l*, *c* (Reuter), 72 *r*, 131 *t*; © Mail Newspapers plc: p. 20 (Solo Syndication); Graham Portlock: pp. 11 *tl*, *bl*, *br*, 12, 19 (shirt, sun-tanned man, freckles, young man, wrinkles), 24 *r*, 31 *t*, *b*, 34 (flowers), 46 *r*, 54 *l*, 55 (all except *tl* & shirt on line), 59 *ct*, *cb*, *b*, 69 *tl*, *br*, 81, 83 *tr*, *cl*, *br*, 101 (hairdresser), 113 (coat), 125 (table), 139 *d*; David Robbins: p. 108; Tom Scott: p. 37; David Simson: pp. 11 *tr*, 19 (sunglasses), 36 *r*, 48 *bl*, 83 *l*, 140; © Thames Television: p. 116; Tony Stone Images: p. 60 *l* (Robin Smith); Topham Picturepoint: pp. 60 *tr*, 60 *br* (Associated Press), 74, 139 *cr*; Mike Wyndham Picture Collection: p. 59 *t*; Yorkshire-Tyne Tees Television Holdings plc: p. 62 (photo © Justin Slee/Guzelian).

t = top, *b* = bottom, *c* = centre, *l* = left, *r* = right

Design and production by Gecko Ltd, Bicester, Oxon.
Picture research by Callie Kendall.
Sound recordings by Martin Williamson, Prolingua Productions, at Studio AVP, London.

The authors and publishers are grateful to the following for permission to reproduce photographs on the cover:
Life File, *tl* (Dave Thompson), *ct* (Jeremy Hoare), *tr* (Joseph Green), *bl* (Andrew Ward), *cb* (Mike Evans), *br* (Andrew Ward).